P9-EGB-903

River of No Return

River of No Return

Tennessee Ernie Ford and the Woman He Loved

A memoir by

Jeffrey Buckner Ford

CUMBERLAND HOUSE
NASHVILLE, TENNESSEE

RIVER OF NO RETURN
PUBLISHED BY CUMBERLAND HOUSE PUBLISHING, INC.
431 Harding Industrial Drive
Nashville, TN 37211

Copyright © 2008 by Jeffrey Buckner Ford

All rights reserved. No part of this book may be reproduced or transmitted in any form or by any means, electronic or mechanical, including photocopying and recording, or by any information storage and retrieval system, without permission in writing from the publisher, except for brief quotations in critical reviews or articles.

All photographs are the property of Jeffrey Buckner Ford or Tennessee Ernie Ford Enterprises.

"Tell Me You Remember, Betty Jean" by Jeffrey Ford. Published by RightSong Music, Inc. c/o Warner/Chappell Music, Inc. BMI. Used with permission by Alfred Publishing, Inc.

"River of No Return" by Kenneth Darby and Lionel Newman. Published by Simon House / Len Freedman Music. BMI. Used with permission.

Jacket Design: Bruce Gore Studio, Nashville, Tennessee
Jacket Photo: Courtesy of TEF Enterprises, LP

Library of Congress Cataloging-in-Publication Data

Ford, Jeffrey Buckner, 1950–
  River of no return : Tennessee Ernie Ford and the woman he loved / a memoir by Jeffrey Buckner Ford.
       p. cm.
  Includes index.
  ISBN 978-1-58182-653-1 (hardcover)
1. Ford, Tennessee Ernie, 1919-1991. 2. Singers—United States—Biography.
3. Country musicians—United States—Biography I. Title.

ML420.F7F67 2008
782.421642092—dc22
[B]
                                                                          2008008268

Printed in the United States of America
1 2 3 4 5 6 7 — 12 11 10 09 08

For Bet & Ern,

Murph and the kids,

and Pack

There is a river called the River of No Return
Sometimes it's peaceful and sometimes wild and free
Love is a trav'ler on the River of No Return
Swept on forever to be lost in the stormy sea

I lost my love on the river and forever my heart will yearn
Gone, gone forever down the River of No Return

And she'll never return to me....

Lionel Newman
Kenneth Darby

ACKOWLEDGMENTS

This book would not be in your hands, opened to this page, were it not for the help, faith, support, encouragement, hard work, ass-kicking, love, determination, attitude, editing skills, sharp eyes, cajoling, patience, and trust of the following souls: Jim Loakes, Paul Corbin, John Siamas, Ken Thompson, Dale Sheets, Todd Gerringswald, and Jo Bill Cook.

To Elizabeth Lyon, for the structure, the patience, and for not adding interest.

To Ron Pitkin, Lisa Taylor, Chris Bauerle, and Paige Lakin of Cumberland House—for the belief and the willingness.

To Sharlene Martin, for being the gutsiest, hardest working, most considerate literary agent in the business.

To Susan Schwartzman, for being the Navy Seal of publicists.

To Murph, Jesse, Tucker, James, Pack, and Bet and Ern—it would not have happened at all without you.

JBF
February 25, 2008

River of No Return

ONE

IT WAS TWO DAYS after his death before we learned where Dad's body was. We would be forced to wait a third before we would finally learn where the service would be. Even then, the funeral directors were under strict orders not to divulge any more information to us than was absolutely necessary and required by law. It was beautiful, really. The next, but not last, logical step in what was clearly a well-laid plan, long in preparation, aimed at isolating an ailing father from his only sons—before and now after his death.

Three weeks earlier, Beverly had called the house—an occasion of note in itself. Curt, breathless, she dispensed with any formalities. "Your father collapsed at the airport. He's unconscious." She briefly recounted the limo ride from the hotel to Dulles (they'd dined with the president and Barbara Bush the day before) and Dad's complaint of stomach pains en route. The driver checked the baggage curbside, they made their way into the terminal, and just outside the doorway to the Admirals Club, he fell to his knees, bathing the marble tiles gracing the entry with nearly a quart of blood. Critically weakened, he was rushed to HCA Hospital in Reston, Virginia, just a few miles from the airport. That was Saturday, September 28, 1991.

Three years before, he'd suffered two nearly identical attacks, the latter hospitalizing him in Nashville for nine days. Mom was still alive then, and against her long-distance advice, I took up residence in the room with him, unwilling to leave him completely in the hands of those other than family. For the first thirty-six hours of that stay, he was comatose, unresponsive, and hovering perilously close to death. When he regained consciousness, he was told bluntly by his doctors that he was pouring himself into a grave. Karl VanDevender, his lead physician, was unequivocal. "Another drink—another attack—and you will probably not make it to the phone, Ernie." The look on Dad's face was one I had seen thousands of times before—vacant, careless, and clueless.

The week I'd spent by his bedside and the knell of Dr. VanDevender's warning took their toll at home later that evening. Dad needed a shot glass full of reality, and I needed intervention help. Grasping at straws, I called Larry Gatlin, remembering that Dad had visited him in rehab a number of years earlier. I embarrassed myself, crying so hard— the words were coming out in gasps and gulps for air. Sacking pride, I begged him to please come to the hospital. He booked his flight that night. Larry also suggested I call Minnie Pearl, who was one of Dad's closest friends and someone I knew—or at least I truly believed—he would listen to. I was wrong, of course, but I was nevertheless buoyed by the hope, promise, and friendship Larry and Miss Minnie gave unselfishly. For a brief moment their visits seemed to bring him out of the antiseptic haze he'd been in, but their gentle admonitions brought the same look to his face that I'd seen when his doctor was laying the law down—clueless denial.

Two days later he was up, packing, shuffling across the hospital room floor, his driver and friend, Bobby Dale, heir to the Martha White Mills empire, in tow, gathering his bags. I stopped to talk briefly with Dr. VanDevender as Dad called Mom at home in the Bay Area.

"I made him promise he'd talk to the doctors about detox," she told me when he handed the phone to me. He promised us both he would. He didn't. I had it on unassailable authority that he was tossing back a Cutty and branch by the time the wheels on the westbound DC-10 lifted off the runway.

"Your father is intent on killing himself," she told me some days after he'd arrived home. "He refuses to do what the doctors have told him to do. He hates my bitching, and I can't stand being in the same house with him anymore. Tell the kids Grandma Bet loves them, and that their Christmas presents are coming early."

Four months later Mom was gone; she'd engineered a massive stroke by downing a handful of tranquilizers with a water glass full of Smirnoff, lightly tinted with just a splash of V-8. She did not die as quickly as I suppose she'd hoped, but by her own hand, as I knew she'd wanted. The three failed attempts preceding this—one by razor and two by pharmaceuticals—were evidence enough. I don't believe she had any intention whatsoever of following him in death, nor did she have the strength to watch him die.

Less than four months after scattering her ashes, Dad married the woman who was now on the other end of the phone in Reston, Virginia. Two years later, he, too, was gone; his mind and body deteriorated beyond repair after thirty years of alcoholism, tempered with a depression that had grown steadily, concurrent with Mom's descent into her own shadows, a depression magnified by a disease that he'd been diagnosed with nearly a year before Mom took her own life, but chose to keep to himself, until his own body and mind betrayed him. By then, though, it was likely he'd forgotten that he'd ever been diagnosed with it. It's also likely that he'd forgotten a great deal more. *Hepatic encephalopathy* has a tendency to work that way. "A progressive brain disorder triggered by acute liver failure," is how his doctor put it. Untreated, you slowly lose your memory, you gradually lose your resolve and volition, your personality changes, and you become disoriented, even around those places and people most familiar to you. By the third stage, you're unable to perform even the most basic mental tasks, but by the time that stage sets in, you don't *know* that you can't.

It's possible that Dad's illness *had* been diagnosed in time and therefore could have been reversed, if he had so chosen. But that would have meant changing his life radically, and I have no illusions even today about the odds of that ever having been high on his List of Things To Do. Even in the last months of her own life, Mom could see that he was wasting his. And she believed he was doing so willfully.

For a brief moment, notwithstanding suspicions that would later prove true, it appeared that marrying again had maybe given Dad some kind of renewal. His moments of clarity appeared sharper, and his memory keener. But it was just that—an appearance, and a short-lived appearance at that. If anything, he became more distant, more withdrawn. In those last days and months there was a vacancy in his eyes, and he seemed . . . empty. Not sure where he was, who these people at the table were, where he'd been . . . where he was going.

Betty was gone, and even in those brief moments when Dad went out of his way to convince anyone who cared to listen that marrying again had released him from the demons and bitterness that marked their last years together, anyone with eyes could see that he'd lost the love of his life, and with her, he'd lost his way and his will.

Through the earpiece of the cordless, the clipped, quivering intonations in her voice told me that Beverly—alone, a stranger in a strange land, her husband lying unconscious nearby, his shirt and jacket a dark, beet red—was hovering perilously close to panic, but not so close that her disdain for me was diluted or softened. On the contrary, there was a definite edge to her tone.

"We're probably going to have to *borrow* money to pay for this," she said between breathy pauses. "We can't afford for you or your brother to come all the way up here." She said the word *here* as if she was searching for exactly *where* she was, knowing she'd be terribly put out when she found out.

I know that witnessing traumatic incidents involving another person can generate almost as many different reactions in people as there are different people. The degree of relationship one has with that person enhances one's reactions commensurately. I was aware of the symptoms of Dad's condition—keenly so—and aware of Beverly's tendencies toward melodramatic displays, which were the stuff of legend in the Ford family, actually. She'd become a caricature of herself over the twenty-plus years she'd known us. Every one of us could do Beverly better than Beverly could do Beverly. Notwithstanding the two years that preceded this call from her, two years that should have given me a clear vision of what lay in store, I was blinded by my own fear for Dad's life. Acutely aware that seeing him collapse in front of her, vomiting blood as he fell, was no doubt a complete shock, I braced for the reaction I expected—a classic, inconsolable Beverly, sobbing in rising and falling muted ululations, a white handkerchief dabbing at tears that weren't there. I told myself to put aside events of the past twenty-four months and focus on Dad. I hoped, all too briefly after answering the phone and hearing her voice on the other end, that she would be of the same mind. She wasn't. That she had the chutzpah to mention money, let alone file this scurrilous claim of near-bankruptcy when Dad was lying near death a few feet from her, was evidence of another mind-set altogether.

"The last thing he needs is for either of you to be anywhere near him. I've told his doctors the same thing." *And I've told them what monsters you both are.*

I heard her say something inaudible to someone nearby and then she was gone, the line dead.

Fourteen hours later, Brion and I were at Dad's side in Reston. For two days we watched, holding our breath, as he slipped soundlessly beneath the waves of the coma that washed over him; his eyelids fluttering occasionally as his consciousness dipped in and out of clarity. For two days we struggled alternately with our desperation and with the desperate measures Beverly employed in her campaign to keep us as uninformed and disconnected as possible. With each passing hour we were there, she became more hostile, more demanding of the staff, more hysterical. It was, regardless of the gulf of hatred that separated us by then, embarrassing. It was telling that once we'd arrived, the first thing Dad's lead physician asked was if he could have my permission to sedate her—that her hysterics (even before we'd arrived) were disruptive to everyone in the ICU. Sedate her? Hell, I felt like telling him to put her to sleep. Over the next two days, he twice suggested that I try to secure an emergency order of conservatorship there in Reston, and he would testify to Beverly's instability. At one point she demanded that a security officer be present in the room any time either Brion or I was in the room with Dad. The implications were obvious and gruesome.

After two days had passed, it appeared that Dad's condition had leveled off some, and the doctors convinced us both that while the wait would probably be lengthy, once he reached a point of relative stability they would make arrangements for a specially equipped plane to fly him home, and from there, he'd be taken to Stanford. Brion and I left for Nashville the following morning. Dad was in a deep sleep and unresponsive when we said good-bye.

Seven days later I was awakened by a phone call from Brion, who'd received a short message from Beverly a few minutes earlier. Dad was gone. After a brief, conscious rally lasting a couple of days, he'd begun bleeding internally again the night before, and his body simply could not fight any longer. He died at 6:15 on the morning of October 17, 1991—thirty-six years to the day after the release of "Sixteen Tons."

The first call I made was to Jim Loakes, who had been Dad's personal manager for forty years, until he was replaced by Beverly's daughter, Stephanie, a part-time dental hygienist—a career change Jim learned about from the press. It was a brief call—Jim had been expecting the news—interrupted by a second call from Brion. He'd tried HCA in Reston almost immediately after he called me. Beverly was not on the premises, and information on the disposition of Dad's body was private—limited to Beverly. They could tell us nothing about where he was, where he was going, or when he was going there. They had no connecting number to Mrs. Ford. She was expected to call them later. Could they give her a message?

There were several rolling around in my head as Brion relayed the story to me. None were appropriate, and I was in a fog.

My second call was to Paul Corbin, at the time director of programming for the then-successful Nashville Network cable channel, and one of the industry's most influential executives. Above and beyond his station, Paul had become one of Dad's closest friends in the business and out. During the weeks ahead I would lean on him mercilessly, desperately needing his help and skill as an advance man.

In less than a half hour, the major press lines had picked up on the story, breaking on radio first and then television. Our phone line was connected—uninterrupted—for more than six hours. For the remainder of the day, we alternately fielded calls, wires, faxes, and journalists, sparing ourselves any time for grief in the process. You couldn't very well do six minutes with CNN if you were gasping for air between every fifth or sixth word, blowing your nose, and bathing the phone with tears. That would come later, in receding and advancing waves; unlooked for and overwhelming, washing me away when I was least prepared, laving my cheeks and neck and throat with salty rivers from a spring that seemed to run unabated. Then, as quickly as it had swelled and broken, the tide would ebb, recede, and eventually stop, leaving me beaten and washed up, my eyes barely visible between swollen lids.

It was late the following morning before we learned that Beverly had Dad's body transported to Dulles and then flown west to San Francisco International. Beyond that, Brion and I were embarrassingly ignorant of any further developments. We hastily concocted stories over the phone to use in order not to seem completely so, but nevertheless, we felt awkward as hell. *"Well . . . as of now, services are going to be held on the West Coast, but we're still working out the logistics. We'll contact you when we know more."* The truth, of course, was we had no idea when that would be or what more we would learn. Moreover, we were both becoming fearful just imagining the stories we would have to create explaining why we weren't at his funeral. Thankfully, we were spared the latter by a phone call from two close friends of the family in the Bay Area with their ears to the ground.

On the morning of the nineteenth, Brion and I and my wife, Murphy, caught the 8:30 American nonstop to SFO. Still ignorant of any plans, we kept our eyes on the airport television monitors and bought papers from every major city, hoping to hear or see some news blurb that might fill in the blanks. We telephoned Holden Court—the Portola Valley house Dad and Beverly had purchased with funds from Mom's trust—intermittently from Nashville International, and then again from the seatback phone in the cabin of the DC-10. For all but one of those five calls, we were told summarily by Beverly's daughter, Stevie, that her mother had "no desire to talk to you or your brother." No kidding, this was the almost verbatim identical closing to *every* call but one; Stevie sounding for all the world like she was *reading* her reply. We imagined it written down in Beverly's flowery handwriting on a Post-it Note and stuck on the wall next to the phone, Beverly pointing to each word with her Pentel pen, mouthing the lines as Stevie robotically read them off. It was the only laugh we allowed ourselves. In each case we were given no time for retort, the in-flight line silently disconnecting, wasting another swipe of the surely-by-now-maxed-out Visa. By the time we landed at SFO and settled in with friends in the valley, we didn't need to search for lines anymore; we'd seen, or rather heard, our script and memorized our parts:

Well-meaning acquaintance: *Have you spoken with Beverly yet?*
Brion/Myself: *No. She has no desire to talk to me or my brother.*

Two days later we were driven to the funeral home where we had learned Dad's body was in repose. Just doing *that* took advance planning worthy of military incursions of note because Beverly, we'd learned, had attempted to bar us from viewing or any visitation at all. As long as I live, I will never forget sitting across from John Hapgood, the attending funeral director, watching as he literally trembled in his seat, mopping curtains of sweat cascading down his forehead. I'd asked to meet with him to request a small vase of a portion of Dad's ashes after the cremation.

"I'm under strict direction to refuse any such request. From you or your brother," he stammered. Add beading tears in the corners of his eyes to the liquid already on his face. This was someone our family had known for more than fifteen years.

"There's nothing I can do. The law says I have to follow her directions. To the letter." Covering his eyes with a handkerchief, he swiveled away from me in his leather office chair and wept openly but silently. I rested my hand on his shoulder then quietly left his office.

The following morning, we arrived at the First Methodist Church of Palo Alto, at one time one of the most beautiful churches on the coast. A cross between classic Spanish stucco and middle European design, in the 1970s it was razed (for the second time), and now it was a building that looked like a boat—an ark—that had been capsized, then reconsidered as an avant-garde piece of architecture.

On the tree-lined sidewalk in front of the entrance some thirty people milled, none of whom Brion or I had the pleasure of inviting, because we wouldn't have known where to tell them the service was going to be held. Their faces were familiar yet unknown to me, and I wondered whether I'd remember everyone's name when it mattered.

Some I recognized, certainly. There was Cliffie Stone, the man who'd discovered Dad, being ably but gamely assisted out of a limousine by his wife, Joan Carol. Here was Paul Corbin, arriving solo from Nashville. Mom's niece, Laura, was here, and of course Jim Loakes—steadfast and true, loyal and heartbroken.

To the right of the big double doors leading into the church, we were greeted first by an announcement board, laying out the day's events at the chapel. *Welcome to the First United Methodist Church of Palo Alto. Today's Events: Services for Ernest Jennings Ford—The Beloved Old Pea Picker—Tennessee Ernie Ford.*

Below the board, under a small arts-and-crafts mission-style table, someone had placed a banker's box containing several rubber-banded groups of five-by-seven, double-folded programs. Like everything else, the programs had been designed and printed without our knowledge or input. Had I the benefit of either, I would have protested the ridiculous picture on the cover, the one of Dad holding the ukulele. A *ukulele*, for Christ's sake. In all her blinding brilliance, Beverly thought it was a guitar. If Mom had been alive, she'd have shot her. Enough wishful thinking. We were lucky to be here at all. Otherwise, we would have missed meeting Beverly's legal representative, who was standing just inside the narthex; a mousy little man accompanied by someone much bigger, who my fifteen years of teaching martial arts to police officers told me was carrying a concealed weapon on his left side. The smallish man stepped forward, barring me from entering the church.

"Jeffrey Ford? My name is Ron VandenBerg. I represent the executor of your father's will. I've been instructed to deliver this order to you, granting your stepmother full authority and power over his estate. I'm really very sorry for your loss. Of everything. Have a nice day."

His friend never said a word but never took his eyes off me, even as they both exited the church.

Trust me, it gets better. Positively Shakespearean.

Anchored on Murphy's left and right, Brion and I were guided to our seats in the pew just behind Beverly, her pale throat within easy reach of my hands, which were now perpetually clinched. To my left, I discovered I'd somehow earned the added good fortune of drawing a seating card alongside Beverly's twin sisters, Emily and Dorothy, neither of whom appeared conscious of our arrival, their eyes riveted to the tiny, circular mirrors of their matching makeup compacts that were open for nearly the entire service.

I looked around the chapel and realized there were fewer than two hundred people in attendance, and I knew or barely recognized only forty to fifty of them. Craning my neck as much as I could without appearing to be doing exactly what I was doing, I surveyed the pews, and brought my eyes back to the podium when I realized that one of Beverly's sisters had closed her compact and was staring at me with all the concern of a Doberman. She snapped the compact closed and slowly swiveled her head around to her sister, whispering something to her I couldn't hear.

As I turned my attention back to the service, Cliffie Stone was at the lectern, being supported on his left by his wife, Joan Carol. He was recalling the salad days, the years spent on the road, the first seasons at NBC, and the early days in the studio when Dad first began with

Capitol. His voice was wavering, and he was clearly having difficulty maintaining his composure.

Pausing for what seemed a full minute to gather his words and his strength, the church fell silent as Cliffie had, many now leaning forward in their pews. In the silence, Beverly looked at her watch, turned to my old math teacher, Robert Halterman, who had accompanied her to the service, and in a voice thick with impatience and undoubtedly heard by two-thirds of those in attendance, she said, "Why is he taking so long, for God's sake?"

Churches are known for their superb acoustics, and the First Methodist held true. The words "for God's sake" floated out of her mouth and up into the nave, hovered above the pews, then soared upward toward the clerestory, before echoing down through the chancel and finally coming to rest on the ears of all, like scraps of thin paper torn from a hymnal and let loose from the rafters above, lazily drifting from the ceiling to the floor.

From my right, Murphy's hand found mine, and her fingernails dug trenches into my palm. At my left, Beverly's sisters opened their compacts again and checked their makeup.

Closing my eyes, I did my best to turn inward, to close my ears and eyes to the bizarre spectacle surrounding me, and tried to connect with Cliffie; to connect with the time and the place he was casting his memory back to—a time and a place when all was right and good in the world. When the lights were bright and the promise of another day in paradise lay just ahead.

Inside, though, like the aftertaste of a bad order of moo goo gai pan, I could not shed the nagging question that crept upward from the pit of my stomach into the inner chambers of my heart.

How did we end up here? How did our family, and such a life, come to this?

TWO

MY MOTHER MARRIED MY DAD on a Friday afternoon, the eighteenth of September, 1942, at the First Methodist Church in San Bernardino, California. At two thirty Pacific time, they were pronounced man and wife by the Reverend Donald S. Ford—no relation. It wasn't big, as weddings go. It was a short, single-ring ceremony; short on folks attending and short on excess. The country was at war, and wedding bands, silk brocade, and silver were being used rationally, like aluminum and rubber.

Mom wore a tailored suit of RAF blue, with a cranberry corsage on the lapel and a cream-colored blouse underneath. Its collar was fanned over the suit's lapels, "giving the bride," according to the story that ran in the San Bernardino *Sun*, "that smart, military look so popular today." Pulled back and braided behind, her dark hair resembled a pilot's cap, slightly cocked to one side and held in place by a simple pin on the right, which was adorned with a single dark-blue amethyst rose.

Dad shaved his mustache, the first of only two instances in his life when he did so, and wore his Army Air Corps dress browns. The pants were creased razor-sharp, the jacket epaulets and collar tabs pinned per regulation; and his airman's cap was tucked sharply under the wing of his left arm, the bill shined to an obsidian black.

The story in the *Sun* gave their wedding two columns and a two-column-wide picture, the first piece of press in what would become,

23

over time, a set of three volumes; massive scrapbooks measuring two and a half by four feet, each between twelve and fifteen inches thick, covering nearly half a century and weighing almost two hundred pounds. I know this because when the books arrived, I happened to think, *Damn, these are huge. I wonder what they weigh?* And I weighed them: 173 pounds, covering forty-seven years and a couple hundred pounds of truth, gossip, guesses, recipes, sightings, schedules, raves, rips, pictures, drawings, and letters that chronicled our family until the end of the eighties.

Most of the ink, understandably, is about Dad. Most of the focus, naturally, is on him. Theirs was a married life celebrated and chronicled, after all, because of him. But it was not a life lived only by him. What I cherish most about this clipping is that it's the first piece of press after their marriage, and it's about *them*.

But the picture is also unusual. Unusual because it was 2001 when I saw the shot for the first time, and unusual because it's completely different from the stock shot supposedly taken the day they were married; the shot I'd seen hundreds, if not thousands, of times. The shot in all the press books, in all the tour programs, and in all the fan magazines. The shot that showed them looking off-lens, slightly to their left (I hate pictures like that, always have. All I can think of is, *What the hell are they looking at?* It's a forced pose, severe and close. I imagine that the shooter for the *Sun*, or perhaps the wedding planner (if there was one, other than Jesse, Mom's mother), went for poses like that, holdovers from the daguerreotype era—stoic and unemotional—two qualities never championed or shown by either Betty or Ernest Ford.

Markedly different from that stock shot, the photo from the *Sun* shows two people I actually recognize, looking straight into the lens, their eyes telling a singularly poignant story of the lives that lay ahead of them, and the lives that brought them to each other. Strength, love, and hope shine in those eyes—the very same qualities that would, over the years, slowly diminish and then eventually evaporate completely.

Less than a year earlier, on the afternoon of December 7, 1941, Dad was in the studios of WROL Radio in Knoxville, Tennessee, preparing for the three o'clock news when the flash came over the wire. It was just after 2:00 p.m. eastern time, and he was pulling copy when the Teletype machines began ringing. Doing double duty as on-air jock and news director, the task of breaking the first news in the region of the attack on Pearl Harbor fell to him. As his coworkers scrambled to calm worried callers and pull late-breaking copy from the UPI and AP machines, Ernest Ford was forced to sit calmly behind the mic and patiently, professionally read a news flash that would ultimately alter his life and the world forever. The balmy shores of Honolulu surely seemed like a world away for this twenty-two-year-old from the hills of east Tennessee, but the bombing and the news of the devastation in paradise very quickly absorbed the miles, and brought the Islands and WWII to everybody's Philco and everybody's front porch.

Dad was born in February 1919 in Bristol, Tennessee; second, last, and youngest son of Thomas Clarence and Maude Lee Ford. Little brother to Stanley Haskell Ford, born two years earlier in 1917.

Bristol is a state-line town. If you're facing east on its main drag, State Street, the left side of the dividing line is Virginia and the right side is Tennessee. I hold few but precious memories of the trips we made there when I was a boy. It was a town of old men in bib overalls, trading knives and talking tobacco. They gathered in knots at the counter of Paty's Hardware, wads behind their cheeks, moving and talking slowly; every word paced and deliberate. It was a town of short-sleeved, crew-cut clerks who wore creased gabardines and button-downs, armed with plastic shirt-pocket penholders, neatly stocked with personalized ballpoints. And it was a town of strong women who wore crisp cotton dresses, did not hide the calluses on their hands, and went to quiltings after church on Sunday, "stitching a square for one in despair."

Known simply as T.C. to family and neighbors, Clarence Ford was a fourth-generation Tennessean, his forebears traceable back to a German-Dutch clan named Brandstutter from the Netherlands, who found their way to the Americas sometime around the early 1600s. He was a tall, quiet man, known for his quick smile, his patience, his friendship, and his steady trustworthiness, qualities that he no doubt needed to rely on and regularly employed during his thirty years with the U.S. Post Office. However, you sensed a powerful current of strength under his calm, placid nature, and although I never intentionally tested those waters, I instinctively knew as a child that angering him would be a grave mistake for anyone who so dared. Twenty-one years after T.C.'s death in 1970, Dad still referred to him as his hero.

Maude Lee was not as tall as Clarence, but her height had nothing to do with her stature in the family or in the community. Descended from Britain's Long dynasty, second daughter of Walter and Nancy Long, she was the rock that both sides of the family clung to. T.C. clearly deferred to her, and she just as clearly doted upon him, trusting his every word and deed as best for her.

When she was felled by a stroke early in 1969, T.C. cooked and cleaned, bathed and clothed her, never faltering, never wavering in his care or love. When that time became darkest—before his own heart finally broke—Maude would call to him from the bedroom daily, pleading with him to take her home. Gathering her up in his arms, her bedclothes draped around her, he would carry her to the car, drive a few miles down the Blountville Highway, then back up the driveway to the house.

With an effort belying his seventy-seven years, T.C. would lift her gently out of the car, carry her up to the porch, and help her into the swing. Slowly, recognition and familiarity would dawn across her eyes, and as he carried her the last few steps across the threshold and back to her bed, she'd thank him for bringing her home.

His strength finally faded in June 1970. Six months later, with no one to carry her home, Maude quietly followed him for the last time.

Less than a month after breaking the news of the attack on Pearl, Dad was standing naked in the Knoxville courthouse with about a hundred other men, preparing for his physical before enlisting as a private in the Army. In his mind he was about a year behind his older brother, Stanley, who he believed had enlisted in October 1940 at Fort Jackson in South Carolina. As usual, his big brother had seen the writing on the wall long before little brother Ernest, and there was no telling where he was now—probably commanding a detachment of men and on his way to the front.

What Little Brother didn't know was that Stanley, exhibiting signs of the jealousy that marked their relationship as children and would separate them later in life, had decided he could do much better than a *radio announcer*, and tried to pass himself off to the recruiting office as both a film director *and* an actor on his application. And, of course, when they dug around a little, nobody could find even an RKO short that Stanley'd had anything at all to do with, let alone acted in or directed. That and other circumstances led them to escort him to the door.

Six months later, after a string of odd jobs throughout the Southeast, Stanley found his way to a naval recruiting station and eventually—somehow—to officer's training school on the eastern seaboard. It was the beginning of nearly five years in the Pacific theater, and the beginning of the end of his life.

Serving on the USS *Sumter* attack transport, he found himself in the middle of some of the most intense naval campaigns of the war, including the Battle of Leyte Gulf in 1944, where he delivered hundreds upon hundreds of Marines to the beaches of those islands, and to their deaths. When he wasn't ferrying ground troops and landing parties, he directed launch craft under enemy fire after dark through the inland waters, red with the blood of dead or dying soldiers and sailors, vainly searching for bodies the tide was pulling out to sea.

After the war he returned home a broken, psychologically fractured soul who heard men screaming in shark-filled waters, the sound drowned out only by the report of ship's cannons blasting across the stern and bow in his sleep and his wakefulness. A victim of what was then called "shell shock," he'd become a hollowed-out image of his former self, anchorless amid a sea of well-meaning but largely ignorant family members who didn't understand.

He spent long hours at the Hammond organ in the family living room, playing hymns and dirges, and burning the finish off the Hammond's dark mahogany veneer with half-smoked Lucky Strikes he'd lay on the console, forgetting to finish them as he played on, lost in whatever nightmare he found himself in. He spoke in low murmurs when he did speak, difficult to understand, always just outside the circle. Family members began to shun him, and in later years, the anger and bitterness that grew out of his illness would earn their enmity. He would never be the same again, and the bond that once tethered the two brothers would eventually stretch to breaking, leaving each without the other and gray with bitterness.

Though I don't doubt he was prepared for the worst, time in the service was kinder to Dad, due mainly to a decision he made that day in the Knoxville courthouse. Many years later he still vividly remembered a new, unfamiliar recruiting officer coming through the door of the temporary psych office, where he and a group of recruits were poring over makeshift Rorschach tests or the like, and asking if anybody wanted to fly.

It was the second time in his life that he'd been asked that question. The first time was four years earlier, on November 5, 1937.

Most of Bristol had turned out that day to celebrate the ribbon-cutting of McKellar Field, later known as TriCities Regional Airport. Besides the usual boring speeches from local and state politicos, taking as much credit as they could for bringing commercial aviation to Bristol, Kingsport, and Johnson City, the highlight of the day was the arrival of the *Southerner*; an American Airlines Ford TriMotor Skysleeper. Sleek, gleaming, and luxurious, the aircraft captured Dad's imagination the moment it taxied to a stop and its captain, O. M. Goodsell, a World War I ace drafted for commercial transport, climbed out of the cockpit and onto the freshly poured tarmac. For the rest of the day, at a cost of fifty cents, Captain Goodsell gave anyone adventurous enough a twenty-minute flight over Bristol and the Tri-Cities. Ernest Ford was the first in line and the last to leave that day. The romance and exhilaration of flight never left him, and he dreamed of the day he might recapture that first sensation of the wheels lifting off the runway.

Four years later, when that new recruiter came through the door and asked who wanted to fly, Dad had been waiting for him since that day at McKellar Field, and his was literally the first hand in the air.

Unfortunately, he knew his chances of making the cut for pilot's training were slim. Entrance into the elite new wing of the Army—the Air Corps—required two years of college minimum, and he knew that his short stay at the Cincinnati Conservatory of Music to study voice wasn't enough. His disappointment was alleviated, though, when he learned that taking the Air Corps exam would not only qualify as the equivalent of the two years' college he needed, but qualify him for cadet school as well. Now all he had to do was pass it.

Four hours and forty-five minutes later he became Aviation Cadet Ernest Jennings Ford, bound for basic training and flight school at Maxwell Field in Montgomery, Alabama.

At Maxwell the focus was on pilot navigation and bombardier instruction. By the fall of 1941, thousands of cadets from all over the country and a specialized group of British Air Commando trainees called the base their home. Through intense physical conditioning, classes in military law, aviation history, aircraft operations, and more, the brass used the results of the course to determine who was going to drive the planes, who was going to read the maps, who was going to open the bomb-bay doors when the time came, and who was going to be packing their gear and transferring back to infantry somewhere.

When the postings went up and the orders came down, his dream of flying came down with them. Cadet Ford would not be piloting air-craft anytime soon, but as a bombardier cadet second class, he'd by God be in the plane, and just a few seats behind the driver. His orders had him shipping out in less than a month to an undisclosed location to report for undisclosed duties. The classification was Top Secret.

That May, toward the end of a brief leave he'd spent at home in Bristol, a sealed package containing his orders arrived by government courier. Scanning the contents, he learned that while his assignment was still classified, his destination was not. Two days later he boarded a Greyhound out of Kingsport and began the three-thousand-mile trip west to Victorville Army Air Base, located in the desert mountains of Southern California. It would be many years and the war's end before he would once again see his brother, the hills of east Tennessee, or T.C. and Maude. When that day finally came, he'd become a Californ-ian by sheer osmosis.

Victorville lay just north of Los Angeles proper, a desert town nestled squarely in the middle of Apple Valley, watered by the Mojave River, bisected by the Santa Fe Railroad, and, until it was paved over by Interstate 15, fed a daily regimen of travelers via Route 66. In the twenties and thirties it was no bigger than a wide place in the road, most of its people cut from ranch or mining stock, eking out a sun-parched living on horseback, in the granite quarries, through the fruit tree groves, or on the river.

But on July 23, 1941, the town's economic forecast brightened con-siderably when construction of the airfield began. Almost overnight and mere months following the attack on Pearl—Victorville, Needles, Indio, Coachella, San Diego—virtually every corner of California was transformed by the defense industry and the war effort. For the first two years of the war, strategists (armchair and legitimate) were bank-ing on the certainty of a similar attack on the California coast. Con-tinental *defense* became the watchwords, and defense contractors, soldiers, sailors and air corpsmen were swarming into and across the state at the rate of a thousand or more every day.

By the time Dad arrived in Victorville, Mom had already been on the base for nearly two months. Her official title was "Secretary to the Wing Commander." She landed the position after graduating from the National Youth Administration School in San Francisco, which was a New Deal agency within the WPA (Works Progress Administration), created by Roosevelt in 1935 and designed to address what Eleanor saw as a national epidemic: the growing problem of unemployment among Great Depression–era youth. The defense industry's growth in the state required an unprecedented labor force, and much of California's under-eighteen population became part of the war effort overnight, albeit on the home front.

Eventually the base would be home to some six thousand troops, but when Dad arrived with the newest class of cadets that May, there were fewer than one thousand, and the young brunette secretary from San Bernardino was the only woman.

She was born Betty Jean Heminger on October 6, 1923, to Charles Dallas and Jesse Etheline Heminger, transplanted Midwesterners of Irish and Scotch-German decent whose families were among the great masses that landed on Ellis Island in the 1800s.

Her father, Charlie, was born in 1883 or 1884, in Indiana. His father, born in Ohio, was named Alvin Heminger. Alvin was a contender in the Cherokee Strip Land Run in 1893. In 1907 Charlie and Jesse were married, and they lived in Medford, Oklahoma, on the ground staked out by Charlie's father in the land rush. Their first child, a daughter, Vayle, was born in January of the following year in the sod house built by her grandfather on that same land.

In 1917 Charlie, Jesse, Vayle, and nine members of their two families loaded everything they had in four Model A's and drove cross-country from the Kansas and Oklahoma plains to California. They slept in tents, and cooked salt meat, potatoes, and canned goods they'd brought. Occasionally, one of the men got lucky, and venison or jackrabbit was added to the night's menu.

Paved roads were rarities, and would not become common even around towns big enough to warrant them until the Road Act of 1918 was passed. They traveled mostly on dirt tracks, broad in some places where traffic was more common, and compacted from years of wagon and livestock passage.

In May of '17, two months after the Hemingers arrived in California, their second child, Wallace, was born. Six years after they settled in San Bernardino, Mom came along.

Her mother was born Jesse Etheline Lynch in Overton, Kansas, in 1887. A first-generation native, her family emigrated from County Mayo in Ireland, sailing out of Liverpool in the late 1880s, fleeing a homeland that had been ravaged twice by blight and continued to be raped economically by the British. After landing at Ellis Island, her father, John Lynch, traveled overland with his wife from New York to Kansas, settling there the same year Jesse was born. Two years later, her mother, Ellen, died giving birth to Jesse's only sister, Kate, leaving father John to raise two girls alone on the prairie.

Jesse grew to be a fiercely independent, physically strong, self-reliant woman, buttressed by the unforgiving life on the plains, and fortified by her ancestral Irish Catholic faith; all of which she stubbornly relied on as John's health declined and his reliance on whiskey increased. By the time extended family followed from Ireland, settling nearby to help raise the two girls, Jesse was more than up to most chores on her own, save for the task of watching her father's slow descent into alcoholism and eventual death. Ironically, she would live long enough to watch helplessly as her only son and youngest daughter descended the same path. In Wallace's case, she lived long enough to bury him.

The gulf of years between Vayle and Mom—seventeen, to be exact—made their relationship more like that of aunt and niece or surrogate mother and child than sisterhood. But fewer years separated her and Wallace, and although he would become a mirror image of the cruel drunk their grandfather Lynch became, Wallace was every bit his baby sister's confidant, her tutor, and in her adolescent years, her protector when Charlie's life took unlooked-for bitter turns inward, and beating his children became his release.

The Heminger household was spartan and strict, ruled with an unforgiving and iron hand by Charlie. Not long after settling in San Bernardino, he took various jobs as a laborer, carpenter, and factory worker, until he took the Civil Service Exam and began a forty-year career with the post office. On his days off, according to the stories Mom used to regale Brion and me with, he beat her and her brother,

Wallace, regularly with a razor strop—a sport Mom inherited no small talent for, although her instrument of choice was usually taken from Dad's belt collection.

While I never doubted Mom's tales of beatings under the strop, I never could quite see how such a man as Charles Heminger could be . . . such a man. He was stoic, quiet, and meticulous in every detail of his life. In retrospect, he had all the earmarks of an artist, albeit possibly a frustrated sort—another talent he conveyed to his daughter. He was a passionate photographer, experimenting with color slides and stereoscopes, when he was not positioning his three children in various poses for numerous portraits he took over the years, chronicling their youth or his talent, I'm not sure which. Possibly both.

Stern, hard, and seemingly devoid of any imagination on his implacable surface, Charlie Heminger left a photographic legacy of an artist of surprising sensitivity, producing thousands of stills and slides from the early 1900s until his death in 1958. Many of his earliest works employed hand-tinting, an arduous, detailed process of hand-coloring monochromatic black-and-white prints. Hand-tinting was elevated to an art form in Japan in the late 1800s, flourished in the commercial production of postcards worldwide until the mid-1900s, and then faded away in the early fifties with the advent of Kodak's color film.

As a child I relished our visits to my maternal grandparents' house in San Bernardino. It held many mysteries for me, as the houses of grandparents do for all children, but I could spend hours on the oval braided rug in the living room, forehead locked onto the Pana-Vue slide-viewer, surrounded by boxes of transparencies. Their depth and beauty transported me into another world.

When Charlie wasn't in his darkroom he was in his garage, bent over his lapidary saw exploring his second passion—cutting rocks of all sizes and shapes, exposing beautiful quartz-like interiors, hollowed and bejeweled, or smoothly veined with ribbons of agate or jasper threading through the surface.

Over time he took thousands of photographs and created hundreds of stone jewels. None remain; all are lost, and with them, a record of the artistry and life of one man. A great loss.

After his death in 1958, Jesse remained for a while in the San Bernardino home she'd shared with Charlie, but the aloneness soon became too much even for her. For a time she was shunted between her son, Wallace, and his wife, Barbara; Mom's older sister, Vayle, and her husband, Tex; and, finally, us. But that didn't last but a few years. Her disappointment in the choices her children had made and, as far as she could see, were continuing to make, was not something she hid well. When she began leaving church pamphlets about the evils of alcohol in conspicuous little places around the house in North Hollywood, like the bedroom I shared with Brion, Mom snapped, and Jesse was moved to a home away from home.

In June 1942, after settling in at Victorville, Dad finally learned what his orders were and why he'd been assigned there. Along with a hand-picked crew of other cadets and one civilian, his unit became one of the first wartime groups to train with one of America's most closely guarded secrets during the war: the Norden bombsight.

An early analog computer, the Norden was designed by a Dutch engineer named Carl Norden, who built the prototype at Rome Laboratories in New York. Using an internal system of gyros, mirrors, trajectory input devices, and a telescope, the Norden effectively changed the science of high-altitude bombing and gave America and its allies air supremacy in the bombing corridors of Europe and the Pacific theaters. Some claimed that its efficiency was overestimated; others claimed it enabled you to damn near drive a sixteen-penny nail with the tip of a two-thousand-pound bomb from twenty thousand feet.

Because of its intricate design and complex mechanisms, the cadre of bombardiers selected to operate the Norden were among the Air Corp's most elite teams. In the spring of 1942, only eighty such cadets had been chosen for that training at Victorville Army Air Base. Among them was Cadet Ernest J. Ford. By the end of his assignment there three years later, he'd graduated to second lieutenant and become one of only twenty-four qualified bombardier instructors on the entire base.

Training with the Norden was conducted in specially constructed hangars, separate from other facilities on the base and under twenty-four-hour armed guard. Cadets would climb into mock cockpit and bomb-bay structures inside the hangar, with an instructor acting as the "pilot," and essentially learn to operate one of the Army's first working battle computers. When in-flight bombing drills were scheduled, the Norden was carried under cover from the hangar to the aircraft, flanked on each side, front and rear, by armed MPs. At the end of training, it was removed and taken back to its hangar in the same way, covered and under guard.

The training was grueling, precise, and mathematical; the tedium broken only by the knowledge that what they were doing would most certainly change the course of the war and, quite possibly, history. Add to that the fact it was no secret the cadets were also competing with one another; you couldn't just learn how to use the Norden, you had to master it. Whether you were testing in the hangar or on airborne runs, your targeting, precision, and math had to be dead-on every time. There was little to no room for mistakes. Scores were kept of each cadet's training runs, and those scores translated into who would qualify for transfer overseas and real-time bombing runs over Dresden or maybe Okinawa, a chance to see real action, even if it was from a couple of miles in the air.

At Victorville, the Norden scorekeeper was a civilian secretary. Her name was Betty Jean Heminger.

Because of her need to know status in the Norden project, she was also one of the first civilians among that group of elite cadets and instructors who were ordered to sign the Bombardier's Oath, swearing with their lives to keep secret their knowledge of the Norden bombsight:

> Mindful of the secret trust about to be placed in me by my Commander in Chief, the President of the United States, by whose direction I have been chosen for bombardier training . . . and mindful of the fact that I am to become guardian of one of my country's most priceless military assets, the American bombsight . . . I do here, in the presence of Almighty God, swear by the Bombardier's Code of Honor to keep inviolate the secrecy of any and all confidential information revealed to me, and further to uphold the honor and integrity of the Army Air Forces, if need be, with my life itself.

Being the only woman on the entire base, I also have it on good authority that, given a choice, a fair number of cadets would've rather put their minds on the prospect of scoring with *her*, and to hell with this top secret crap. Only one would make the cut.

Mom remembered him as being "different" from the other cadets. Focused and hardworking, but not particularly ambitious; handsome and naturally good-natured, but not impressed with himself. There was a simple humility about him that set him apart from the other recruits.

When they met for the first time at the post exchange, he'd come in ostensibly to "borrow" a piece of carbon paper, promising to bring it back when he was done with it. Which meant, of course, he didn't have a clue about its life span. But it wasn't necessarily the right time to give him a lesson in the usability of carbon paper. He was easy to talk to, if not the sharpest knife in the drawer, and he made her laugh, which was something she didn't do much on the base.

When he brought the carbon paper back a few days later, he brought a thank-you gift along with it: a single piece of applesauce cake made by his mother. For Ernie Ford, this was undoubtedly a difficult thing to give up. She'd actually sent him an entire cake, and he'd eaten all of it but this one last piece. Mom remembered that he'd wrapped it in a piece of the tissue paper it'd been mailed in; smeary, and a little torn. When he produced it from his pocket, where he'd kept it on the walk from his barracks to the exchange, any resemblance it might have had at one time to the shape of a wedge of cake was lost. The gesture, however, was not lost on Mom.

When he finally got around to asking her out, she accepted without giving it a thought. Then he promptly stood her up—on four separate occasions over four successive weekends. This was not entirely his doing, and certainly not his intention. On each occasion, he'd no sooner let the words "out tonight?" leave his mouth, than he was brought up short on some minor disciplinary charge of one sort or another. Shoes not shined. Latrine not cleaned to standard; uniform not regulation. So, instead of a movie in San Bernardino with Betty, he was walking the flight line or doing kitchen police. It was, looking back, a miracle that she had the patience to put up with him, let alone wait for him, especially in light of the fact that seventy-nine other recruits were, by that time, waiting in line, waiting for her to give Cadet Ford his dishonorable discharge papers.

Eventually, he got his act and a weekend pass together, and on a hot Saturday afternoon that June, he caught a bus to San Bernardino and walked to the Heminger house at 227 West Tenth Street. After a quick meeting with her folks, who didn't think much of the lieutenant from Tennessee, Mom, Dad, and Mom's niece, Laura, piled into her '39 Plymouth and split for the beach in Orange County.

Other men might have been put off by the niece factor in the mix, but Dad was not. He got along great with Laura, and his amiable nature struck Mom immediately. Over the rest of the day, she grew more interested and more attracted to him. But either he didn't sense it or, if he did, he didn't let on. By late afternoon they had talked the day away, and the only thing on Lieutenant Ford's mind was food.

On the way back to San Bernardino, he thought his dream had come true when they passed one of the many roadside stands farmers erected on the back of their pickups, this one laid out with casabas, pole beans, and fresh ears of corn, the latter a homeboy's delicacy Dad hadn't had since he left east Tennessee. It was the only request he'd made all day—could they stop so he could buy a few ears . . . he hadn't eaten corn on the cob in months.

Now, earlier I painted the picture of Mom's mother, Jesse; stalwart woman of the plains who was running a farm with her own hands before she was twelve. Strong of sinew, self-reliant; as skilled in the kitchen at a woodstove as she was on a milk stool.

Absolutely none of those attributes were inherited by or cultivated by her daughter. Her dream was to be an actress, and she had no plans of cooking any time in the near future.

No problem here, though. Jesse was bound to be home, and Mom knew instinctively she'd be happy to cook corn on the cob for a hungry cadet. Mom also knew instinctively that if her mother wasn't home, said cadet would continue to go hungry, because Betty Heminger hadn't cooked one meal in her entire life, and she didn't have a tinker's clue how to cook corn on the cob, or anything else, for that matter. Not wanting to disappoint anybody, though, Mom conveniently left that little fact of her life out.

Great first date so far, wasn't it?

I love this . . . they get back to her place on Tenth, and the first thing Mom notices is the sinking cold pit of ice in her stomach when she sees that her folks' Studebaker is gone. Any other time, a girl bringing a date home would welcome the fact that her folks were gone. Jesse Heminger gone, though, meant Betty Heminger was going to have to do some serious tap dancing around the corn-on-the-cob issue.

Strapping on her self-reliant genes, she did her best to forget about corn and steer the hungry cadet away from all thoughts of food. She talked about movies, how she was hoping to land an audition for Louis B. Mayer, and was going to have some glamour shots done. She talked about Ronald Colman's latest picture. She talked about the war, she showed him all five scrapbooks of her dad's snapshots, and she was getting ready to show him his lapidary saw, which Dad said would be great—after they ate.

Fearing humiliation but banking on those self-reliant Heminger genes and her hopeful talent as an actress, Betty Heminger gamely gathered up the sack of corn and bravely marched into the kitchen.

Leaving Dad with Laura, who was going on a mile a minute about God knows what, Mom did the first thing that came to mind—she got a couple of pans out of the cabinet under the counter and rattled them around on the stove as loud as she could. Cooks always did that—rattled pans. Next she ran some water in the sink for . . . oh, a good three minutes. Cooks always did that, too. Then she went through every corner of the kitchen desperately hunting for a cookbook—a single recipe—that would instruct her on the three intricate steps of preparing corn on the cob: shuck, boil, and butter.

Half an hour later she came out of the kitchen, untying the apron she'd found off the pantry, and, brushing her slightly mussed hair, announced that this particular strain of corn would take far too long to cook, possibly an hour or more.

Saving face, they found a little Chinese place downtown, and, along with some rumaki, egg rolls, and muu shu chicken, Dad got his wish when he ordered two sides of nothing but bang zhi, those little miniature corn on the cobs.

They'd been married for nearly five years before Dad ever let on he knew what had happened.

By the end of July, they'd grown attached to each other and found more in common; each had an older brother in the Navy, and both their fathers were carving out civil service careers at the post office. The latter finally gave Dad something he could talk about with Charlie Heminger, which, in the beginning, was like pulling teeth. The man was about as comfortable to be around as a tax auditor, except that tax auditors talked more.

On the fourth visit Dad made to the Heminger house, that changed. The "comfortable to be around" part, anyway. From the living room Dad could hear the measured rip of a handsaw and the steady drive of a hammer coming from the back of the house, where Charlie was busy building a third bedroom above the landing on the back porch. Over the next month Dad was by his side each weekend, measuring, cutting, nailing, and framing; working together, the two built a quiet bond that didn't require words. The simple act of working with their hands gave them a common ground that supported, grew, and nourished a lasting friendship that endeared Dad to that strict, hard man and in turn chiseled out a place in his adamantine heart for Dad.

The bedroom was finished late on a Sunday afternoon. After hanging the tools up for the last time, Dad made reservations at the California Room in the California Hotel on E Street, the closest thing San Bernardino had to a four-star in 1942. On long nights years later, when her clarity was way past gone, soaked and floating in a water glass of vodka, Mom could still remember and recount that night as if it had been the day before.

"I wasn't as dumb as I looked," she used to say. "I knew what your father was going to ask me that night before he did."

Seven thirty-foot-tall palms lined the block in front of the entrance to the California Room, casting long shadows across the sidewalk and the cars parked there. She remembered a light breeze coming down E Street and snapping the fronds in the palms above them as they walked back to the car.

"When your father said he had something to ask me, I just answered, 'Yes.' But he asked me anyway, and I answered yes again. There were a lot of reasons a lot of people thought we should wait; we'd only known each other for a couple of months, and the war . . . mainly because of the war. But no one knew—the war might have gone on for years and years. No one knew. What we *did* know was that it didn't matter we'd only known each other for a few months—we both knew we were supposed to be together. The only thing we waited for was for your father to graduate out of his cadet class in September. We just knew."

One month later, on September 18, 1942, four months after meeting each other that day on a dusty airfield in the desert, they walked out of the First United Methodist Church of San Bernardino, Mr. and Mrs. Ernest J. Ford.

THREE

UNLIKE MOST of his contemporaries, Dad didn't land in Hollywood by design. He didn't come to the town with stars in his eyes, dreaming of being discovered at Schwab's. He never pounded the pavement looking for an agent or a break, never camped out at Central Casting, never worked as an extra hoping for a line or a close-up, didn't do time in a chorus line, and was never anyone's second banana. It simply happened. "I fell into this business," was the simplest way he could put it. And it was damned close to the truth.

From the late thirties through the early fifties, he was fortunate to find he could make a living in radio. After he and Mom were married in September 1942, he was regularly tapped for AFRN (Armed Forces Radio Network) broadcasts and public service announcements while he was stationed at Victorville. The brass was aware of the time he'd spent behind the mic at WOPI in Bristol, at WATL in Atlanta (where he went by the name of Bob Carroll—go figure), and at WROL in Knoxville, where he'd delivered the first news flash in that area of the attack on Pearl Harbor. Of the thousand or so personnel on the base, he was the obvious choice for the assignments; he had an innate talent for communicating with people, the baritone timbre of his voice was a natural fit for the medium, and best of all, he could read government-issue radio copy without putting people to sleep.

In addition to keeping his announcing chops up for what he hoped might lead to steady work after the war, the duty had another cool benefit—the base didn't have broadcast facilities—no studio, no mics, no control board. They were on the cutting edge of technology in air warfare, but their radio gear—not counting tower-to-aircraft—amounted to little more than a couple of tin cans and a piece of string. This was a benefit because it meant the brass had to find a real radio station to do the broadcasts from; a station with enough buttons, whistles, and antenna power to get the signal to a relay tower, and from there to the men and women overseas. Dad suggested a station he knew a little something about: KFXM, a valley-based outfit in San Bernardino that broadcasted from studios on the second floor of the California Hotel on E Street—the same hotel where he'd proposed to Mom in July of '42.

It was an auspicious choice; KFXM fit the bill to a tee, and before long became the Air Corp's radio base of operations and a feather in Dad's cap. It later became the second station he worked in after the war, and where the character of Tennessee Ernie was born.

Like most other young couples during the war, Mom and Dad's life together was simple, uncomplicated, and, because they were both attached to the Air Corps, regimented to a certain degree. After their marriage they lived for a brief time with Charlie and Jesse, sleeping in the room Dad had helped Charlie build on the back of their house in San Bernardino. When the house got just a *little* too crowded for Dad, they moved to base housing in Victorville, where they stayed until he was transferred to Carlsbad, New Mexico, in the middle of 1944.

Government housing for married couples was in short supply in Carlsbad, and there wasn't a big building boom going on in the New Mexico desert. The best they could find on short order was a two-room-with-a-shared-bath, which had been a commercial chicken coop before the owner went out of business and converted it to what he advertised as an "apartment house." It was furlongs from anything that even remotely resembled a civilized world; isolated and dust-bound, an outpost twelve miles from the closest restaurant, theater, and sidewalk—all of which just thrilled Betty Ford to no end.

Cooped up most of the day (pun intended) with nothing to do but give nicknames to the Gila monsters and scorpions out the back door, and "imagining all sorts of dire things that could happen to your father," Mom would bide her time buried in movie magazines, novels, and a diary she began keeping. Around five o'clock or so, she'd throw something in the oven for dinner, "usually forget about it, because I still didn't have a clue how to cook," and then climb the windmill at the edge of the property, where every night she'd watch for the dust trails and headlights from Dad's Plymouth as he made his way home from the base.

They lived there for three months, sharing the building and the bathroom with another couple in the coop next door, while Dad looked for something that they didn't have to share or pick feathers out of before they could move in.

After a short trip back to Victorville in August 1944 for cadet training, Dad came home to the roost with what he said was great news.

"Your father thought he'd found the perfect little house for us," Mom remembered. "He was so damned excited." It was close to the base, he said. The rent was manageable, and best of all, "it was on the river. Naturally, the way your father described it, it was like a god-damned Norman Rockwell painting. And I was just naive enough to get taken in by it. He didn't tell me the half of it."

Okay—in Dad's defense, it *was* a single-family dwelling. They wouldn't be sharing the bathroom with anybody. And it was on the water. Literally. That was the half he hadn't told her. The perfect "little house" he'd found was a house*boat*. Floating on the Pecos River.

The first week, they actually thought they *had* found the perfect place for themselves. The river was quiet, there was no traffic, and it was peaceful on the water. A week went by, Mom hung pictures and clothes, decorated with what few things they had; they got the water running from the dock service . . . they were in business. Their little houseboat felt like a "homeboat." To celebrate, they had a small house-warming get-together with a couple they'd become friends with from the base.

It was Dad who first noticed they might have a small problem. The wine he'd poured to go with the spaghetti Mom had made was . . . listing in everybody's glasses. "Listing," for those of you not nautically literate, is a term used to describe a vessel's angle of lean or tilt to one side or another. In this case, the port wine he'd poured was listing to starboard. Have you got this?

It was a minor problem, the owner told them the next day. It had simply slipped his mind. All you needed to do was check the engine room about once a week to make sure the leak hadn't filled the compartment too badly, turn on the bilge pump, and everything would be fine.

This, of course, thrilled Betty Ford to no end.

In December of '44, Dad was granted a transfer to undergo flight training in the B-29, the Air Corp's newest bomber, built by Boeing.

Called the "Flying Fortress" because of the wealth of armaments on board, its payload capacity, and computerized defenses, the B-29 set the standard for long-range bombers, able to carry its immense tonnage of explosives, crew, and equipment more than five thousand miles on a single tank of gas. It was the apple of General Curtis LeMay's eye, and the plane that Colonel Paul Tibbets would drive high above the encircling hills surrounding Hiroshima on the morning of August 6, 1945.

After three months of gunnery training in Vegas, followed by a brief layover for navigational and avionics classes in Nebraska, Dad was given his orders to report to MacDill Field in Tampa, Florida, on May 1, 1945. If you'd been learning how to fill *any* seat on a B-29, MacDill was the final phase, the last stop of training. Making it that far meant two things: You were cleared for the duty you'd been training for, and you were on your way to the Pacific or the European theater. You were on your way to war.

Seven days after Ernie and Betty arrived in Florida, Germany surrendered.

Over the next two months, the elation over Germany's resignation was tempered by the continuing escalation of fighting in the Pacific. There were rumors in the B-29 hangars that a mission was being developed around a decisive bombing run planned for sometime before the end of the year—a run the rumors said would dramatically alter the landscape of the war. Every crew tightened their training posture, shaved seconds off flight operations and weapons readiness. Every crew member, from navigation to gunnery, was sitting on go, preparing their minds, their bodies, and their spirits for the task they'd been training for.

In June Mom and Dad sensed there wasn't much time. They decided that if a mission took him overseas, she'd stay in Florida. They'd found comfortable base housing in Tampa in a two-bedroom tract house with a little yard in the back, in a nice neighborhood, and close to two other couples they'd become friends with; both the guys members of Dad's B-29 crew.

But there were loose ends that needed tying up back in San Bernardino. And they both knew Mom would have to plan, prepare, and execute that mission solo.

Near the last few days of July, using the security clearance she still held from Victorville, she landed a jumper seat on a troop transport flying west to San Diego. She'd telephoned her folks and enlisted their help in selling the car and storing everything she wouldn't need in Florida with them. Then, with the proceeds from the Plymouth, Mom would grab a one-way ticket on the first train back to Florida.

The year before she died, she remembered that day on the tarmac at MacDill, before her plane taxied down the runway to take her home to San Bernardino.

"We tried not to think about it, but we both knew your father might be called before I'd had a chance to come back to MacDill," she said. "He was bluer than I was, but we knew we had to keep a stiff upper lip. We really weren't sure we would ever see each other again."

Home in San Bernardino, it took her just over a week to move everything into the room they'd lived in when they first got married, pack their clothes and a few belongings, and sell the coupe. With the $400 it brought she had her ticket eastbound, and on August 14 she said good-bye to her folks at Union Station in Los Angeles, grabbed her bags, and was getting ready to board the big streamliner when the whistle began blowing. And blowing. And blowing. Passengers started streaming out of the Pullman cars, and porters were running pell-mell down the turnstile rows, colliding with newsboys dashing alongside the train.

Japan had surrendered. The war was over.

Closer to Tennessee than California, Mom and Dad left Florida for Bristol in the last few days of August 1945, after his discharge from the Air Corps. It was a happy reunion not only with his folks, but also with his older brother, Stanley, who'd returned a decorated ensign from bloody duty in the South Pacific.

Dad was rehired as a staff announcer at WOPI, where he'd started in radio in the late thirties, and for five months he stuck it out, trying gamely to reintegrate himself as a Tennessean and make Mom feel at home; neither of which was successful. The Pacific Coast had claimed him as one of its own, and it had never released its hold on Mom, who was about as comfortable in the hills of east Tennessee as a long-tailed cat in a room full of rocking chairs.

It wasn't all bad. While he ran the boards at WOPI, he and Mom met a young brunette named Judy Tilford, who, for all practical purposes, ran the station for the guy who ran the station. She wrote copy, sold advertising, answered the phone, pulled news from the wire services—everything but spin records. Perhaps more important, at least from Mom's viewpoint, she knew where to find a good, cheap bottle of red wine in the wet county just a few miles away. She and Mom became instant best friends. They liked the same movies, they both loved Tommy Dorsey, and, over a bottle of merlot one night when Dad was doing the graveyard shift at the station, discovered they both shared a unique talent—a gift, really—one rarely bestowed upon ladies or, if given, rarely employed, at least by proper ladies.

They discovered they had the vocabulary talents of lumberjacks, of longshoremen, of out-of-work prizefighters, of stevedores routing lazy crews under their command. These were women who discovered they could swear with a profanity that would have sent the good people of Bristol to their root cellars and armed the local constabulary. These were women who found a calling, who had obviously reached a logorrheic breaking point; they had grown bloated with excess word-weight gain over years of steadily building female frustration, exacerbated by their hesitancy to use such vile verbiage in public, fearful of the repercussions it would bring upon them and their families' good names.

These were women who could cuss.

It happened innocently enough—a glass tipping over and spilling wine on the carpet in the little flat Mom and Dad were renting, staining the rug and their chances of holding on to the lease, as drinking was forbidden in the building. An unguarded slip of the tongue from Betty Ford, and they were off to the races. By the time Dad got home, they were both in the bag, long past your average profanity; they were creating whole new facets of the lexicon, each of them knee-deep in guttural gab, verbally toiling to outdo the other.

I am not sure whether Judy kept the epithetical faculty she discovered she had that night tuned up over the years. I haven't asked her, and probably should. I can tell you, though, that Betty Ford not only continued to employ what was obviously a God-given talent, she became famous for it, gaining no small degree of notoriety among family and friends, and—with a few drinks under her girdle—first-time acquaintances.

She didn't merely swear; she honed this fluency to a razor-sharp edge. She painted with vulgarity, creating beautiful minimalist works of enduring simplicity, and canvases slung with great swaths of blue and purple language, as if Jackson Pollock had used words and not colors. She weaponized profanity, delighting in taking aim at the uninitiated or unprepared, punctuating with the Lord's name in vain, and throwing in a few choice anatomical references for good measure.

While I certainly inherited many traits—good and otherwise—from both my parents, any predilection for swearing that I might have today, any urge I might have for reaching down into the verbal mud, I owe solely to my dear mother, and herewith—albeit belatedly—I offer my deepest gratitude. Thanks, Mom. You were the best.

Within three months after arriving in Bristol, homesickness for California began to take its toll on Mom. She wasn't exactly hitting it off famously with Dad's folks—T.C. and Maude—and she was growing more leery by the day of Dad's older brother, Stanley. She longed for the sight of the Pacific and for the citrus-scented breezes blowing through the San Fernando Valley. Both seemed light-years away from Sullivan County, Tennessee, and she was burning the long-distance telephone wires to her folks daily. It wasn't long before Dad began to realize he may have made a mistake by coming home, and Mom's new best friend, Judy, began to sense their unhappiness, which delighted her immeasurably.

For years Judy had dreamed of making a break, of leaving Tennessee to try her luck in Hollywood or Chicago or New York; where the big shows were broadcast from and where the stars were. Where the opportunities for a sharp girl with stars in her eyes were way more than she'd ever find in Bristol. Her fiancé, Elmer Hicks, was still overseas with the Army, unsure when his discharge would come through, so there was nothing to hold her in Tennessee. And now, praise God, here were two refugees from Southern California who talked incessantly about the sun, the movies, the opportunities, the beach, and the life they missed. And they'd dropped right in her lap, homesick for San Bernardino—wherever the hell that was.

Her daydreaming was all Mom and Dad needed.

In February of '46, Dad said good-bye to his folks for the second time in four years, loaded what few things they'd brought with them in a four-door Plymouth he'd bought (I don't know where this attachment to Plymouths came from), added Judy Tilford's gear to the trunk, and the three of them headed west. Oddly enough, they dropped Judy off in Texas, where she decided to stay on with her fiancé's folks until he returned from the front. A few years later, however, in the early fifties, both Judy and Elmer did move to the coast, where Judy took a job as a production assistant on Dad's ABC Radio series from Hollywood. With just the briefest of detours, her dream came true.

When they arrived home in San Bernardino, moving back in with Mom's folks was a necessary evil until they could find a place of their own. But that wasn't going to happen without a paycheck. When he learned that KFXM was scouting for an afternoon staff announcer, Dad applied that very day, interviewing with the same manager who'd arranged for the Air Corp's AFRN broadcasts during the war. He remembered Dad and hired him on the spot—an hour before he went on the air.

The signal from KFXM's tower on the roof of the California Hotel gave it a broadcast area that covered most of San Gabriel Valley and the Inland Empire. On a good day you could pick it up as far west as San Diego and clear to Palm Springs, but that was rare. Its audience covered an equally varied demographic, but its core listeners were blue-collar folks—defense industry workers, citrus growers, road crews, and waitresses in diners along Route 66. Many had immigrated to the state throughout the thirties and during the war years, found the land and its people to their liking, and settled, becoming Californians by choice if not by birth, and in some cases because they had no other choice. They were working-class, ordinary folks; the backbone of a burgeoning, expanding coastal economy.

KFXM knew their audience and recognized the value that audience had not only to the state's economy and growth, but also to the station's ratings. In fairness, they probably gave more thought to the latter. They tailored their playlist to appeal to that core group of folks, running the gamut from Sinatra to Homer and Jethro, from Kate Smith to Gene Autry, tending to lean more to folk and western than Broadway and pop. In the twenty-five years it had been on (and off) the air, its ability to tap into and recognize its audience, becoming a voice for them, had made it one of the fastest growing, most popular stations in the state. Ratings were up, the big markets were taking note, and stars arriving in town for premieres at the Fox or vacationing at the Arrowhead Hot Springs Resort began tuning in and dropping by, catapulting its image, boosting its signal, and jacking up the advertising rates.

None of that was too awfully important to Dad; he didn't pay a lot of attention to signal boost or advertising rates. He paid attention to what he enjoyed, and to what the folks enjoyed listening to. He made it a habit not to get much more complicated than that. Paying attention to signal strength and demographics was too much like real work. And he simply didn't view what he was doing as work. He couldn't be having this much fun if it was work.

Ernie Ford was never known for having a passion to succeed. He worked for the reasons most of us tell ourselves we're working—to finance what we really want to do with our lives, which usually amounts to . . . not working anymore. He didn't have that broad of an agenda. In fact, he didn't have any agenda—beyond spinning a few records during the week and lying around during the weekend—unless the fish were biting somewhere or there was a new picture in town to take Mom to. He was not ambitious, wasn't driven, and didn't feel the need—then—to start socking away dough for the future. The future was Saturday and Sunday, and that was about as far ahead as he cared to look. He was operating on EFST: Ernest Ford Standard Time. The war was over, he was having a ball, and he was making sixty-five dollars a week. No need to get excited. Relax. Don't overdo it. Everything in moderation. Take your time. We'll get there tomorrow.

All of this infuriated Betty Ford to no end. She was practical. She was driven. She was trying to start some kind of a nest egg. She was climbing the walls living with her parents, and she was going nuts trying to raise a twenty-seven-year-old husband—a husband who thought sixty-five bucks a week for a job in radio was like a ticket on the U.S. Gravy Train.

It was a difference in philosophies that would mark their lives, and define their relationship for the next forty-three years.

But as much fun as Dad was having on the air, a staff announcer's afternoon shift—even in the high-pressure, fast-lane world of 1946 San Bernardino—could make the leap from fun to boring in about the time it took to play a Spade Cooley record. The job required massive intravenous feedings of black coffee, a wholesale account with the local Lucky Strike distributor, an ego matched by an unabashed desire to entertain people, and (perhaps most important) an acute need to entertain yourself—something Ernie Ford never had any problem doing.

To break the tedium, he reinvented himself, splitting his personality in the process, creating a character that would immediately resonate with his audience and become an alter ego he would be associated with for the rest of his career. Like Edgar Bergen's Charlie McCarthy, it was a character that would become like his second skin, a twin that had somehow grown out of him.

But the character was only one part of a larger concept; one borne out of several ideas, all inherently integral to the medium of radio in 1946. It was a medium of imagination, a theater of the mind, that allowed for a spontaneity television would be hard-pressed to imitate. There were, to be sure, scores of tautly scripted and tightly timed dramatic serials. But for the biggest part, there was a freedom and an intimacy that existed on the air that lured, hooked, and magnetized listeners.

Although 78's remained the primary source of the music programmed and played on radio, live entertainment was an important staple. Stations all over the country featured shows that put the spotlight—figuratively—on local and regional talent: singers, musicians, bands, soloists, comedians, and actors. Occasionally somebody would book a juggler, or a magician, on a show without an audience. Careers were made and lost overnight. *"He's putting his hand into the hat. Now he's waving his magic wand, and . . . yes! Here it comes! He's pulled a rabbit right out of the hat, folks!"*

I told you . . . it was a medium of the imagination.

Drawing on that concept, Dad created not only a character but an entire illusion. He stopped being Ernest Ford and became Tennessee Ernie, proprietor of the Bar Nothing Ranch, where you could come in for a spell, eat some home-cooked food, and listen to the latest and greatest on the Hit Parade.

For thirty minutes every day, his alter ego took the mic; a loud, obnoxious, crazed hillbilly from Tennessee who turned the stolid afternoon shift on KFXM on its ear and into an all-out bunkhouse party. Adding his own props and sound effects, he expanded on the illusion with cowbells and livestock sounds to punctuate the craziness. And in a moment he couldn't have known would be looked back on as inspired, he did something that would change his career and his life. He turned his mic on during one afternoon's show and sang along with the records he played. Not all of them, of course; only the songs he knew and could lend harmony to.

Like the station *Bar Nothing Ranch* was broadcast from, Dad and his alter ego knew his audience. He identified with them and related to their calloused, sweat-of-the-brow lives. They were people much like Betty's family, hardworking folks who'd been part of the vast numbers of migrants who'd fled Oklahoma, Kansas, or points farther east, looking for but never finding the Golden State that beckoned to them from postcards and billboards.

In the late 1930s entire communities formed throughout the Southern California valleys; camps swelling with families who'd left everything believing that a land of plenty awaited them. Driving from San Bernardino to Ojai, you motored past the outskirts of those camps, past smaller sites marked by makeshift lean-tos or tents, past foremen's lines, where the men, women, and children who were old enough waited for the chance to work the fields.

They were the second great wave of American refugees. In 1937 their faces, lives, and deaths were etched forever into the American psyche through the lens of photographer Dorothea Lange, who was commissioned by the Farm Services Agency to chronicle their plight. Her powerful images in turn inspired Steinbeck to pen his classic *Grapes of Wrath*.

By '46, many of those sprawling camps had thinned. And although migratory labor was still a vital subindustry, the postwar boom offered the immigrants from the plains a far more stable environment for finding regular work and raising their families.

In Southern California's Inland Empire, the fields in which many of those families sought a day's wages were noted for a variety of crops. Of those crops, one in particular grew abundantly, didn't require the vast reservoirs of watering that other crops did, and didn't impale your fingers when you threshed the rows. It grew low to the ground, lush and green, and when it was ripe, the pods stretched to the bursting point; the seams taut and rich. A hungry worker could spread a ripe husk and eat a handful of the sweet things inside without getting sick and without getting caught. It grew best along coastal routes, near towns like Nipomo, where Dorothea Lange photographed her famous "Migrant Mother" portrait in 1937, and its abundance required massive labor forces of field hands, whose seasonal camps hearkened back to the camps of the thirties. Great herds of the workers would appear almost overnight, flood the fields during the months of the growing season, and then move on, blown by the dust and winds of need. They worked long hours, lived on barely passable wages, and spent their free time lost in the ethereal world of the radio.

The crop was a basic green garden-variety vegetable, and the workers were simply called pea pickers.

Their prevalence in the valleys, especially during the season, made them a part of the daily press, of the conversations among business leaders, gas station attendants, and reporters. They became objects of derision and ridicule, eventually making the name attached to them and what they did, "pea pickers," synonymous with an entire class of people—a substratum of the working poor not deserving of even the most common respect.

As a man, and as an entertainer, Dad recognized these people; he knew these people and spoke to them directly. Before long, he was opening every *Bar Nothing Ranch* broadcast with a welcome to "all you pea pickers." It became for him as much a part of the show as the skits, music, and sound effects, and would evolve into an integral part of his professional signature, but not for the reasons the world was led to believe.

For nearly thirty years the press and fans believed "pea pickers" was a reference to his life growing up in Tennessee, to a life they mistakenly assumed was spent among unschooled hillbillies who lived in a shack on the edge of a pea patch that grew next to the still in back of the outhouse. Nothing angered me more. It angered me as a boy, and it continues to vex me today. It was a myth that dogged him for much of his life and nearly all his career, perpetuated by his willingness—long after the *Bar Nothing Ranch* and *Hometown Jamboree* days—to be photographed in bib overalls and a straw hat, with a chaff of hay between his teeth. It was a myth that clung to him like a wet cloak.

The truth is, Ernie Ford wasn't raised by, around, or anywhere near hillbillies. Nor was he cut from that cloth.

Google "pea pickers," and you'll find the first ten references have nothing to do with Ernie Ford. Wikipedia defines the term with this entry:

> A Pea-picker is a derogatory reference to poor, migrant workers during the Great Depression. These people were unskilled, poorly educated workers, suitable only for menial tasks, such as harvesting crops, and, as such, received poor wages for working long hours under dreadful conditions. Many of these people were photographed by Dorothea Lange.
>
> The term "Pea picker" is used to distinguish a group as a lower social class from some other similar group, such as the "Pea-picking" Smiths, as opposed to the "Respectable" Smiths.
>
> Temporary communities of Pea-pickers are called Pea Picker Camps and farms that employed them were Pea-picker farms.

Ernie Ford was never a pea picker, never a laborer, never a hillbilly. But he was a man who recognized the innate dignity of those people, and an entertainer who saw the wisdom and value of brightening their lives.

By appealing to them as his core audience, he gave them an identity that brought pride and place to a class of people and made it okay for anyone to be a pea picker.

Ernie Ford: Early, Unsung Social Activist.

Bar Nothing Ranch came to a close every day at noon, and as perfunctorily as he'd brought Tennessee Ernie out, he put him away. In his place was Ernest Jennings Ford, erudite man of the airwaves, respectable voice of reason and good taste, "bringing you the up-to-the-minute midday news from the studios of KFXM, high atop the beautiful California Hotel in downtown San Bernardino."

The change was so abrupt, the difference in the two personalities so radically different, only a few insiders knew it was the same person. *Bar Nothing Ranch* became an instant hit, and a fictitious character became a star.

Rather than pull the curtain back, Dad chose for some time to continue the charade, keeping his two selves separated. That decision would serve to magnify the popularity of one but hamper the attempts he made to gain acceptance as a serious, legitimate singer. He wanted that acceptance; he'd studied classical voice at the Cincinnati Conservatory to prepare for that acceptance. He was making a living doing radio, but he was just twenty-eight and already feeling the constriction of typecasting—with a character *he* created. In one of the first—and last—real efforts he made to distance himself from that character, he booked himself to appear at the Harmony Under the Moon outdoor music series, produced each summer in the little town of Colton, eight miles west of San Bernardino. How far he was willing to go to establish his legitimate self is immediately evident from the Friday, August 29, 1947, clipping:

> Featured artist will be E. Jennings Ford, dramatic bass baritone, who will present a program of classical numbers. Accompanist will be Mrs. Gertrude Engle, pianist. Included in Mr. Ford's program will be "Invictus" (Huhn); "Two Grenadiers" (Schumann); "O Sublime, Sweet Evening Star" (Wagner); "Hear Me, Ye Winds and Waves" (Handel); "Sylvia" (Speaks); "Song of the Open Road" (Malotte); and "On the Road to Mandalay" (Speaks).

In seeking that acceptance as a serious, classical singer, he literally had to create another character: E. Jennings Ford, eliminating the Ernest, so he would not be recognized by his day-job handle on KFXM.

Unfortunately, or fortunately—I'm not sure which—one of his coworkers at the station tipped the Harmony Park Ladies' Auxiliary League, and his secret identity was exposed. They booked him, but he had to promise he'd bring out Tennessee Ernie for the second half. Turned out they liked his classical stuff, but they were all closet pea pickers. Jesus, he couldn't win.

Not deterred, Dad kept the illusion up, the split of the two personalities so complete, so successful, that it captivated even the most jaded of professionals in the business. Among that group was one Loyal King, an impresario of the California radio scene and owner of Pasadena's KXLA—one of Southern California's most powerful and popular stations.

Loyal King made a habit of listening to the competition on the dial regularly. He was a shrewd and competitive dealmaker who was known to have broken some of Southern California's biggest acts, bankrolling more than one. He was big, flamboyant, loud, and dressed like a wardrobe stand-in from the westerns lot at Republic Pictures.

Driving through Rancho Cucamonga on his way to Palm Springs one afternoon, he tuned in KFXM as *Bar Nothing Ranch* was just getting under way. The show and its over-the-top host held his attention from Fontana to Redlands, where the signal began to fade in and out.

Intrigued, he jumped in his Cadillac the next day to try to pick up the signal again. Between Beaumont and Calimesa, KFXM came in strong, and at 11:30 sharp, *Bar Nothing Ranch* was on the air. King was hooked. As he had the day before, he listened to the entire show, captivated, until the midday announcer came on at noon to do the news. Pleasant-voiced guy, Ernest Jennings Ford, but King wanted to talk to this guy Tennessee Ernie, and he wanted to talk to him now. He'd been looking high and low on the dial for somebody with that kind of energy, and now that he was sure he'd found him, he just had to make him an offer he couldn't refuse. And nobody refused Loyal King.

Several days later King met with Dad, learned he was also Ernest Jennings Ford, voice of sophistication, was sufficiently more impressed because he'd been fooled, and offered him a fifteen-dollar-a-week raise to come to KXLA. Eighty-five dollars a week. Pasadena. The big(ger) time.

Unfortunately, Dad was forced to turn down King's offer. Ten days earlier, sensing that a change in the station's ownership was numbering his days there, Dad had resigned from KFXM and taken a job in Reno as chief announcer at KOH. It was less money than King was offering, but the wilds of the untamed West in Nevada appealed to him, and it seemed on the surface that filling the position of chief announcer was the right step up.

Wrong.

Dad and Mom lasted all of six months in Nevada, living in a rooming house with an Italian family of nine, none of whom seemed to have any trouble falling asleep in fully lit bedrooms, bathed in the glare of neon from the casinos next door. Mrs. Nannini's ravioli was about as wild and untamed as things got, unless you counted fighting her children for the bathroom in the morning.

From the moment they arrived, they knew they'd made a bad

decision; something Mom took every opportunity to remind her husband. Yes, they were in love. Yes, they were young. Yes, it was kind of an adventure. No . . . it wasn't. They were miserable. Well . . . Mom was miserable, and she wasn't about to be miserable all by herself. They'd sold everything they could to finance the move, they were living in a rooming house, for God's sake, she didn't give a damn about the Wild West, Ford was making nothing (to speak of), and though pleasant enough as a family, the thought of an entire winter with Filaccina Nannini and her family drove them both into gullies of depression, and drove Mom to Mrs. Nannini's cooking wine.

There are volumes of press devoted to Dad's early career in radio, but very little was written about that half year of their lives. You could count on the occasional obligatory "where he spent six months at KOH in Reno before making his way back to Los Angeles" throwaway, but little more than that. Google any history pages for the stations he did time at, and you'll find one or two paragraphs highlighting the fact he was there. Try that with KOH, and he doesn't exist. He rarely brought it up, and when he did, all you could get out of him was how much he liked Mrs. Nannini's ravioli. It was as if he and Mom took a detour off the map for half a year and just disappeared. In fact, if I hold a portable radio to my ear, I can almost hear Rod Serling welcoming the two of them to the Twilight Zone.

The most ink given was from a fan book written in 1957 by Ted Hilgenstuhler, a stringer for TV *Life* and other fan rags that were prominent in those days. He gave the episode eight paragraphs, and one of those paragraphs is telling, revealing what I believe now to be the beginnings of a descent into depression and addiction that Betty Ford would never completely pull out of.

I realize I'd be a fool to try to reconstruct from a piece of fan press the exact time when alcoholism first wrapped its wet hands around Mom. But the imagery conveyed through that one paragraph is unsettlingly similar to her descriptions of the same period in three to four minutes of audiotape she recorded in 1988 as part of an effort to set down moments of her life she wanted to remember. Much of the tape is difficult to make out, unless you've been tutored in translating Betty Ford's speech patterns when her vocal cords had been lubricated with Smirnoff, but the memories are there. She recalled that period with distinct clarity, remembered it darkly, and forty-one years later, still held Dad accountable for the seeds of anger and loss of hope that I believe were planted and sown then.

For his part, I believe Dad did all he could in those early years to keep both their chins up; that was his nature then. And Mom did not simply slip into darkness one day in 1947 and stay there. There were many times over the years when she would laugh to the point of gagging over the craziness, unpredictability, loneliness, and happiness of their first few years together. But as the years progressed and the darkness claimed another inch of the aura of light around her, the laughter could—and would—be shut off like a spigot, and in its place would come forth a scalding stream of bitter sarcasm and derision, unlooked for, unexpected, and aimed nearly always at Dad. Her loss of happiness, her failings, the kids' lack of direction, the decline of his career . . . she laid it all at his feet. In anyone else's case, with commensurate drink in their bloodstream, the aim would have been wild, unfocused. But her attacks rarely failed to find their mark.

I know he was wounded by those salvos, and yet it was well into the fading years of their lives before I ever detected any pain in his eyes. Until he eventually tired, and sought solace on the deck of the Cutty Sark, he would simply absorb the blows, endure the darkness and embarrassment, and wait for the day to break. When it did, his love for her was never stinted, and he never revealed his wounds.

Just before Christmas the darkness in Reno began to dissipate, magnified by a western current of warm air. Actually, it was a blast of hot air, blowing through the phone. Loyal King was calling from Pasadena, and he wasn't taking no for an answer.

FOUR

MONTEREY PARK sits tucked into the southwest corner of the San Gabriel Valley, seven miles due south of Pasadena if you take a straight shot up Atlantic Boulevard to Colorado. Like the scores of small towns that sprang up from the late 1800s through the end of the 1920s, surrounding Los Angeles and urbanizing the San Gabriel, San Fernando, and Conejo Valleys, it's almost indistinguishable today from its counterparts. The greater L.A. Basin is one long, clotted suburban grid, blanketed with a network of six interstates and dotted with townships that have lost their uniqueness and identity. Take a drive from Whittier to El Monte, or West Covina to Alhambra, and try to find where one town ends and another begins. "*L.A. is a great big freeway. . . .*"

It wasn't always that way.

In 1948, Monterey Park was a quiet, suburban bedroom community, coming to the close of a second real-estate surge that began with the end of the war. Neighborhoods sprang up like mushrooms off its main arteries—Garvey and Atlantic—and the emerging postwar middle-class families snatched up houses as fast as they were built. For about fourteen grand, you could wrap your hands around a genuine piece of the two-bedroom, one-car garage, picket-fence-in-the-front American dream.

The raise Loyal King offered Dad to come to work at KXLA put him and Mom in a slightly higher and more comfortable tax bracket, but they were still shy of the credit they needed for a piece of that dream. And moving back in with Mom's folks was out of the question. Then a smallish two-bedroom came on the market just a block from the duplex they'd been renting since their escape from Reno. When Mom's aunt Emerine took up the slack, took a loan out from her own bank in San Bernardino, and turned around and loaned the money to Mom and Dad at 2 percent, the white bungalow at 430 North Florence became their first house.

Like Hollywood itself—still mourning the sunset of the Golden Age—Mom's and Dad's lives and fortunes were on the cusp of change, but neither Hollywood nor Betty and Ernie Ford had the slightest idea of how rapid and revolutionary those changes of fortune would be, and how dramatically their lives would forever be altered.

Between 1948 and 1954 Dad did five years as a staff announcer at KXLA, headed the cast of the groundbreaking variety show *Hometown Jamboree* for five years, signed with Capitol Records in 1949, hosted a national radio series for ABC for two years, signed for a coast-to-coast radio series for CBS for two years, became the first Capitol act to headline the London Palladium, recorded three number one singles, guest-starred in the first two-part *I Love Lucy* episode ever filmed, taped 260 live fifteen-minute radio shows for national syndication, played more than seven hundred live dates in clubs from the Copa to the Thunderbird, became the first guest host for NBC's *Kollege of Musical Knowledge*, and signed with the network for his own daily series, to begin in January 1955.

In seven short, blistering, blurred years, he went from being a locally known DJ in Pasadena to being one of the most popular entertainers on two continents. Queen Elizabeth told the *Daily Mail* he was her favorite singer, Capitol's Lee Gillette credited him with the creation of rockabilly, and jazz virtuoso Stan Kenton told the L.A. *Times* he might be "the best vocalist in pop music today."

He would not record "Sixteen Tons" until September of '55, and *The Ford Show* would not debut on NBC until October of '56. And yet, in the seven years preceding those events, he was catapulted from relative obscurity to blinding fame. By January 1955, he was already talking quietly—sparsely—of giving it up; of making enough money to flee. The ride had been too fast, the ascent too dizzying, the work too demanding. And for Betty, the lights had become too bright. They shone everywhere, lighting every corner, every room, illuminating every private moment; a part of their lives rapidly disappearing. Where the darkness of the war and the uncertainty of their lives compelled her to seek and cling to the bright outlook that the man she married always seemed to have, she was now seeking quiet corners of shadow, removed from the lights that had invaded their simple lives.

Sanity in those early years—for Dad, anyway—rested largely in the hands of two men he entrusted with his career and, to a large extent, his life. But both would become far more important and integral to our lives as a family than to Ernie Ford alone. Indeed, they would become nothing less than members of our family.

Cliffie Stone is credited with the distinction of having discovered Dad; a credit he was never shy about claiming. When they met on Dad's first day at KXLA, Stone was already a major player in the area, having carved out an enviable career for himself on multiple fronts. History would regard him as one of the singularly most important people in the California music scene for more than thirty years.

He was one of western swing's top bandleaders and arrangers, and one of the architects of the California western-jazz sound of the late 1940s and early 1950s. He was involved in some way on virtually every record Capitol recorded at its Melrose Avenue studios in Hollywood from 1946 through the late 1950s, and worked with all the biggest acts of the day—everybody from Spade Cooley to Frank Sinatra, from jazz guitarist Jimmy Bryant and orchestra leader Billy May to Helen Forrest and the Whiting Sisters. He was the producer and creator of *Hometown Jamboree*, the KXLA show that followed Dad's program, and would become the first variety show of its kind to go from radio to television in Southern California. In his spare time, he became one of the most powerful—and most trusted—music publishers in the business. His catalogs under Century and Central Songs, LTD, contained standards that are still being recorded today. It was an unprecedented career. Anybody who was anybody knew Cliffie Stone, and many owed him *their* careers. He was about as close to being a legend as you can get.

* * *

Unlike KFXM, there were three studios at KXLA; the interior windows of the two smaller control booths overlooking a larger third studio on the floor below. From his control board on the second floor, Dad had a nosebleed seat every day at 11:30 when Cliffie would bring his scaled-down band up to the mics and broadcast *Hometown Jamboree* from 11:30 till 12:30.

It's probably fair to say that Dad was more familiar with Stone than Stone was with Dad; Cliffie's reputation as a musician, writer, recording artist, A and R man, and radio personality well preceded his arrival anywhere. He had released a number of regionally popular singles on Capitol, which Dad regularly included in his playlist on his own morning show, *Bar Nothing Ranch*.

In fact, hearing Dad play those records was what prompted Stone to come to the studio early that day of Dad's first shift; primarily because they weren't the same records he'd remembered cutting. The needle hit the groove, the first notes jumped off the speaker, and in the middle of the song, somebody else started singing harmony. Then they sang a lead verse over the guitar break; neither of which was part of the session Cliffie'd produced. Halfway expecting to find this new DJ playing counterfeits, Cliffie arrived at the station to find Dad in studio three—doing the same thing with virtually everybody else's records: turning his mic on, potting it down to about a four setting, and, just off-line from the microphone's grille, singing with the track . . . on the air. And the damnedest thing about it was, Cliffie would recall many years later, it sounded a hell of a lot better than many of the originals.

Cliffie Stone was a radio warhorse, a veteran of the broadcast trenches since 1937. He thought he'd seen and heard everything. He worked in the same studios as Jim Hawthorne, for God's sake, the hugely popular L.A. announcer history would credit with creating talk radio; a guy most people thought bordered on being clinically insane. But here was something totally off the radar; a guy who was completely changing the way people were hearing what was on the radio. He was out there, with this *Bar Nothing Ranch* thing, for sure, and the show was a novelty hit . . . but what began to hold Stone's attention was Ford's voice.

"There was a dynamics in your dad's range I couldn't put my finger on," he told me one afternoon late in 1989. "He was doing harmony lines all over these western and pop tunes; everybody from Jimmy Wakely to Bob Wills and Bing Crosby. Hell, he was singing circles around Peggy Lee—third and fifth parts that no damn disc jockey had any business knowing how to sing—unless he was trained, you know. From what he was doing on that little show on KXLA, I didn't have any idea what he was capable of. . . ."

That changed one afternoon when Stone invited Dad to come downstairs to studio one and sit in with his quartet for a few numbers on the air. "He had a natural instinct for harmony," he told me. "There wasn't a damned thing he couldn't sing. And it was just effortless for him—like talking. He sat in with the group for three shows and I asked him to join the cast. It was that easy. And I never looked back."

From that first meeting in the Pasadena studios of KXLA, Cliffie and Dad were virtually inseparable. The bond between them was instant, symbiotic, and immediately evident to those around them. Artistically and musically, their tastes were almost identical, and mutually eclectic. If they'd had the broadcasting freedom, they'd have been following a Sons of the Pioneers record with a Benny Goodman side. The fact that they were broadcasting to a largely western music audience, more familiar with Bob Wills than the Mills Brothers, didn't dampen their love for either.

While their friendship would be the primary force that guided their lives for the next forty years, Cliffie's antennae as a producer and A and R man for Capitol were always up in those postwar years—one side set to broadcast, the other aerial set to receive; always scanning for unsigned talent—a new player, a new picker, a new voice. And with each turn at the mic, each informal jam at the piano, each exchange of notes, Cliffie became more convinced of Dad's potential; not just as a singer, but as a complete entertainer. In mere months, he was the most talked about new cast member of *Hometown*, moving from the quartet to solos, to comedy routines that Cliffie began writing for him; from guest, to guest star, to headliner.

Like Dad, Cliffie was keenly, almost presciently aware of who his audience was, where they were from, and what appealed to them. He was completely focused on what worked and what didn't, whether onstage or on the air. And it was clear to him that Ernie Ford worked. "They completely related to Ford," he said in one article. "The people he entertained felt from the beginning that he was one of them—not removed from them. He sang *for* the people, not to them."

Although he still sought acceptance as a serious singer, Dad found in *Hometown Jamboree* the venue for both his personae. Behind the mic and, later, in front of the camera when the show went to television, Tennessee Ernie melded with E. Jennings Ford, synergistically joining the two personalities. After two years of struggling to find a way to keep them separate, he'd found a way to make them both work together, yet independent of each other.

In Cliffie Stone he'd found someone who heard and saw both; who recognized the appeal one had to the current audience, but the potential of the other to reach audiences far beyond KXLA and the Southern California basin.

But apart from all that, Dad had found something much more in Cliffie Stone, something more important than what Cliffie would come to represent professionally, musically, and artistically in his life. More important than the guidance he would give him as a producer or the success he leveraged as his first manager, Dad found a touchstone, a counterpart, a confederate.

He'd found a brother. The wise, patient, loving older brother he'd never known in Stanley Haskell Ford, born just one month removed from Stone. A brother in whom bitter seeds of jealousy had never grown, believing he'd been displaced by the birth of Maude and Clarence's second child—a child who seemed gifted with unending good fortune.

In Cliffie Stone, Dad had found the brother he'd lost forever to shell shock somewhere in the waters of the Pacific, and then to resentment somewhere deep beneath the surface of his own troubled waters, the brother who'd begun a long, slow descent into a darkness from which he would never return and into which Ernest Jennings Ford never reached his hand, and never ventured.

For nine years, Cliffie Stone managed, produced, guided, piloted, and engineered the career and success of Ernie Ford. His insight, talent, instinct, and faith were the primary factors that propelled what many would call one of the most phenomenal and unprecedented success stories in the business. For many years that followed, he would remain a powerful force of good in Dad's career and life, but those first nine years were the years that made the difference. They were the years that established him, made him, and vaulted him among Hollywood's elite.

From 1949 to 1957, every aspect of that career was implemented and overseen by Stone, from Dad's biggest successes in radio to his stunning accomplishments as a recording artist, as well as his virtual overnight claim of television stardom. Together, they literally cut the edge and rode the crest of the Second Golden Age of Hollywood.

It is impossible for me to categorize, compartmentalize, quantify, or overstate the impact that he had on Dad, both as an entertainer and as a friend. But the rigors and demands that Ernie Ford's success placed on Stone dramatically altered the path of his own career, and it would never regain the momentum or direction that he'd given to Dad's. By the end of 1956 the pace was so frenetic, so demanding, Stone knew that to remain effective, he needed to stay focused on the two areas in which he was most qualified and most proficient—the music and the production. He desperately needed someone to take up the slack. Someone he could trust—more important, someone Dad could trust. And like the lore surrounding all great masters of their craft, an apprentice labored in the wings. In this case, literally.

By 1957, Ernie Ford the Act had become Ernie Ford the Small Industry. The family companies—BetFord Corporation and TEF Inc.— employed a board of directors, and teams of accountants and lawyers on retainer. One company issued salaries and covered the bottom lines on directors, producers, and writers. The other, choreographers, conductors, and arrangers.

When the responsibilities of day-to-day management of the man became the minute-by-minute management of an enterprise and a family, Stone handed the duties to a man who had become indispensable to both him and Dad, from *Hometown*'s earliest television days at the El Monte Legion Stadium in 1949. His name was James Loakes, and like the man from whom he learned his craft, he would give up nearly everything in his own life, and devote himself and his life to Ernie Ford, his lovely wife, Betty, and their two sons, Buck and Brion.

Jim Loakes was not a lawyer, not an accountant, not an agent, and I'm confident in saying that I'm sure he never had any desire to be and didn't need to be any of those things, but he nevertheless possessed the instinctive skills of each. You did not argue a case with Loakes, you did not misplace so much as one decimal point on a royalty statement, and you did not take advantage of Ernie Ford—whether it be his time, his talent, or his family. Those skills made him more than merely indispensable to the business; he was vital to Dad's sanity and, on more occasions than this book could list, crucial to our family's stability. He would one day be counted among a near-mythical group of now-extinct show-business phenomena: the personal manager. He would be compared to and talked about in the same breath as Elvis's Colonel Tom Parker and Dylan's Albert Grossman. Over the forty-six years he devoted to Dad and our family, he would become Dad's closest confidant, his most trusted aide-de-camp, my surrogate older brother, Mom's surrogate older son, and the photographic chronicler of our family. For nearly half a century, he was attached to Ernie Ford at the molecular level. When Dad died, I believe something cellular died in Jim. He'd lost more than his employer of forty-six years. He'd lost his best and closest friend.

I have no business, really, directing the day-to-day operations of our family company today. The task should have been delegated to someone else. But as events unfolded and played out after Dad's death, the office of eldest son could not have been delegated to someone else, and the responsibilities that came with that office fell to me.

In many ways, I have apprenticed under Jim Loakes in much the same way he did under Cliffie Stone. Every instinct I have for any aspect of this business, I learned—I absorbed—from him. Any knowledge I have about the half-century-long career I'm charged with managing, I gleaned from him. Even today, he remains possessed of the most singularly intact photographic recall of any human being alive on the planet—at least in Palm Springs. There isn't a damned thing he can't pull up from the memory banks when you need it. Ask him what the track order was on Dad's fifth album, and make sure you have a pen in your hand, because you'll start writing as soon as the question has left your lips. Ask him what color socks Dad was wearing on the night Liberace made his first guest appearance on *The Ford Show*. If he doesn't know, he'll put you on hold while he checks his files.

I've hesitated to ply him too regularly in writing this memoir, for fear I'd have to change the title to *Jim Loakes Remembers Every God-damned Thing About Ernie and His Lovely Wife, Betty*.

These few paragraphs do not do Jim the justice, or give him the honor, he deserves from our family, and the unceremonious, unfair release he was given by Dad's second wife in the months before Dad died compounded that unfairness with a grave injustice, one he never acknowledged having been done to him and one that I hope this book has some part in healing.

Ⓕ

FIV

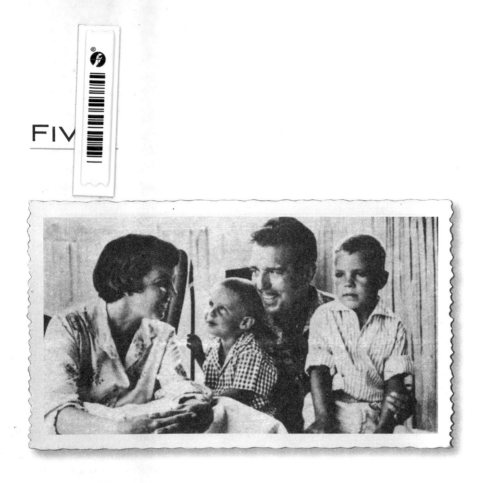

I WAS BORN JANUARY 6, 1950, at St. Joseph's Hospital in San Gabriel, California—seven years and four months after Mom and Dad were married in San Bernardino, a little prenatal fact Mom went to great pains to remind me of throughout my youth. "We waited seven and a half years to have you, buster. Do what you're told."

My given name is Jeffrey Buckner Ford, but before I'd celebrated my third year, the *ner* was all but dropped from my middle name, and most people just called me Buck for most of the rest of my life. Mom was not altogether happy about that. Bucking the trend (pun intended), she continued to call me Jeff, Little Jeff, or Jeffrey, for some time. But it did not last. Eventually even she relented.

Dropping the "ner" was mostly Dad's idea. He originally wanted to name their first, if the baby turned out to be a boy, Buck, after his good friend and hunting partner, Buck Sarten. Mom did not like Mr. Sarten. He was big, ungainly, unkempt, used foul language, and smelled like a cross between gun oil and cheap whiskey—which was natural, because he was usually awash in both. Dad thought of him as a man's man. Buck was a man's man's name. Buckner had an air of . . . something else.

Mr. Sarten shot himself in the ass one year at the annual deer hunt Dad attended just outside Price, Utah. He was out solo, on a ridge above camp, just him, his deer rifle, a .22 pistol he carried in a holster, and a pint of Old Charter. Everything a real man needed in the wild.

According to the legend, Mr. Sarten had removed his pistol from the holster before ankling his pants in order to answer a particular call. Upon concluding his business, he did what many men do after a meeting; he had a drink. And then he holstered his pistol. However, as he slid the gun into the sheath, the hammer caught on his belt loop, and snapped closed, striking the firing pin. That action discharged a slim .22 round at close range directly into Mr. Sarten's right buttock.

As Dad would recall many times in later years, the sound that came from the timbered ridge above the camp immediately following the report of the pistol was difficult to identify at first. Part human, part enraged animal, it sounded like. Only when Mr. Sarten came bellowing down the hill, through the scrub pine and sagebrush into camp, did they realize the sound they'd heard had been made by Mr. Sarten himself.

That sight and sound alone, coupled with the men's eventual knowledge of the events that preceded Mr. Sarten's injury, might have qualified the story as legendary, but the proceedings that followed gave the story a quality and memorability that etched that day indelibly into the mind of each man in attendance for the rest of his natural life.

According to Sharpe Bryner, wizened Utah rancher and patriarch of the family of the same surname, Mr. Sarten was in some danger, albeit not the life-threatening kind. The bullet, it seemed, had entered Mr. Sarten's buttock at a downward angle, and due to the prodigious size of the flank, and the goodly amount of fat layering it, did not travel far, but lodged about one-inch just under the surface.

"You could feel it, plain," Sharpe remembered. "No bigger than a little rock, but you could feel it."

Feeling it, of course, meant that one had to place a portion of one's hand on a portion of Mr. Sarten's exposed heinie. Not a job for the squeamish. And while the layering of suet insulating Mr. Sarten's posterior had all but eliminated the likelihood of any dangerous loss of blood, a purplish bruise of some size was beginning to form around the entry wound, and infection was becoming an issue; an issue magnified by the fact that the hunters were a good half-day's trip from Price and any medical facility.

It was clear to Sharpe and his younger brother, Holly, that emergency field surgery was in order.

"That round had to come out, plain," he said. "And we needed to get in there soon, while I could still feel it, before the swellin' come up too big."

A quick inventory was made. Anesthesia: check. There was a fifth of Cutty in the Plymouth. Surgical tool: check. Holly's skinning knife was rumored to be sharp enough to cut deer bone. Suture: check. Sharpe always carried his tackle box, and at least two rolls of fishing line. Ten-pound test—the trout were good-sized in that part of Utah.

Gingerly, Dad and the two brothers moved Mr. Sarten to the back of the Chevy paneled station wagon, where sleeping bags had been quickly piled to provide the patient with as much comfort as he deserved. Reclining on his left side to diminish the pain and speed of swelling, and under the stern and welcomed direction of Mr. Bryner, Mr. Sarten began the process of self-administering the anesthesia, his mouth glued to the bottle of Cutty, and his eyes glued on Holly as he honed his skinning knife, occasionally wiping the blade down with a whiskey-soaked bandanna.

In roughly half an hour, Mr. Sarten had finished roughly half the bottle, and, though known in questionable circles for an ability to hold his liquor, began to have some noticeable difficulty speaking clearly and holding his head up.

When his consciousness finally appeared to lapse, Dad, Sharpe, and Holly carefully unbuckled Mr. Sarten's pants, rolled him to his stomach, and, as Dad remembered, drew straws to see who would pull the britches down. In retrospect, this task may seem to the reader as being relatively tame. However, as the Bryner brothers and Dad recalled, the significant amount of scotch taken in by Mr. Sarten, coupled with the camp's breakfast that morning, had created the near-perfect conditions for internal gas, which was emanating from Mr. Sarten with remarkable force and, like a geyser in Yellowstone, when least expected.

Flatulence notwithstanding, the surgery was performed, the round removed, the wound cleansed and sewn shut. Surrounding and walling in his body with the camp's gear, Dad and the Bryner brothers climbed in the woody, and by dark they were in Price, watching proudly as orderlies trundled their semiconscious, still-flatulent patient into the clinic.

Mr. Sarten reportedly kept the expended .22 round wrapped in Sharp's whiskey-soaked bandanna as a memento. It was found in an empty can of snuff among the wreckage and blood some three years later, when he killed himself and his only son, Gary, by driving off a cliff while in a high-speed chase with the Bakersfield police and the California Highway Patrol. Dad, I believe, was thunderstruck. Mom, I believe, felt vindicated.

Dad was on the road when I was born. Actually, that's not altogether true. He was in the air when I was born, somewhere over Oklahoma, or Ohio—no one is really sure—on his way to Nashville for the CBS radio show *Sunday Down South* and to do his first guest appearance on the *Grand Ole Opry*.

By that time he'd been with Capitol for a few weeks more than a year, and while he wasn't burning down the house, sales were more than respectable. The label had renewed his contract just a few weeks earlier, mainly on the strength of "Anticipation Blues," a funky number he'd written with Cliffie Stone, detailing the travails and woes of Mom's pregnancy with me—from a man's point of view, of course. It was just loopy enough that radio was giving it strong play from Chicago to Miami and points west, putting him—and now yours truly—on the charts. Him, of course, for the second time, after "Mule Train" hit number one late in 1949.

Being in the air and all, over Oswego or wherever, he had no clue that Mom was on her way to St. Joseph's in San Gabriel, water breaking in the backseat of our next-door neighbor's Chevy, with Cleo behind the wheel, tearing breakneck through Monterey Park, Mom holding on to the armrest, trying gamely to keep herself from rolling onto the floorboard as Cleo rounded corners, pedal to the metal and sucking Pall Malls down like they were made out of hollow paper.

I should mention here that, just before she was manhandled into the backseat of Cleo Bradley's four-door, Mom had the presence of mind to calmly call Cliffie Stone so someone would get in touch with Dad, who was in the air over Oregon, or Omaha, or someplace.

Always conscious of the value of a great publicity gimmick when he saw it—or, in this case, heard it—Cliffie got on the horn right away with Capitol's Lee Gillette, Dad's producer at that time. Almost immediately, the Capitol publicity department swung into high gear and into the fast lane. So fast, when Dad landed at Berry Field in Nashville just before dark later that day, Frank Jones, the Capitol man in Nashville, handed him a telegram from the home office announcing my arrival, the second he stepped off the DC-9.

My younger and only brother, Brion—christened Brion Leonard Fabian Ford—was born September 3, 1952. As was the case with my delivery, Dad was on the road again. Literally on the road, as opposed to in the air. Manic fame was still three years away, but three hit singles, his growing popularity as a radio star, and heightened visibility on the *Hometown Jamboree* television show had already earned him more than a hundred club and theater dates a year, and a Command Performance at the London Palladium scheduled for April the following year. When he wasn't on the road, he was in the Capitol studios, in the booth at KXLA, writing with Cliffie, rehearsing with the band, or doing *Hometown*.

In those months and weeks he was absent, Mom relied heavily on her organizational skills to keep the house up, regularly on the neighbors for companionship, grudgingly on her mother, Jesse, for maternal advice, and habitually on a slow, but steadily increasing regimen of Gilbey's. She was in her gin period then—martinis mainly. Her appreciation for vodka developed as a gradual, acquired taste—not coming to full fruition for some years.

From her youngest days, Betty Ford prided herself largely on her sense of self-reliance and self-sufficiency. In the first years of marriage, that skill became a need, a survival mechanism, operating on overdrive in the face of war and the uncertainty of the future that lay ahead. When the war ended, Mom and Dad's life together took on a sense of benign adventure, heretofore-unseen vistas opening up before their eyes. Granted, one of those vistas led them to the Nanninis' boardinghouse in Reno, but we won't go there again.

Returning to the coast brought a renewed hope, better money, and needed grounding. When she became pregnant with me in March 1949, all the positives were on the plate. Life, while perhaps not good, was definitely better. It hadn't taken the turns she'd envisioned for herself, but it was good nonetheless. This need to rely on the kindness of others, however, was contrary to her sensibilities, and it irritated her. She didn't like it, but she had little choice.

Breaking the tedium and uncertainty of the life she was coming to grips with, she joined Cliffie's wife, Dorothy (her new best friend and soul mate), and accompanied Dad on a few road dates, including his sold-out two weeks at the Thunderbird in Vegas opposite Irene Ryan— the first date with Cliffie in his official role of manager. She and Dorothy tried to make it to the Legion Stadium in El Monte every weekend for *Hometown's* broadcast on KCOP and the dance afterward, but as she grew closer to term, partying became a chore. Moving from the couch to the damned car became a chore. "All I gave a shit about was what was in the fridge, and when your father would come home so I could complain to somebody besides Cleo, Dorothy, and your grandmother. Your father would never say so, but I was a grade-A bitch."

So she dreamed little dreams to take the place of the big dreams she'd set aside. After this baby, she'd slim down a little, have the chance to get a little closer to Ernie, become a little more involved in his career, maybe travel a little more with him. Maybe worry and bitch a little less.

Then, somewhere near my second birthday, after shepherding me through my colicky phase, my introduction to teething, her mother's insufferable lessons in child-rearing and all those other wonderful moments that make parents of even the toughest fiber strongly consider the finer points associated with sterilization, adoption, and matricide—about the time I entered the terrible twos, she discovered she was pregnant again.

Brion was a small baby who, in the weeks immediately after his birth, looked more like an old man than a child. In the earliest photos I have of him, his eyes seemed out of proportion with the structure of his face. Big, ovaloid, and penetrating, they could have been prestylistic studies for Margaret and Walter Keane's famous doe-eyed portraits of their daughters. Like a wizened, shrunken old Nepalese, eyes holding the wisdom of the ages, he sits partially cradled in the crook of Mom's arm, seemingly at peace with the world. Who could have known, in those early, infantine months, save for perhaps Mom, who was given advance notice in utero, that underneath that deceptive, outwardly placid, monkish demeanor slept a human dynamo, storing, readying, and priming a physical energy that would soon test all of us; Mom, Dad, Jim Loakes, me—hell, everybody. An energy that none of us seemed capable of containing, harnessing, or channeling. An energy that earned him a familiarity with Saint Joe's emergency room far too early in life. An energy that would drain the natural resources of patience one would expect in even the most even-tempered of parents or siblings. An energy that no retribution, however severe—threatened or real—seemed sufficient to counteract. Although "hyperactive" was the clinical term for the condition he was diagnosed with early on, it seems, in retrospect, too tame a description for Brion's first twelve years. He was cyclonic; he was indefatigable. He was nuclear.

When he was three, he showed the first signs of having inherited a predisposition for controlled substances as he developed a taste for baby aspirin, which he acquired following a game of trampoline in our bedroom late one afternoon.

In the fifties and sixties, trampolines were huge deals. Thousands upon thousands of families had them, their ubiquitous popularity exceeded only by the all-American swimming pool. More fortunate kids had both, one usually adjacent to the other, so you could practice flipping from the trampoline to the pool; which we used to do at Bill Thetford's place when we moved to North Hollywood, until Mom got wind of it and put the kibosh on the fun.

Trampolines seemed innocent enough, but of course, kids didn't pay attention to the reports of rising instances of cranial injuries and broken limbs that began circulating. This was long before the invention of the safety-net walls that are now almost required with assembly. This was during the time of the trampoline parks; asphalt lots pocked with rectangular pits six to eight feet deep, each with a trampoline anchored around the perimeter, flush with the surface of the lot. You didn't need to climb up on and into the trampoline; you simply stepped right onto its surface. With equal parts skill and luck, one could bounce away for the fifteen-minute minimum without careening off to one side or the other and splitting one's head open on the blacktop. Those were the days.

At any rate, Mom refused to even consider the thought of a trampoline, which left two choices for Brion and me: trampoline at our friends' house, which Mom also forbade, or, convert our beds into indoor versions! And until one particularly bloody afternoon, we thought the latter choice was brilliant.

In our indoor trampo-bed park, we didn't measure skill merely in height, but in multidirectional springing; corner to corner, side to side, corner to side, back to front. The faster and more complex the combination of trajectories, the more accomplished the tramper . . . or is it trampist? To reach the pinnacle of tramperfection, though, it was critical that the bed be made just so; the covers and sheets tucked tight, something you had to stop and do repeatedly, but something Brion neglected that afternoon.

It was like I was watching a great athlete at the peak of his performance. He was going faster, higher, and in more directions than I'd ever hoped to. And he was laughing—hysterically. And then it happened. In retrospect, I see it in slow motion, now—like the famous footage that used to accompany Jim McKay's voice-over at the beginning of ABC's *Wide World of Sports*—"the agony of defeat"—the shot of the downhill slalom skier's tip catching the hard-pack, launching him into the air before hitting the slope at about eighty, his body slamming the moguls, ass over tea kettle, before he finally came to rest.

Now, here was Brion's foot catching the rumpled blankets, his body pitching forward at an awkward angle, legs netted in the covers, arms akimbo, his hysterical laugh freezing in his throat. At that same instant, his head struck the heavy wooden headboard, just above the western carving that adorned its frontier facade, and his body dropped like a sack of flour.

When you're not quite six, seeing such a thing happen to your brother can cause any number of reactions, from paralyzing fear for his safety to paralyzing fear for the god-awful trouble you're going to be in for allowing him to have done such a stupid damned thing in the first place. Both now coursed through me, rooting me to my own bed, the spell broken by a scream so loud, it surely registered on sonar scopes off the coast. It also registered with Mom, and her mother, who was visiting for the day. Big surprise, Grandma—Brion's cut his head open!

It actually looked a lot worse than it was, requiring only a few stitches, and two launderings to get the blood out of his shirt and the bedclothes. Most entertaining was the deep-blue-colored mound that swelled across his forehead, giving Brion the appearance of having been raised by that tribe of South American Indians who give their children those welts at birth; a sign of beauty.

For three weeks, Brion received daily cold compresses and a regimen of St. Joseph's Baby Aspirin, which looked remarkably like Sweet-Tarts. They had a thin film of sucrose on the surface, so they had a taste that was not at all unpleasant, and they made you feel good, to boot. It stood to reason that if Mom gave you two, and you felt a little better, more would make you feel a lot better.

So went Brion's logic, which, after Mom had removed the compress one afternoon, given him his dose of the sweet pain relievers, and made her way back to the living room, led him to the bathroom, where he climbed on top of the commode, opened the medicine cabinet, found the source of his relief, and ate the entire bottle's worth. I know this because I came upon him just as the container was leaving his lips, allowing two of the pills to fall to the floor, which he quickly scooped up and devoured, along with the rest.

When you're not quite six, seeing such a thing being done by your brother can cause any number of reactions, from paralyzing fear for his safety to paralyzing fear for the god-awful trouble you're going to be in for allowing him to have done such a stupid damned thing in the first place.

Having learned my lesson the first time, I shoved the amazement from my mind, grabbed the bottle from his hand, and ran screaming for Mom as fast and as loud as I could—an act that firmly established me as Responsible.

I was only weeks away from my sixth birthday, but Mom obviously felt I was capable enough to hear, absorb, and follow through with the directives she was drilling me with as she manhandled Brion to the station wagon.

"Tell your father what happened. Tell him I've taken your brother to the hospital. Tell him they're going to have to pump his stomach out. Tell him to take the chicken out of the fridge, and put it on the rotisserie. Lock the doors." Brion was limp, a pinkish foam coming from the corners of his mouth. And then another sort of foam erupted from Mom. "Jesus *Christ*. God *Almighty*. Where in the goddamn *hell* is your father? *Goddamnit*, Brion!"

And then she was gone, flying down Las Pasadas, the Lord's names echoing in vain down the driveway, Brion retching in the backseat.

Later, under Dad's concerned and intense gaze, I recounted the episode in all its urgent detail, wisely choosing, however, to omit Mom's prayers that God damn everything and everyone, including Brion and Dad.

"And she said to tell you that Brion was going to have his stomach pumped out," I said, concluding my report.

And then, as if hit between the eyes with inspiration, I added my own postscript, ensuring that my final entry not cause him any undue panic.

"But don't worry, Dad. I'm sure the doctors will put it back in before he comes home."

As he grew, the wizened old man's countenance left Brion, and he took on the distinct features of Betty Ford: high cheekbones, umber eyes, a brilliant, disarming smile, and an infectious sense of humor matched only by an abrupt anger that could be relentless. And while both of us inherited her predilection to addiction, his mannerisms, physical attitude, and voice were Ernie Ford reborn—something he was told often as he matured from his teens into his twenties and began to think about a career in the business. By Brion's mid-twenties, he found he could do Ernie Ford better than anyone else, and almost better than the original. He had his voice down so pat that if you closed your eyes when he sang, only those intimately familiar with Dad's phrasing could tell the difference. It was spooky.

I know that's not unusual, regardless of who you are or what family business you're thinking of going into. We all naturally remind others of our parents. But if you take after a parent who's a carpenter, or a pilot, or a millwright, you do so in an arena that's usually far removed from a 6k spotlight and the court of public opinion. You're cool with knowing you're holding the hammer the way your elder did and comfortable to continue doing so. You might drive the nails a bit differently, but for the biggest part, you don't fall far from the tree. While children of entertainers inevitably face the same comparisons, there is a need to develop a style, a voice, a range, an identity that at once acknowledges your debt and your genes, but also a need to separate yourself. Completely. To do otherwise invites professional suicide, or worse, being cast as your parent.

While Brion went through a musical period where he seemed intent on finding that separate identity, it was short-lived. After he moved to Nashville, he took a job for a brief period in one of the musical revues at Opryland, USA, where he was called upon to sing "Sixteen Tons," and later he joined a traveling gospel group that used his name for every dollar they could squeeze out of every tent show and church social. He put together a folkish duet with his late brother-in law, Don Gay, but it was also unrewardingly brief. Likewise, his on-camera ventures did not bear fruit beyond a few local commercials every now and then.

Not achieving success in the business became an albatross around Brion's neck, and even when the thing threatened to drown him, he refused to take it off. He was embittered by the failures he'd experienced and the advantage others took of him, because, in his mind, he was Tennessee Ernie Ford's son, and fame was bound—destined—to come to him. "Someday," he told me once, "someone's going to knock at my door, and just look at me and say, 'Brion Ford, come with me. I'm going to make you a star.'"

While it was not always so, Brion and I spent much of our youth, our formative years, and our young adulthood in a culture of intoxication. The life we were blessed with was intoxicating. The love that bound us as a family was intoxicating. But we believed inherently that to get everything we could from that life, we needed to *be* intoxicated. We had everything. It was just better stoned.

Above all, the fame that gave us everything was intoxicating. It was an intoxication that took me years to find my way out of, but one that I still know intimately. It held me in its sway for long years of my life, and without the wife and children I've in turn been blessed with, I would certainly still be hearing its siren call. It is a cruel drunk, fame; false, careless, shameless, and without pity. The more you crave it, the less it cares about you.

Brion clung to that false dream, and it sucked much of the life out of him. In the wake of Dad's death, that vacancy was compounded by the ensuing years of litigation that surrounded and followed it, resulting in the eventual depletion of nearly all the financial legacy left to him. When that was gone, Brion became an embittered soul, living in perpetual denial, unhappy and grim. But still—still waiting for someone to knock on his door and make him a star.

As I see these words appear on the monitor in front of me, letters traveling left to right on the digital paper, more than a year has passed since I last spoke to Brion. We live less than a half hour from each other, but it may as well be a continent, a vast ocean that separates us. We hold a mirror, but the images it projects are not of us. In its glass are the reflections of our father and his only brother, estranged, silent, and alone.

I wish it had been different. I wish him peace. I hope his dreams come true.

SIX

ERNIE FORD WAS EITHER a chameleon or a schizophrenic or both. Maybe neither. Like a method actor, he was able to immerse himself in whatever role he found himself, and lose himself in the man he was, or felt he needed to be at the moment. On the set, in the studio, or onstage, he was a consummate professional musician and entertainer. On the ranch he was cowboy laborer. In Hawaii he transformed himself into a beach boy and a surfer. At the lake he was a fisherman. If he was required to meet with a U.N. delegate at any of those places, he became a diplomat; erudite, not even the faintest trace of an accent, seemingly literate in all manner of worldly doings, and willing to advise on the political ramifications of the situation, say, in Rwanda, gracious as he did so. He was as comfortable with a chain saw as he was with a spatula, or a microphone, or a gavel. I have some classic shots of him piloting a catamaran in Hawaii. God, the truth is I don't know which of those people my dad really was. I suppose I need to possibly accept the fact that he was all of them. Or that he had the ability to *become* all of them—to morph into each of them at will when the situation called for it. Like Woody Allen's human chameleon, Leonard Zelig.

I'm not complaining. I loved my dads. All of them.

Betty Ford was completely the opposite. She did not change who she was regardless of whom she was around. Actually, that's not completely true. She did change, but the change that befell her was usually commensurate with the ratio of vodka to boredom. From dinner with the neighbors to a network cocktail party, she would go from brilliant maven of modern life to scathing distributor of honest insight in a blink—make that drink—of an eye. No one was safe, from the maid to the president of J. Walter Thompson. If Betty Ford had something to say to you, she did so, privately or publicly—it didn't matter.

She was who she was, and she never—in all her life—regretted one damned thing she'd ever said to anyone. To hell with them if they were thin-skinned enough to be offended.

Together, they were the life of the party. One never knew who or what Dad would morph into during the evening; what Mom would say, or whom she would say it to.

As the years progressed and Dad's fame grew, his talent for morphing melded into his hope of escaping, and Mom's natural gift for insight blossomed. But where Dad could sense, and change, and control his personalities, Mom could not. As the lights illuminating our family grew brighter, she drank more, and started earlier in the day. And her keen, disarming insights into people—into their lives, their wardrobes, or whatever—would become barbed lances of sarcasm, instantly. This earned her a kind of fame completely different from the sort she saw being achieved by the man she loved, changing him and transforming the family we had been. Those who knew her best loved her for it, and I know for certain that many wished they could be as unflinchingly honest, but they wore their best shields around her nonetheless.

Two months after Brion was born we moved from Monterey Park to Whittier, a town that would forever hold the dubious distinction of having been the birthplace of Richard Nixon, and where Brion's tramp-o-bed and baby aspirin incidents occurred.

The house was a long, low, single-story ranch, set in a pocketed hollow that had been subdivided and developed at the end of the war. It was nestled at the end of Las Pasadas, a short, arced cul-de-sac that ran off Colima Road and Mar Vista. In the surrounding distance, beyond the sloping lawn and the pool, the Whittier Hills orange groves rolled, like quilted ground swells on a citrus ocean, the peaks and valleys broken only by the occasional ranch house, anchored amid the verdant seas.

While the primary catalyst for moving to Whittier was Brion's birth, and the primary reason for a bigger house was the need for more room, the move to a bigger house probably would have happened regardless. Fame, up to that point itinerant and tentative, had moved in, and it was a demanding and hungry boarder. A larger house in a more affluent neighborhood befitting its appetite was in order.

By the end of September 1952, Dad had recorded nearly forty singles for Capitol, including his second hit with Kay Starr, "Oceans of Tears," and "Blackberry Boogie," an original rocker that was his tenth Top Ten record for the label. A grueling road and recording schedule, broken only by his loyalty to Cliffie Stone and *Hometown Jamboree* every week, had long since made continuing at KXLA impossible. Nevertheless, in January of the same year, he accepted a deal with CBS Radio to do a daily variety show from Columbia Square in Hollywood, on their coast-to-coast network. And while it wasn't getting the national notices that regularly came in for Crosby or Benny or Hope, listenership was steady, a fan base was there and growing, and the numbers kept getting better with every broadcast.

Unfortunately, nearly everyone on both coasts knew that radio's signal was fading—slowly, to be sure, but inexorably nonetheless—and it was just a matter of time before it would eventually segue into the era of television.

Commensurate with Dad's growing popularity, the occasional story in the occasional local paper became regular features in all the media, and Mom had to make room for a second boarder to join Fame: Publicity. Together, the two became as common to the house as colic and pipe tobacco; as gin and tonic. Writers, stringers, photographers, broadcasters, and gossip columnists became regular visitors, like neighbors, but neighbors who had a deadline. The pool of light had expanded beyond its single-spot illumination of Dad and was now widened to include Brion, me, and Mom. Fame had brought baggage with it. Baggage it had apparently kept hidden—baggage that seemed to be everywhere; hangar bags, suitcases, massive steamer trunks . . . crap that Fame expected us to lug around whenever it needed moving. We had arrived at a moment in our lives as a family where everything we said, everywhere we went, everything we did, everyone we were, was written about, commented on, scrutinized, printed, and aired. The walls of our house disappeared, replaced by transparent plates of glass.

To live a normal life behind those panes was impossible, but from the beginning trying to do exactly that became *the* primal urge for Dad, and the main hook for any of the press that he could influence. If Publicity was going to invade our family, it would see a family unchanged, unscathed, unblemished by Fame. It would see a family no different from any other wholesome American family. It would see the family Dad wanted them to see, even when that family had become the antithesis of the family he wanted desperately to believe we still were.

As the years progressed and his career ignited, Fame and Publicity became harder to control. They outgrew the little room Mom had prepared for them, and spilled out into the every corner of the house. They ate and slept with us, they rode in the car to the hardware store with us, and they lounged around the pool with us. Dad knew they came with the property, and he endured them, but he made every effort, nevertheless, to hide them from neighbors and guests. For Brion and me, they were like two uncles we weren't supposed to hang around. They couldn't be trusted, and they were bad influences. Ignore them. Don't pay any attention to them, don't talk to them, and for God's sake, don't encourage them. Eventually, they'll leave you alone.

Right.

In February of '53 London called, and Dad was booked for a Command Performance and two weeks at the London Palladium. Brion was not quite a year old, and I'd turned three just a few months prior. Nevertheless, Mom made the decision to tear herself away from the joy and immeasurable exhilaration of teething, dirty diapers, and the croup to go to Europe with Dad for three weeks.

Normally, a trip of that importance would have required Cliffie Stone's management. But commitments to KXLA, his growing music publishing interests, and his duties to Capitol precluded his accompaniment. Second in the chain of command was Loakes, but having just been discharged from his stint in the Army, he was needed more at Cliffie's side in the States than back across the pond, where he'd been stationed in Germany for two years.

These were major gigs—Dad's first European concerts. These shows could make or break him over there. Someone needed to organize the itinerary. Someone needed to schedule and screen the press. Someone needed to pack the sheet music, confirm the orchestra, and arrange the rehearsals. Someone needed to make sure the lights worked and the sound was hot. Zero Mostel was on the same bill, for God's sake! Someone needed to be Ernie Ford's roadie.

Okay, the word *roadie* didn't exist in 1953. But somebody needed to do all the stuff that a roadie would be doing when they'd be called roadies sixteen years later.

There was really only one choice—one candidate. One person who could manage to keep Dad in line and on his mark.

So, in April of that year, Ernie Ford departed for his first headlining tour of England, accompanied by his secretary, travel adviser, press agent, and tour manager, Betty Ford. An entourage of one.

It was the first and last time she'd be a part of Dad's work.

In '53 the Palladium was managed by Val Parnell, a flamboyant act of his own, who became senior manager of England's Moss Theaters dynasty in 1945. By 1950 Parnell had earned himself a seriously controversial reputation by loading the Palladium with big-time acts from the States, to the limitation of Britain's staid and standby vaudeville stars. Traditional troupers like the Crazy Gang, Cicely Courtneidge, and others were dropped from—or to the bottom of—the bill, and replaced by Judy Garland, Danny Kaye, Sophie Tucker, Bing Crosby, and Johnnie Ray, the act Dad followed into the hall.

Most of those acts, though, including Dad, were not booked by Parnell. They were packaged for Parnell by Grade Brothers, England's premier talent agency, run by Leslie Grade and his older brother, Lew Grade.

Sir Lew, as he would be called twenty years later following knighthood, would rise to become the single most influential entertainment impresario in British history, partnering with Parnell and literally creating England's television industry, among other things, from scratch. In 1953, albeit knightless, he was no less powerful as Britain's equivalent of Swifty Lazar or Lee Hayward; the agent's agent—cigar between his teeth, phone glued to his ear, dealing his way to fame and lucre, radar up, scanning for the next big act.

With three singles each reaching the million-selling mark, his country boogie melting jukeboxes from Battersea to Liverpool, Ernie Ford had become a major blip on Lew Grade's screen.

No one, especially Dad, was prepared for the response when he opened on the night of April 7. Every seat had been sold two days earlier. It was standing room only for two weeks—every show. It was the single biggest two-week date for Varnell, Grade, and the Palladium since 1945. Reviews were extraordinary, ticket buyers formed a queue ten-to thirty-deep daily, and bobbies were turning crowds of fans away—almost all of whom were under thirty. Ernie Ford was the closest thing to a teen idol to hit the hallowed hall since the end of the war.

His impact onstage was mesmerizing. Cream-white dinner jacket and slacks, black string tie and boots, backed by a full ten-piece orchestra punching out rhythm lines that had been covered with just a five-piece band on record. Virtually every song brought the packed house to its feet, and virtually every night closed with encore after encore after encore.

It was an unqualified success, galvanizing his arrival as an international star.

Like the lion's share of his career, the record of the Palladium date and his tour of northern England that followed were chronicled and kept in the press books. Newspaper clippings and black-and-white shots from backstage and under the spotlight fill a volume dedicated to that tour.

But unlike the volumes of press covering the twenty years that followed, many of the shots in this chronicle include Mom side by side with Dad. Backstage with fans and Dad. Signing autographs in the dressing room with Dad. Arriving at Heathrow with Dad. Posing with the tour's publicists and Dad. Sightseeing in London with Dad. Confident, strong, and beautiful, she is positively beaming in every shot. Not standing in Dad's shadow, but very much casting her own.

They were more than just husband and wife on that trip. They were partners. Yes, it was him onstage. Yes, it was his voice—I know all that. But it was their partnership that starred. And while the act wouldn't break up for many years to come, it was their first and last show as a team.

When Dad began his work in television, it seemed evident to virtually everyone around him, almost immediately, that the medium had been developed specifically for him—that Milton Berle had been merely an afterthought. That in creating the tube, Philo Farnsworth did so knowing that someday it would glow brightly, and beam Ernie Ford through the ether into millions of living rooms across the fruited plain, from sea to shining sea.

From his earliest appearances on *Hometown Jamboree*, when KCOP was broadcasting the show throughout Southern California, his performances on-camera seemed effortless, a natural extension of himself. There was no "stretching." No reaching. No cheating for his good side. He didn't have one. It was all good. From the time of his legendary 1954 turn in the first two-part episode ever filmed of *I Love Lucy*, there was no looking back.

By fifty-five, he had established himself as a recognized star in radio, racked up a string of Top Ten singles as a recording act, was becoming one of the most in-demand nightclub and showroom acts on the road, and was on the brink of capturing television audiences everywhere.

My earliest memories of Dad are of him inside the screen. Inside the big Magnavox console in the little living room in Monterey Park. *Hometown Jamboree* was still being televised in the very early fifties, and for me, it became synonymous with where I knew I could find my Dad. I didn't expect to see him in other rooms at home. Home was the place inside the Magnavox. And I knew that *h e* knew I was there with him, because he never failed in his promise to wave from inside at the end of each show.

When the daily NBC series *The Tennessee Ernie Ford Show* began in January 1955, I was transported to the other side of the screen. Two to three days a week, my mornings were spent with the crew and cast in the Hollywood Playhouse (briefly renamed the El Capitan Theater, then, later, the Hollywood Palace), where the show originated.

Originally, NBC scheduled the show to be broadcast from their new studios in Burbank. But in 1955, Burbank was about as far from the crossroads of the world and Hollywood Boulevard as you could get. Tourists had no idea where it or the studios were, so the decision was made to move the show to the El Capitan, in the center of Hollywood. An hour before showtime every morning, NBC would send uniformed pages bearing free tickets down to the corner of Hollywood and Vine with instructions to rope an audience for that day's show. Glen Larson, who would go on to become one of the Four Preps, and later create and produce *Magnum, P.I.*; *The Fall Guy*; *Knight Rider*; *Quincy, M.E.*; and scads of other properties, was one of those guys.

I spent many mornings on the set, roaming the theater, hiding in the wings, and distracting the production staff at crucial times. The cast and crew of the show became as familiar to me as if they were family. On the surface it has all the trappings of a privileged youth, but frankly, there was nothing heady about it, because I didn't know any different. Riding into Hollywood with Dad, spending the morning on the set, in the booth, or in his dressing room watching the show was just part of a normal day. I was just going to work with my father— learning the family business. Granted, learning it at an early age, but learning the family business nonetheless. In fact, just two months before my seventh birthday, I made my debut on the show and earned my AFTRA card when I was cast in three live commercials for John son's Baby Shampoo. Three days running, Dad picked me up and sat me in a big, high-backed leather chair, wrapped a towel around my shoulders, and on live TV, shampooed my head—praying to God, I'm sure, that he wouldn't get any in my eyes, bring tears to them, blow the product's hook ("No More Tears"), and blow the account.

When the show first went on the air, it was classified as a "sustaining program," one of the many network shows broadcast between the late forties and mid-fifties without commercial sponsorship. David Sarnoff, William Paley, and other early television leaders used the time to push affiliates around the country into purchasing their equipment and buying time on their network. Dad, *Howdy Doody*, *The Colgate Comedy Hour* (Dean Martin and Jerry Lewis's series, which was also broadcast from the El Cap), and many others were first broadcast as sustaining shows until sponsors became involved.

As a half-hour morning show, the target audience was primarily housewives. When sponsors finally did come on board, the show's popularity had risen so sharply, so fast, that everyone from Blue Bonnet Margarine to Royal Gelatin and Johnson & Johnson clamored for commercial time. It became harder to find time for a song than for a spot.

One of the chief reasons for that was Dad's natural skill as a salesman; a skill and talent that would factor in mightily when Ford Motor Company launched *The Ford Show* the following year. He could literally sell anything. Primarily because he didn't try to. He didn't put his foot in the door. He wasn't obnoxious; he didn't press. He used the product at home—he shampooed his son with it, he ate it for dessert, he spread it on his toast. And he just . . . sold it. Because they believed him. And because several million housewives had fallen head-over-heels for him, they were swinging at everything he pitched to them.

Sponsors loved Ernie Ford almost as much as the housewives did.

Morning show notwithstanding, Dad's growing popularity among fans and colleagues alike made it a favorite show among some of Hollywood's most famous people, many of whom made more than one guest appearance. Bob Hope was a favorite; Julie London did the show several times. Jack Benny, George Gobel, Dinah Shore, Rosie Clooney, Dean Martin, and on one hilarious morning still being talked about today, Jerry Lewis.

This is a classic story . . . Mom and Dad had been invited one night in August of '56 to conductor and arranger David Rose's place for dinner, and to screen a film of Martin and Lewis's act from that July in Las Vegas. No one, except perhaps Dean and Jerry, knew that it was a film of their last appearance together. But that's beside the point. (*Damn*, I would love to see that footage—show-business history . . . but that's beside the point, too.)

It was an exclusive A-list party. Everyone who was anyone in Hollywood was there.

Jerry, it seems, had long been a closet fan of Dad's, and over after-dinner drinks told him how much he loved the show. Dad was gracious but not bluffed. "Jerry," he scoffed, "you haven't been up at 9:00 a.m. in twenty years. You wouldn't know from 9:00 a.m."

Jerry's lower lip fell and those eyes drooped to his cheeks. "I have so. I watch your show every day, Irving!"

"Ernie."

"I'm Jerry."

"No, you said 'Irving.'"

"I thought I said 'Jerry.'"

That's how their friendship began. And for as long as they remained friends, Dad was always Tennessee Irving. If I have time, remind me to tell you the story of when Dad and Pat Boone dressed up as bellboys at the Royal Hawaiian on Oahu in '58 and schlepped every one of Jerry's bags to his room before he recognized them. He was crying, he was laughing so hard. And he was laughing so hard he "forgot" to tip them—something I think Mr. Boone is still riled about today.

Anyway, Jerry turns to Dad and says, "Why don't you have me on your show sometime, Irving?"

"Jerry," Dad says, "I honestly don't think we've got the budget for you. We spent it all on Hope and Gobel." Jerry wasn't fazed.

"I don't care. I'd love to do it."

Dad knows he's not going to win this. "Okay, Jerry. Let me talk to Milt [Hoffman—the show's producer] and see what we need to do."

Jerry put his drink down. "Thanks, Irving! I'll be there tomorrow."

The next morning, Dad pulled Milt Hoffman aside and told him about the dinner at David Rose's and the conversation with Jerry.

"I have no idea if he's on the level, Milt. I mean, it's Jerry Lewis . . . I don't know what to expect."

Together, they decided that they'd rehearse as if he wasn't going to show, but keep a backup plan to use if he did.

At eight thirty, the pages started herding the audience in. At eight forty-five, the band ran through the scales and tuned up with Jack Fascinato. At five till, Dad came out of makeup, and at 9:00 a.m. sharp, the studio doors opened, and Jerry Lewis walked on the set, threw his arms around Dad, and shouted, "It's the Tennessee Irving Show!" The audience sounded like one long laugh track for the next thirty minutes.

He stayed for the entire show, did the Royal Gelatin spot with Dad, called it Jell-O—*twice*—and cemented a friendship that lasted more than twenty years.

Dad had only been doing the show for six months when Berle Adams, his agent at MCA, brought news that Ford Motor Company was planning to throw their hat into the prime-time ring to compete with Dinah Shore's *Chevy Show*. They'd assigned their longtime ad agency, J. Walter Thompson, to begin the search for a star to host the show, and the agency's West Coast man, Corny Jackson, had called MCA.

Ford Motor Company wanted its own identity during prime time. They wanted a host who was unlike anyone else in Hollywood. Someone they could claim as their own. Word was they wanted someone with the star power of Crosby, the charisma of Sinatra, and the all-American appeal of Kate Smith.

Berle Adams told them they wanted Ernie Ford. There simply wasn't anyone else. In point of fact, MCA's head, Lew Wasserman, suggested to Adams that the agency not pitch anyone else. They were that certain—knowing if it didn't work, J. Walter Thompson would look elsewhere.

Jackson did his homework, flew to Honolulu where we were vacationing, took one meeting and a dinner with Mom and Dad, and was convinced. "I knew immediately he was our man," he said. "The real work was going to be convincing Detroit."

As the legend holds, Henry Ford II was not happy that his ad agency would suggest someone with the last name of Ford to host the show. It would look like they were reaching, desperate. Like they weren't serious. And they were *serious*. The company wasn't thrilled with the records he'd released, and while they were all aware of the splash he'd made hosting *Kay Kyser's Kollege of Musical Knowledge*, guesting on *I Love Lucy*, and the respectable numbers for the daily series, they weren't anywhere near sold on his ability to hold a prime-time audience for the world's biggest automaker. Moreover, Ford himself was rumored to have suggested—and none too quietly—that it was not Dad's real last name. He wanted to see a driver's license.

At Jackson's urging— and buttressed by the involvement of his superior, Danny Seymour; MCA's Sonny Werblin, and NBC's West Coast president, Tom Sarnoff—MCA convinced Ford to meet with Dad, Cliffie Stone, and Berle Adams and his people. In the meantime, Corny Jackson suggested to Henry II that he and the board set their watches to catch the morning show every day. "You will love this guy," he told him. "America will love this guy. They already do."

The meeting was set for Saturday, August 24, 1956.

The story is it took Dad some fifteen minutes before Henry Ford and the rest of the board of directors were in tears at the conference table. Expecting a long siege, MCA and J. Walter Thompson had come prepared for lengthy negotiations. Before Dad sat down, he took his driver's license out of his wallet, handed it to Corny Jackson, and told him to "take this down to the man at the head trough." It was over in little more than an hour.

The Ford Show debuted on Thursday night, October 4, 1956, to lukewarm reviews. From the beginning, despite their certainty that they'd picked the right host, NBC, MCA, J. Walter Thompson, and Ford thought it critical that Dad have a complete image makeover in order to compete and succeed in prime time. They didn't discount the growing popularity and overnights the daily series was getting; they simply didn't believe—none of them believed—that whatever might be working for him with housewives from nine until nine thirty in the morning would work with entire families at 9:00 p.m.

He needed a more defined sense of polish, an air of sophistication. Their first step was to cast British stage and film veteran Reginald Gardiner to play opposite Dad. Clipped, elegant, and poised, they thought him the perfect foil for Ernie Ford's Everyman. He was insufferable.

He lasted one show.

They immediately cast character actor Gil Stratton to replace him. Sharp, quick, and likable, he seemed a far better fit with Dad's natural and relaxed demeanor.

He lasted two shows.

By the time the fourth show was in rehearsals, Cliffie Stone and Dad had made their point. This was Ernie Ford's show; he alone would carry it, or drop it. Don't force him to interact with a foil he can't work with. Each guest would become his foil. Build the skits around them, and let Ernie be himself.

Decades later, when Cliffie was being interviewed for the documentary I produced on Dad, he elaborated: "They wanted him to be something he wasn't. They wanted him to be an actor. They wanted to write repartee for him. You didn't write repartee for Ernie Ford. It came out of his mouth naturally. He wasn't an actor. He was just a guy. He was just a guy who knew how to entertain people."

That kind of philosophy made Dad, Cliffie, and Jim Loakes more comfortable, to be sure, but it gave everyone else ulcers—starting with the show's producer and director, Bud Yorkin, and chief writers Howard Leeds, Danny Arnold, and Norman Lear. Lear and Yorkin would later form Tandem Productions and bring *All in the Family* and *Sanford and Son* to television, Howard Leeds developed *Diff'rent Strokes* and *The Facts of Life*, and Danny Arnold (one of the funniest men who ever lived) went on to create *Barney Miller*.

Already one of the medium's most celebrated directors, Bud Yorkin was like an antenna for what worked on prime time. Norman Lear, Howard Leeds, and Danny Arnold had an innate gift for writing bits and mini-plays that were hilarious. Together, they were in large part responsible for the show's success. One of the primary reasons for that was their willingness to mold the show around Dad, and not force him into positions that would betray his discomfort. Nevertheless, each week was an antacid commercial waiting to happen.

Add to that the fact the show was live, a demand that Cliffie and Dad made before one pen was put to one contract. Playing to an inanimate camera in an empty studio was about as far as possible from what Dad and Cliffie believed show business was, and they just couldn't— wouldn't—consider it. "This was show business, for Christ's sake," Cliffie remembered. "Our business was to put on a *show*. For an audience. We wanted to see who we were entertaining. We wanted to know if a joke really worked or not. God forbid that we'd ever get to the point of relying on a laugh track, or canned applause. Sullivan never did, and by God, we never did."

But for many in television, success lay in safety. *Anything* could happen on live TV, and that scared the hell out of producers, directors, writers, and—perhaps more than any other group—advertisers.

The J. Walter Thompson guys' first allegiance was, of course, to Ford, and the competition between them and Campbell-Ewald—the GM ad agency for *The Dinah Shore Chevy Show*—was fierce, uncompromising, and ruthless. The JWT guys lived on cigarettes, Pepto-Bismol, and Anacin, sweating each week in fear their newest prime-time star would decide to toss the script.

Which, of course, he did on a regular basis. Not intentionally, and not every time, and definitely not to make the product or the agency look bad. He just didn't attach the same life-or-death critical meaning to a two-minute spot for a convertible that they did. That was reality check number one. Reality check number two was that Ernie Ford sold more Fairlanes, Galaxies, Country Squires, Thunderbirds, and Falcons than any showroom in the country.

The people believed him. He was just a guy who knew how to entertain people. By the end of the first season, Ernie Ford was J. Walter Thompson's new best friend.

From October 1956 until June 1957, Dad was doing both the daily series from the El Capitan five days a week and *The Ford Show* from the NBC studios in Burbank every Thursday night. Once the audience had been herded out of the El Cap, he and the cast would quickly rehearse the numbers for the next day's show. Then he and Jim would grab a quick, late breakfast before heading to rehearsal for Thursday night's show. Five days a week.

Compounded by his recording schedule, guest appearances on the shows of everybody from Perry Como to Dinah Shore and Steve Allen, and a rapidly filling concert calendar, the pace had become frenetic, grueling, and insane. At the end of *The Ford Show*'s first season, it was evident something had to change, and the decision was made to drop the curtain on the daily series at the conclusion of its second year. Doing so allowed him to devote more time to prime time, as well as get an extra hour or so of sleep every night.

In its 192 airings, *The Ford Show* brought Dad and his supporting cast, the Top Twenty, into more than forty million homes every week, setting broadcast milestones and standards that literally changed the face of live television production. It ran for five consecutive seasons until its last curtain on June 29, 1961, and save for the first few broadcasts, consistently ran in the Nielsen Top Five. For the last three seasons, it was the number one show in its time slot, and became the only show to unseat *Playhouse 90* from that vaulted perch.

Although there were phases of the series when it seemed trapped in a gulley of formulaic sameness—hackneyed bits from predictable guests followed by expected musical numbers—those phases were few, and more apparent during its last weeks on the air. For the biggest part, each week was fresh, each production crisp. Reviews were consistently strong in middle-American cities, but especially so in the markets where they needed to be: New York, Chicago, Los Angeles, Detroit, St. Louis, and Dallas. When the *New York Post*'s John Crosby became a fan, it was in the bank, baby.

Scattered through those 192 half hours were shows of stellar brilliance; classic moments of timeless entertainment that still shine fifty years later. The best of those moments occurred when predictability was thrown out, when Dad took chances with the show *and* his image. When he defied convention and went against popular opinion and type, and against the judgment of the powers that were, who thought they knew his audience better than him. The show's '59 production of Gilbert and Sullivan's operetta *The Mikado* was a perfect—if not *the* perfect—example.

The popularity of musicals and opera on Broadway has experienced a resurgence of late, but from the fifties to the sixties, they were the toast of the town. Hit songs were coming from musical scores, and opera stars like Lily Pons were A-list guests on shows like *The Ford Show*. What am I saying . . . Lily Pons was a guest on *The Ford Show*.

The Ford Show's production of *The Mikado* began as an idea for a musical sketch, built around a three-song medley from the opera arranged for the Top Twenty. As production discussions progressed, however, the sketch continued to expand, and, eventually, Dad suggested they consider doing their own condensed version of the opera, with full costumes and sets. The idea took hold and within days, storyboards and a rough draft of the modified script were ready. But while Dad, the Top Twenty, and the crew were becoming more excited over the concept, the network, J. Walter Thompson, and Ford Motor Company were not. *The Ford Show* was holding the number one spot for half-hour variety shows in the Nielsens and was consistently higher in the ratings than its closest competitor over at the Tiffany Network, CBS. An *operetta?* Set in *Japan?* Starring . . . *Ernie Ford?*

"Obviously, we'd never done anything like this before," Dad told *Variety*'s Army Archerd. "It was an experiment we all knew could blow up in our faces. . . . We were fooling with our own success and we knew we could hurt ourselves."

It didn't matter that Dad himself was covering every dollar over *The Ford Show*'s usual bottom line, that he was trained in classical voice, or that he was familiar with the opera, having done the show while at the Cincinnati Conservatory. To the brass on Madison Avenue, in Detroit and Hollywood, this wasn't the time to experiment, nor, for that matter, was it the kind of show to experiment *with*. An operetta. Jesus H. Christ, Ernie. What in the name of *God* are you thinking?

Adding to the pressure, word had leaked to British, Canadian, and American Savoyards—traditional Gilbert and Sullivan players' groups—who publicly skewered the idea and Dad, and demanded that true devotees boycott NBC and *The Ford Show* that night. Concurrently, the press had learned of the planned show and seriously questioned the wisdom of condensing one of the world's great operas to thirty minutes, and the wisdom of such blasphemy being committed by E. Jennings Ford.

The *New York Times* April 17 review pretty much settled everything:

> Tennessee Ernie Ford came up last night with a charming little sleeper; a thirty-minute version of the Gilbert and Sullivan operetta "The Mikado." The result was a delightful sampling of G&H, presented with professional taste and style worthy of a major production. The Top Twenty, regular singing group on Mr. Ford's program, showed themselves to be much more versatile than might be expected. The costumes and sets

can only be described as absolutely beguiling. The only complaint about last night's "Mikado" was that it didn't last twice as long. Mr. Ford certainly fooled those who might tend to think of him only as a Pea picker.

Variety's review came out the same day:

Viewing a half-hour version of "The Mikado" is like making a one-week tour of Europe; it leaves one thirsting for the rest of it. Tennessee Ernie Ford managed to compress the Gilbert & Sullivan into thirty minutes, and to Ford's credit, it was one of the most entertaining half-hours of this season.

The following season, in January 1960, the cast produced their second Gilbert and Sullivan opera, *H.M.S. Pinafore*. The press was equally effusive, and Savoyards the world over sang the praises of *The Ford Show*'s treatment.

The series' ratings, production values, and Dad's affability and professionalism made *The Ford Show* a magnet for Hollywood's greatest stars and personalities, 130 of whom appeared as guests over its five-year run. Douglas Fairbanks Jr., Charles Laughton, Carol Channing, Liberace, Zsa Zsa Gabor, Johnny Cash, Minnie Pearl, Lee Marvin, Odetta, Cesar Romero, Hedda Hopper, Danny Thomas . . . many of whom became and remained dear, close friends to both Mom and Dad for years afterward.

For most kids my age, Friday and Saturday nights were what you lived for during the week, and I was certainly no different. But for me, Thursdays were equally paramount. By the time I was eight, I knew the preproduction, showtime, and postproduction schedules of *The Ford Show* as well as any member of the cast or crew, including who the guest was going to be any given week. Call-time: 4:30 p.m. Run-through at 5:00. Makeup at 5:30. Audience in at 6:00 p.m. sharp. Curtain up at 6:30. (Taping was done then, in order to run live on the East Coast three hours ahead.) Say good night at 7:00. Out of makeup by 7:30. Dinner at China Trader at 8:00. Home by 9:00 for drinks and to watch the show on channel 4 at 9:30. Sometimes with that night's guest as Mom and Dad's guest at home after the show.

Huddled at the top of the staircase, Brion and I would wait until our cue—a call up from Mom or Dad—then troop into the den for a good-night kiss, a pat on the keister, and a hug or tousle from Mr. and Mrs. Gobel, or Cliff Arquette, or maybe Mrs. Clooney and Mr. Ferrer. Then, under the watchful gaze of Beatrice, our long-suffering housekeeper in the Hollywood years, we'd troop back up the stairs to bed.

Granted, most of those nights I was already *in* bed, or in pajamas by nine thirty. But on perfect Thursdays, the heavens would open, and Mom would take me to NBC with her, where from the booth high above the soundstage I'd watch, rapt with unbroken attention and unbridled excitement as the show unfolded below me. Dad under the lights, partially obscured by the boom. Cameras focusing, gliding across the polished soundstage floor. Harry Geller's orchestra. The din of applause. A brief glance upward from Dad, and . . . there! His smile, and then, striking the chords of my memory from those earliest days when I believed he lived inside the Magnavox, a wave. In the midst of and surrounded by all that, he saw me. And he waved.

SEVEN

IN FEBRUARY 1992, I was coproducing a documentary on Dad for the now-defunct TNN cable network, and Cliffie Stone was in town to be interviewed for the film, along with music historian Rich Kienzle, TNN's programming director Paul Corbin, and Lloyd Wells,  who'd taken over as Dad's conductor in the later years. Jim Loakes would be interviewed in Burbank the following week. We'd turned Paul's offices into a location base for shooting interviews, and the lobby had been transformed into our "greenroom."

I'd brought a couple of hours' worth of restored audiotapes from a syndicated radio series Dad hosted in 1953. There were 260 fifteen-minute live-to-tape shows from Western Recorders in Hollywood that were broadcast on more than a hundred radio stations around the country and overseas on the AFRN—Armed Forces Radio Network.

It was a standard fifteen-minute "coffee-klatch" show of the day, the kind airing from rooftop lounges and radio studios all over the country. What made this show stand out, though, was the band—and Dad. Most shows like this got the budget for a full orchestra. *The Tennessee Ernie Ford Show* had a six-piece rhythm section. But it was the hottest band on the airwaves from coast to coast. His voice was incredible. He was completely on, and the groove he cut with the guys backing him up still ranks as perhaps the best stuff he ever put down on acetate.

The band had been assembled largely by Cliffie from the *Home-*

town days, and the members were as familiar with Dad's phrasing and vocal arrangements as anyone could be. But they'd also worked with everybody from Nat King Cole to Betty Hutton. By the time they were hired to do this series, they were widely regarded as among the most talented, fluid, versatile, and in-demand studio cats in the business. They could play anything and back anybody.

Led by jazz accordionist Billy Liebert, the group included Billy Strange on rhythm guitar, George Bruns on bass and trombone, Speedy West on pedal steel (the only cat I know who could do entire horn lines on a steel), Jimmy Bryant on lead guitar, and Harold Hensley on clarinet and violin—or fiddle, depending on what he was playing at the time.

In those 260 shows Dad and the group covered everything that had come out of Tin Pan Alley or Hollywood in the past fifty years, from Hoagy Carmichael to Cole Porter, from Smiley Burnette to Loerner and Lowe. More than a thousand songs, recorded in less than three months.

Each show's format was identical: the opening theme, a solo number from Dad, an instrumental number from the band, intro the girl guest, solo from her, duet with Dad, closing number, and out. All of it broken up twice with a spot from the series' sponsor, Griesedieck Brothers Brewery. Makers and bottlers of GB Beer. It was the first and only time Ernie Ford was ever sponsored by a brewery.

The spots were harmless enough—some trite copy about what to ask for at the market, what to bring out of the fridge when company comes over . . . a jaunty little theme song, and then the tag: "Remember . . . say GB, please—GB means Good Beer. Griesedieck Brothers Beer."

Now, the German name is pronounced Gri-sea-deek, but out of Ernie Ford's mouth, it came out, *Greasydick.* I swear to God. Every time, 260 shows nationwide. To this day, I still can't believe it got past everybody, especially the sponsor. I can see offices full of little German beer makers in St. Louis, cringing every time the show came on. *The Tennessee Ernie Ford Show*—brought to you by *Greasydick Brothers.*

Because only a few walls separated the greenroom from the room the interviews were being shot in, we had to keep the volume down on the little cassette player I'd brought, but it didn't diminish the power of the music coming from the tape. Forty years after it was recorded, it still sounded better than 90 percent of the crap that was

Bristol (Tennessee) Elementary, 1929

San Diego, August 1929

Graduation from Bristol High School

Graduation from San Bernardino High, 1941

Home from the Cincinnati Conservatory

The War years—Victorville Army Air Base

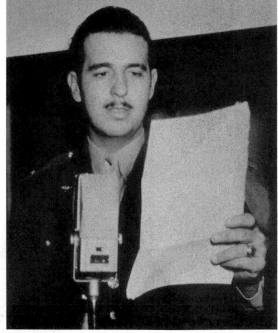

Reading Air Corps copy at KFXM in 1942

Home to Bristol after the war

Bristol, 1946

Picking the playlist at KXLA in Pasadena

With Doris Day on ABC Radio

Mom with Jesse and Charlie in San Bernardino

San Bernardino, 1951

Cabo San Lucas

On the cliffs at Cabo

London, 1953

On stage at the London Palladium, 1953

Backstage at the Palladium

Together in Paris

On the Arc de Triomphe, overlooking
the Champs-Élysées

First trip to Hawaii, 1953

Production still with Lucille Ball and Desi Arnaz

At the Thunderbird in Vegas with Cliffie and Dorothy Stone, 1954

Jack Fascinato, Doris Drew, Molly Bee, and Skip Farrell—the cast of the daily NBC series

Backstage at the El Capitan in Hollywood with guest Jerry Lewis

My debut on the daily series from the El Cap

Family time in Whittier

Arriving in Honolulu, 1956

On Clear Lake

At The Brown Derby with Bob
Cobb, artist Nick Volpe, and
Capitol's Lee Gillette

On *Person To Person* with
Edward R. Murrow

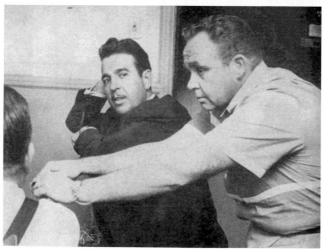

In the studio with Cliffie Stone

Mom and Dad with Ralph Edwards on the set of *This Is Your Life*

At her makeup table in North Hollywood

With label mate Nat King Cole

Cocktails in New York

With Oscar-winning actress Miyoshi Umeki

At the Emmys with Bob Cummings, Rosie Clooney, and Art Linkletter

North Hollywood

Sunday fashion in North Hollywood

On the back nine at Lakeside

Brion and me in a still from the Kodak ad campaign in North Hollywood

Brion, Mom, and me in North Hollywood

being passed off as popular music on the radio in 1994.

We must have looked like we were expecting something to crawl or jump—or materialize—out of the cassette player; me, Cliffie, his son Steve, and Lloyd Wells, hunkered down over the little machine on the coffee table in musical supplication.

After a half hour or so, the assistant director came through and let us know that Cliffie was up next. He straightened up and slowly stood (the norm, he was approaching his late seventies).

"That's still incredible stuff," he said. "Maybe the best stuff your dad ever recorded."

Steve helped Cliffie up, straightened his jacket, and adjusted his tie. Cliffie brushed his hand away.

"We recorded some later stuff that came close, but *that* stuff"—he gestured to the cassette player on the coffee table—"that was his best. Before everybody else got their claws in him, you know. Before he lost his soul."

His words hung in the air over the tape machine as Cliffie meandered down the hall with Steve and the AD for his interview. Lloyd and I stared blankly at each other—but only for a moment. He was late for a meeting, and after a hug, booked out to the parking lot.

I saw Cliffie twice again after that shoot; the last time at an awkward meeting he'd been asked to attend, dealing with the dissolution of our family company he'd been instrumental in creating in 1955, but I never asked him what he meant. *Before he lost his soul.* Did Dad do a Robert Johnson and give it all up at a crossroads somewhere? Or did Cliffie mean something else—that he'd lost his *soul* . . . his mojo. His edge. His groove?

In my heart and in my own soul, I knew it was a little of all the above. And if you listened close enough, you could hear the trail of that loss in the recorded legacy he left behind.

I have no problem saying this: Ernie Ford may have been one of the greatest singers ever recorded in American history. World history, for that matter. He knew no boundaries as a singer. He moved across all genres effortlessly, making whatever he was singing at the time uniquely his own. There were very few songs he couldn't wrap his baritone around and make it sound like it was written for him. What Capitol, and virtually every one else around him didn't get, though, was the material he was most *comfortable* singing. He needed to have fun singing . . . he needed to enjoy what he was singing. Once it started to become work, he completely lost interest, and that loss began to become most evident around 1970.

The first inkling I had that things were starting to go south musically (and I don't mean he was recording in Nashville) was in September of that year when Capitol drafted David Axelrod to produce an LP called *Everything Is Beautiful.*

David Axelrod had become something of a wunderkind at Capitol, having been shown the ropes by veteran Lee Gillette and apprenticing under executive producer David Cavanaugh. He was a different cat, mainly into jazz, and a protégé of sorts under Nat Adderley. His arrangements tended toward a cross between jazz, blues, funk, and soul, and he'd shown his biggest talent for blending those elements into a fusion that worked incredibly well with Lou Rawls. Ernie Ford was not Lou Rawls, though, and it would soon become evident that what worked for Lou wouldn't necessarily work for Ernie Ford, no matter who was producing.

Judging the entire album on the Richter scale of LPs, it's actually among the weirdest. It was—and still is—obvious that Capitol was reaching, trying desperately to make Ernie Ford palatable to the music-buying public of 1970. To remake him into an image of the musical giants of the day. To make him *relevant.* So, they paired him with Axelrod, who had produced Lou Rawls and the Electric Prunes, among others, and picked twelve relevant and contemporary hits, and three not so.

But they couldn't leave it to only the music to make him relevant. His image needed relevancy, too. And what better hook for image relevancy in 1970 than to give him that mod look. So they put him in a snappy corduroy blazer with leather elbow patches, and tucked an ascot into his shirt, to give his new mod look a British flair. But, in their wisdom, Capitol's image gurus knew instinctively that they couldn't completely separate him from the image they felt—knew—he conveyed, so, in that infinite wisdom, born of, I'm sure, *hours* of research, they had the brilliant idea of putting him in a rural setting! Next to a tree! Brilliant. But the rural setting needed something . . . something bucolic, something that spoke to the farmers they still assumed made up the lion's share of the Ernie Ford audience. So again, in a blinding example of marketing brilliance, they leaned a horse collar against the tree. My God, these people were beyond brilliant. They were prescient, for God's sake. They knew him. They knew what would convey that new image, that relevance. An ascot, a tree, and a horse collar. Damn brilliant.

He wasn't like an old dog who just couldn't learn the new tricks. He didn't *want* to learn the new tricks. There's a big difference. He was a product of his generation, and try as hard as they might, the people around him just couldn't get him to see the comparison between Hoagy Carmichael and Carole King, or whoever. He said regularly that he had no problem with new music, but I didn't buy it then, and I don't now. It just didn't work for him. The melodies didn't fit his phrasing, instrumentation was changing, and the production techniques were becoming far too reliant on technology. It left him cold, and you heard it in his voice.

I was on my way home from a voice-over session one late afternoon on February 13, 1995. It was Dad's birthday. Had he lived, he would have been seventy-six.

I was listening to NPR, and Garrison Keillor was doing his daily five-minute "Writer's Almanac" commentary. I was (and I suppose still am) a regular listener and fan of *Prairie Home Companion*, but the Writer's Almanac thing always left me a little nonplussed. Garrison reminding everyone with their radios on how intelligent, well spoken, and erudite he is. I endured it, because he usually closed with a piece of verse or poetry that reminded me why I favored Public Radio.

"Today is February 13," Garrison droned. "The anniversary of Charlemagne's ride into Vichy [or some obscure piece of history], and today is the birthday of gospel singer Ernie Ford."

I wanted to reach through the dashboard and throttle him.

Ernie Ford was *not* a gospel singer. It's a testament (pun sort of intended) to the power of those who believed they controlled his career that he's referred to as a gospel singer by so many people today. Capitol Records and others who lined their pockets and wallpapered their banks off his royalties cast him as a gospel singer. Truth is, he was a singer—period. He loved singing gospel, but for that matter, he loved singing Broadway, he loved singing blues, he loved singing pop, he loved singing country, and he loved singing opera. People that call him a gospel singer have been duped. Jesus H., he was a *singer*, for Chrissakes.

When he recorded *Hymns* in 1956, nobody really expected the record to do as well as it did. And he didn't cut it because of some grand plan dreamed up to introduce inspirational music to the mainstream record-buying public. It was just music he enjoyed singing. That it became the phenomenon it did was not due to design. It wasn't due to anything, really. It was a natural next step, set in motion years earlier when he'd joined the cast of Cliffie Stone's *Hometown Jamboree*. One of that show's staples, one of its signatures, was that it closed each broadcast (when it was a radio series, and when it went to television) with a hymn, or a spiritual. It was Cliffie's idea, borne of the fact that he was tuned directly in to the audience for that show; farmworking families, blue-collar folks—people who relied on their faith, and largely lived by it. It was as natural a part of the show as the skits and cowboy jazz dance numbers that brought listeners to their Philcos in the living room, and filled the El Monte Legion Stadium every Saturday night. Regardless of how rowdy the show—and the crowd—might get (and they did), you brought it all back home, and *sent* everybody home with hymn. Almost like a closing prayer. Everybody left peacefully . . . everybody got home safely. You never read about any fights in the parking lot of the hall afterward. It was brilliant. I've often wondered if maybe eminem or Suge Knight shouldn't take the cue.

When NBC signed him to do his first series for the network—the daily show from the El Capitan Theater in Hollywood—Cliffie produced that show as well. Banking on bringing a large part of the crowd that had become fans because of *Hometown*, they naturally decided to close this morning network series with a hymn as well. It worked. Housewives (the target demographic of the show) loved it, and sent letters in saying so.

When he was signed by Ford Motor Company to do *The Ford Show* the same year, he brought several of his own ideas to the table, including some that came from his days with the cast of Cliffie Stone's *Hometown Jamboree*.

When he and Cliffie suggested the idea of closing the show with a hymn to NBC, Ford Motor Company, and J. Walter Thompson, there was a collective intake heard round the advertising and marketing world, followed by successive near-coronaries. They didn't just balk; they thought he was out of his mind. This was going to be a primetime network variety show. This was Ford's debut in prime time. Their counter to The *Dinah Shore Chevy Show*. And you want to close it with a hymn?! New York will kill you. L.A. will change the channel.

Cliffie and Ford didn't blink. Dad told them plainly (something he repeated often throughout his career), "We're not doing this show just for people in New York and Los Angeles. We're playing all the houses in between."

By the end of the first season, the closing number was generating around fifteen hundred letters a week. The network and Ford began to worry when he *didn't* close with a hymn.

The recording of *Hymns* was largely due to the popularity of the closing number on *The Ford Show*, but not solely. Dad went in with Jack Fascinato, a handful of contracted backup vocalists, and a fairly minimal group of studio musicians to cut some music he grew up singing in church back in Bristol. Seven years later it was still on the Billboard charts, and was honored by his label as the most successful LP ever recorded by a Capitol artist—277 weeks straight on the pop charts. A *hymns* album. He was typecast forever. When it came time to record his next LP for the label, it was more of the same—*Spirituals*—a pretty cool record arranged by Jack Fascinato, and a little more contemporary. It always struck me as odd, though, that an album of spirituals didn't have any black folks involved. It was white bread through and through, but pretty cool arrangements nonetheless. I hand that to Jack Fascinato, who really didn't know from spirituals, but knew good music and even better arrangements.

Jack was an amazing cat; he grew up in Chicago and did a lot of NBC radio shows, then went on to be the musical conductor for *Kukla, Fran and Ollie* when television was in its infancy. The show was the brainchild of puppeteer Burr Tillstrom, who came up with the brilliant idea of doing adult comedy skits, but with puppets. A lot of the material went straight over the heads of the initial targeted audience—kids—and the show became a bigger hit with moms and dads, as well as New York's show-business elite. Jim Henson took many of his cues from Burr Tillstrom, and the Muppets' off-the-wall humor remains a continuing tribute to the show.

Jack came to Dad's attention by way of the arrangements he was doing for *Kukla, Fran and Ollie*, as well as the writing he was doing for commercials (*Northwest Orient . . . gonnnngggg . . . Airliiiines*) and some other great, minimalist stuff. He was probably a genius; always on the outer edge of stuff. Gave me a book when I was ten or eleven that took you photographically from a mosquito on your arm into the cellular structure of the body, then out of your body, off the globe, and into the solar system, then back again. His daughter, Tina, married Jimmy Messina of Loggins and Messina fame. Jack died of Alzheimer's, the disease reducing and diminishing him before his family. In a few short years he went from being a man overflowing with vitality and a love of life to flailing away physically at demons only he could see as he aimlessly wandered the streets of Palm Springs alone at night. He was a great man, and a great friend to the family.

Spirituals didn't do as well as *Hymns*, but it went gold. By that time *Hymns* had already gone platinum (one million units sold). All that Capitol and Dad's "people" could think about was how many of these they could wring out of him before the well ran dry. They *turned* him into their own private, in-house gospel singer. And no matter how hard he would try later (which wasn't all that hard), he'd never shake the label of "Ernie Ford, gospel singer."

The fact that he closed *The Ford Show* every Thursday night with a hymn or a gospel song of some kind didn't help. I'm not saying it was a bad thing, because it wasn't. I don't want anybody reading this book to get the idea that I'm complaining. Actually, I am, but I don't expect anybody to care or give much of a damn. We lived off the sales of those records and others that would follow, and lived royally. But the powers that were (and still are) cast him as a gospel singer, and he never shook it. Within a few years he was under the cow with everybody else, milking it for all it was worth, and it sucked him creatively as dry as a bone. He lost the edge in his voice, the urgency and the freedom that allowed him to float across styles and genres, giving each his own sense of timing and uniqueness. He stopped being an artist and became a celebrity. He'd allowed—given—Capitol and others the power to decide what they believed was best for his career, and ended up becoming their vision of him.

For a time I thought maybe it was just me, that I was selfishly trying to imagine him being the singer he really wasn't; that the plodding, repetitive dirges and unimaginative arrangements that filled LP after LP were what he really loved doing, really loved cutting. But it wasn't just me, and a pattern *was* emerging. Of the forty-nine stand-alone LPs he recorded for Capitol, there are maybe six that musically shine, that show his talent as a vocalist that I believe from the beginning set him apart, that remind you why he shot to the center of the spotlight as fast as he did. Why he was on every other artist's list as a singer that couldn't be touched.

The other albums? It was evident he was just going through the motions. Capitol dictated when and how he recorded, and he was just fulfilling his part of the contract. He was recording because he had to. As the years wore on, instead of maturing into what I believe could have been incredibly rich years for him as a singer (Tony Bennett is in those years now), he drank more, lost more of the vibrancy in his voice, and the label began to lose interest in really promoting him at all.

Not every record was lackluster—there were a handful that echoed his love of singing and went beyond the sameness that pervaded so many of his other sessions, or in the later years, the misguided efforts to bring him into the contemporary fold. His second effort with the Jordanaires, *Great Gospel Songs*, was a standout in its simple bread-and-butter harmonies, and was 1964's Grammy winner for Best Inspirational Recording—the only Grammy Dad ever won.

The best of those, in my opinion, was an LP he cut in 1964 at a little studio called Coast Recorders in the Bay Area. It was called *Country Hits . . . Feelin' Blue*.

What set this project apart was that it allowed him to be a singer again, to sing simple, uncomplicated tunes that he could relate to and convey. The production itself was minimalist genius: Dad on vocal, jazz bassist John Mosher on upright, and Dad's old friend Billy Strange on acoustic guitar.

In two four-hour sessions, they had the entire LP in the can. Twelve classic heartbreakers from ten classic writers who knew the value of simplicity in a great lyric. From a genre-specific standpoint, they'd be categorized as "country" songs, but Dad gave each of the twelve a completely new identity, a new meaning and imagery. Listening to *Feelin' Blue* even today, you can almost see Dad, Strange, and Mosher, lights down, smoke curling in the air above them, the room laced with blues. There's almost a jazz feel to the LP as a whole, and it still stands today as timeless a piece of great music as has ever been recorded. Capitol's failure to see the same was evidence of their shortsightedness and unwillingness to promote him beyond what they erroneously believed him to be. Released today, with the right promotion, I have no doubt it would utterly captivate people all over again.

After *Feelin' Blue*, Dad cut twenty-six more LPs in the twelve years he had left with the label. Three stand out, but the rest were throwaways, musically. None of them but one really fit him, and, ironically, it was a valiant but incomplete attempt to recapture what had happened on *Feelin' Blue*.

Produced by Steve Stone—Cliffie's oldest son—it was called *Ernie Sings & Glen Picks*, and paired Dad with Glen Campbell. Cut in May 1975 at the Capitol Tower on Hollywood and Vine, Steve did his damnedest to re-create the intimacy, immediacy, simplicity, and effortlessness that marked *Feelin' Blue*—with a couple of exceptions: he added overdub lead breaks from Glen on a second gut-string guitar, and Glen sang harmony lines on one of the tunes. As was the case with *Blue*, the material chosen was mainly country, but this time from more contemporary Nashville writers including three Kristofferson tunes, which was a mistake. Kris was cool for Ray Price, and for sure Cash, but trying to fit his lyrics and phrasing to Ernie Ford's style, voice, and, most important, his personality, was like putting a bouquet on a vinegar barrel.

Adding to the clutter was someone's idea that it would be cool for Dad and Glen to "talk" to each other during and after the songs, little asides that you would expect to hear between the two of them when they were listening to playback. Used within the bodies of the tracks, though, made them sound scripted, and because of that they sounded unnatural, a forced effort to imply the camaraderie (old man, young picker; elder statesman, new kid) between them. Genuine artistic exchange between the two would have been enough had it been real, but it misses the mark.

Most unfortunate (again, in my opinion) is that you can hear Dad *trying* to sing these tunes, trying to sound country, trying to match what he thinks a country vocal should sound like, and that's the primary drawback to this LP. That and the fact that I can hear and smell the Cutty Sark and Smirnoff in every vocal on every track.

He felt every song on *Blue*. He's just *doing* every track on the LP with Glen.

In his twenty-seven years and two months with the label, Capitol released a total of eighty-three singles by Dad. Of those eighty-three, seventeen charted Pop, and twenty-nine charted Country. All together, nineteen were Top Ten singles. Between 1949 and 1958, he recorded the lion's share of that collection: sixty-three in all, but between 1960 and his last session in May 1976, Capitol released only twenty. His cover of Billy Joe Shaver's "I Been to Georgia on a Fast Train" was the last, released in July 1976. It peaked at number 95, and after three lonely weeks, disappeared.

By the time long-playing albums became the norm, Dad was never marketed aggressively as a singles artist by Capitol, and yet the stuff he cut and released on 45's between 1949 and 1956 stands today as among his best, and was the stuff that put him on the map musically. Many of those early records were his own original songs, and they established him as a musical force to be reckoned with—a classically trained voice, cool with any genre; writing boogie-woogie and country-blues stuff that was totally different from anything on the radio. And therein lies the rub. I don't think Capitol had a clue what to do with Ernie Ford as a recording artist, until he cut *Hymns* in 1956. After that, they couldn't think of anything else he was good for. Jesus, they were such idiots, and so blind.

I'm probably being a bit harsh. There were moments in the string of singles when Lee Gillette had his head on straight and heard Ernie Ford for what he was: a great singer. Putting him in the studio with Kay Starr was a stroke of genius. She was sultry, steel-edged, and just bluesy enough to fit Dad like a glove. They sang like they were meant to record together; an effortless, harmonic blending of two distinctly unique voices. Together, they cut a total of four tracks in two sessions each in 1950 and 1951. The first of those four, "I'll Never Be Free," was a classic record then, and still stands as strong today.

On the strength of the Kay Starr duets, Capitol started looking for other ballsy female vocalists to pair him with; including Molly Bee (from *Hometown Jamboree*), Ella Mae Morse, and actress Betty Hutton, who, at the time, was dating Capitol's president, Alan Livingston.

Although Dad cut only two sides with Betty, they were completely off the wall and off the charts—figuratively and literally. Mainly due to the fact that, in their search to broaden his audience and establish him firmly in the pop market, they put him and Betty in the studio with one of the most notoriously inventive, popular, and wild arrangers and conductors around: Billy May.

May had done time as a trumpet player and arranger for Glenn Miller and Charlie Barnet, produced Yma Sumac's "Mambo!" smash, and had been arranging exclusively for Capitol since the label's Paul Weston signed him in the late forties. Known for his glissando sax lines, wraparound big-band sounds, unconventional arrangements, and (if you believe the back-story) an ability to conduct and arrange stone drunk, Capitol thought he'd be the perfect band leader to kick-start Dad into the pop market, and booked him for three sessions in March and April of 1954.

Those sessions produced eight tracks, released as four singles, including "River of No Return," the theme from the Marilyn Monroe, Robert Mitchum picture of the same name. It was a great single, a great arrangement, and one of Dad's most memorable vocals in his entire career. "Somebody Bigger Than You and I" also came out of those sessions; a glistening pop arrangement, powerful and yet understated—of, essentially, a hymn. It was the first "inspirational" number Dad ever recorded, and it was fabulous . . . the arrangement and Dad's performance are both incredible.

But the track that stands out is also the track that never made it to the charts; one of the two recorded with Betty Hutton, a kick-the-doors-in, blow-your-socks-off, try-*this*-on-Sinatra, big-band smash by Ed Pola and Allan Copeland called "This Must Be the Place." It was the first and last time Ernie Ford would record with an orchestra led and arranged by the likes of Billy May, and one of the highlights of his twenty-seven years with Capitol. Naturally, it didn't last. Unfortunately, neither did Betty Hutton. She married Alan Livingston the following year (her fourth), but at the time, she was signed to RCA. Her career went into a nosedive, she divorced Alan Livingston after five years, and within six, she was being treated for alcoholism, drug addiction, and a suicide attempt. She was a totally unique American talent, and one of a kind. What a loss.

With only one track out of the Billy May sessions reaching the charts, Capitol was getting nervous. They knew they had something in Ernie Ford; they just didn't know what it was. They'd tried everything to cross him over, to find the niche, the market, the box they needed to put him in so they could decide exactly what the hell he was.

By the fall of 1955, things hadn't really improved. In fact, they were poised to get worse. Coming off the road on a Sunday night from an extended string of nightclub and state fair dates, Capitol welcomed Dad home with news that he needed to cut four sides by the following Tuesday, or they'd have no choice but to fine him for breach of contract.

Hastily, he met with Cliffie and Jack Fascinato and dug through material, none of which, in their haste, felt right. On top of that, Dad was dog-tired, road-weary, rode hard, and put up wet. He needed a break, and he put the decision in Cliffie's hands.

The next day, Cliffie met with Lee Gillette, and together they decided on the selections for the session on Tuesday. Moreover, Gillette was excited . . . he'd picked the first single out of the group, one he was sure was the breakout they'd been looking for. It was a country-flavored tune from Terry Shand and Bob Merrill called "You Don't Have to Be a Baby to Cry," but Ernie's conductor, Jack Fascinato, had given it a new touch, with horns, electric guitar, and a definite big-band feel. It would be perfect for Ernie Ford. Then, before the meeting was over, Gillette picked the B side: a song he thought would balance "Baby" nicely, and be good enough for filler.

It was called "Sixteen Tons."

Every popular singer has or dreams of having a moment in their recording career that establishes them, pushes them into the spotlight, and defines them in the ears, hearts, and minds of the public. That one track, that one song, that kicks them into the Top Ten. For Crosby, it was "White Christmas"; for Sinatra, it was probably . . . oh, hell, pick one. For Rosemary Clooney, "C'mon-a My House"; for Dean Martin, "Amore"; and for Dad, it was "Sixteen Tons."

In August 1946, Capitol Records' Lee Gillette assigned Cliffie Stone the task of putting Capitol in the folk music business. The success of Burl Ives, Pete Seeger, and a few others was noteworthy enough to warrant the label making its own effort to capitalize on what Gillette saw as a potential trend, and Cliffie's knowledge of the burgeoning western scene exploding out of Southern California made him the natural choice to lead the search. The problem was, Cliffie didn't know any folksingers, and he wasn't exactly sure what made something a folk song. "Besides, Ives, Woody Guthrie, and Jimmy Rodgers were the only folksingers I knew anything about," he recalled. "Rodgers was dead, Woody Guthrie was on a freight train somewhere, and Burl Ives was on Decca."

Someone did come to mind, though; a young guitar player and singer named Merle Travis, recently arrived in town from Cincinnati. Travis's talent as a player and writer had brought him to Cliffie's attention, and had resulted in his signing with the label earlier that year.

His first release was a double-sided hit—not unusual in those days—but only one of the two songs interested Stone in his search for a folksinger: a topical song Travis had written called "No Vacancy," about the hardship veterans faced at home when returning from service. No one knew at the time, of course, but it was a harbinger of future compositions to come from Travis's mind and pen, caustically taking the powers that be in America to task, and championing the plight of the working poor and forgotten masses.

Travis was thankful for the prospect of another session, but dubious about the material they wanted. He reportedly told Stone, "[Burl] Ives has sung every folk song there is."

"Then write some new ones," Cliffie told him. "Tonight. I've got the first session of four songs scheduled for tomorrow."

The completed album was one of the earliest formats of a boxed set; four 78 rpm discs encased in an accordion of thick, cardboard sleeves. It was called *Folk Songs of the Hills (Back Home/Songs of the Coalminers)* and included thirteen songs in all. Eight were well traveled: "Barbara Allen," "I Am a Pilgrim," and other standards you'd expect on a folk album. The remaining five, however, were Travis originals, all of which he penned in less than a week, looking back to his boyhood home and the mines of Harlan County, Kentucky, for his inspiration. One of those five was called "Sixteen Tons."

Recorded with just Travis and his guitar, the album was probably twenty years ahead of its time and was, in retrospect, exactly what Lee Gillette had asked for. But its purity as a folk album guaranteed its commercial failure. There was no possibility of its competing with Burl Ives's jaunty, tame "folk ballad." This was hard-core—grim tales of oppressed people, unadorned with any contemporary production. The record-buying public just wasn't ready. After a brief life span on the shelves, it all but disappeared, along with Capitol's hopes of gaining a foothold in the folk music market. Ironically, it would become one of the genre's most important milestones, influencing everybody from Bob Dylan to Joan Baez, Chet Atkins to John Lennon.

Dad knew the song from working with Travis on *Hometown Jamboree*, and knew the story behind Travis's inspiration for the stark images portrayed in its powerful lyrics. His father worked the deep mines in Harlan and Hazard his entire life, held in virtual serfdom like thousands of others who couldn't quit and couldn't die, because he "owed his soul to the company store," where food and supplies for a miner's family were doled out on credit. "You didn't work for pay," Merle told Dad one afternoon. "You worked to pay off your debt to the coal company."

But although Dad was familiar with the song, he could not have known the controversy it would generate or the long-term, worldwide impact it would have as a social statement, let alone as a hit song. On the brink of the emerging Cold War, the political climate in the late forties was volatile; J. Edgar Hoover and many others in the government saw songs dealing with workers' woes as potentially seditious, and the singers who sang them were investigated as agitators, or communist sympathizers.

Travis had already come up on their radar when he wrote "No Vacancy." Now, the FBI was surreptitiously and quietly but firmly advising stations around the country not to play Travis's records, because they considered him a subversive. It was classic Hoover hysteria, and bullshit, of course, but nevertheless, the campaign guaranteed the album's demise.

The song lay fallow on Capitol's shelves until June 1955, when Dad and Jack Fascinato dusted it off during a search for material for the daily NBC series, then in its fifth month from the El Capitan Theater in Hollywood.

Taking Merle's straight guitar melody, Jack brought the Travis-picking tempo down, and built a spare, jazz instrumentation around it that completely altered the feel and mood of the song; transforming it musically and theatrically, allowing Dad's vocal to bring a sense of drama to the arrangement that was only hinted at in Travis's original version.

Backed by Jack's small seven-piece band, the song generated far more response than anticipated. In fact, neither Fascinato nor Dad anticipated any response. They'd picked the song because of Dad's friendship with Travis, and performing it on television would give his publishing income a needed shot in the arm. They had no idea.

Within three days, NBC received more than twelve hundred letters from viewers asking about the song and requesting that Dad perform it again. Over the next week, another two thousand letters would swell the network's mailbag.

Pleased with the response, Dad and Jack added it to the road repertoire and performed it for the second time at the Indiana State Fair later that summer. The crowd of thirty thousand was at capacity for the first night's show, and by the fade of the last four notes of "Sixteen

Tons," the crowd's decibels had risen to capacity. The response to the song was nothing short of deafening.

Lee Gillette was aware that the song had scored nicely on the morning show, and Cliffie Stone padded his pitch appropriately by bringing in boxes of mail and recounting the reaction it had received in Indianapolis. But Gillette was not impressed enough to make it the A side of the upcoming session. Moreover, the failure of the album that the song had originally been a part of was—ten years after the fact—still fresh in his mind. "You Don't Have to Be a Baby to Cry" was the A side. Period. He'd cut "the Travis thing" as the B side, but he had no hopes for it.

On September 17, 1955, both songs were recorded at studio A in the Capitol tower in Hollywood, with essentially the same band Jack conducted on the daily series. "Baby" was finished in three takes, and in the can. Gillette was excited. This was a hit song, the song they'd been looking for—the song that would put Ernie Ford on the map and in the bank. He began making phone calls and told Cliffie to go ahead with cutting the Travis thing.

With Gillette's mind off the session and on promotion, Cliffie gave the green light to the engineer, and the tape began rolling. To kick off the tempo, Dad did what he had always done in rehearsing the song; he began snapping his fingers. When the first take was done, Gillette heard the playback, but heard it cued up just past the finger snapping. Everybody was satisfied—why do another take?—and they called the session for the day. When the finished track was mastered, the engineers mistakenly assumed that the snapping was part of the track and kept it on the finished disc, giving it what one musical historian would later say was "a hipness beyond anything in the country field," or on pop radio at the time.

On October 17, Capitol shipped the new single to distributors nationwide and to deejays around the country, confident that "Baby" would be a hit. But inexplicably, radio stations coast-to-coast began "flipping" the single and playing the B side. Purely by accident, music history was being made.

In the eleven days following its release, four hundred thousand singles were sold. Demand for the song was so great, Capitol geared all its pressing plants nationwide to meet the deluge of orders. In twenty-four days, more than one million records were sold, and "Sixteen Tons" became the fastest selling single in Capitol's history. By November it had captured the top spot on every major record chart in the country, and by December 15 (less than two months after its release) more than two million copies had been sold, making it the most successful single ever recorded.

Merle Travis was nothing short of immortalized by the song. In later years, whenever he performed the song himself, he'd change the last line, and sing, "I owe my soul . . . to *Tennessee Ernie Ford.*"

I was hesitant to include the story of that song's genesis in this book. It's been told thousands of times, and still occupies print and media space and time worldwide. As recently as 2005, it was the musical bed under a major General Electric television campaign focusing on new technology to make coal burn cleaner. It became a rallying cry, sung like a hymn, following the Sago mine disaster in 2006, and is still held up as an anthem for every working stiff who's "another day older and deeper in debt."

That the song has generated as much lasting impact socially, musically, and politically as it has, warrants its place in this book, I suppose. But the impact it had on Dad's career, and on our lives as a family, was much more immediate and much more personal. The blur of the past seven-year ride from virtual obscurity to where he was now would seem like a walk around the block.

It changed everything forever.

EIGHT

WE MOVED to North Hollywood from Whittier in December of '56—two months after *The Ford Show*'s premiere on NBC. It was a grand house, a two-story Cape Cod–ranch–Georgian in Toluca Lake, next door to Bob Hope and his family. Six blocks up the street, the Warner Brothers lot sat at the corner of West Olive and Riverside, and just a few blocks beyond, the Disney Studios fronted Buena Vista Drive.

Tucked away and over the hill from Hollywood proper, Toluca Lake and Burbank were quiet, safe neighborhoods between 1956 and 1961. Narrow streets meandered through manicured neighborhoods that looked like the back lot of the Republic studios where Beaver Cleaver and My Three Sons lived. Stars with families moved there because it gave them the sense of community that was missing in Bel Air or Beverly Hills, yet it was still close to the studios. For Dad, that was paramount (not the studio, the degree of importance). From the driveway to the gate at the NBC lot on West Alameda and Bob Hope Boulevard, it was less than ten minutes, and no freeways.

I have no memory of the move to the new house. Only waking up there one morning, and finding Brion and myself in a very different bedroom from what I'd remembered going to sleep in the night before.

It was on the second floor, much bigger than Whittier's, with our own bathroom and a bay window with a bench seat overlooking the backyard, which was flat and seemed as expansive as a football field. Within a few months, dump trucks, skip loaders, bulldozers, and work-men would be carving a pool out of its center.

To the right of where the pool would eventually be was a playhouse, built by the previous owner, a doctor who moved his family and prac-tice to Ventura. A carbon copy of the big house in every detail, from roof to trim, it had been his daughter's dream playhouse. For Brion and me, Bill Thetford, Chuckie Jedica, and Chris Noonan, it was a com-mand center, a base of operations—the neighborhood's coolest fort. Impregnable. Unassailable. Perfect for our five-year-long game of war.

When I was nine, I used the playhouse as a laboratory of sorts, to see which struck a larger flame; book matches or wooden kitchen matches. The Diamond Brand kitchen matches won out handily, very nearly burning the playhouse—I'm sorry, *fort*—to the ground. An unintended consequence of scientific progress . . . an excuse that held no water whatsoever with Mom or Dad. Brion, Thetford, Jedica, and Noonan bought it, however. Unfortunately, we lost our base of opera-tions in the conflagration—another unintended consequence. Ah, the misspent adventures of youth.

There were two additional bedrooms upstairs, flanking the one I shared with Brion; Mom and Dad's master, which was to our right at the end of the balustrade, and the guest bedroom to our left, which was connected to ours and shared the same bath.

Directly underneath our new bedroom was a room Mom and Dad called the "lanai"; bamboo-ish wallpaper, tatami-esque flooring, lou-vered windows, and a glass patio door that led to the backyard. Funny—I remember the lanai better than most rooms in the house. I can't say precisely why. It has an organic sort of memory—I hear a Martin Denny sound track when I picture it, accompanied by our Pearl cockatiel, Billy, welcoming you whenever you came in—or walked by—proudly proclaiming his aviary self-esteem, or perhaps his sexual orientation: "Hello! Hello! I'm a pretty boy. I'm a pretty boy."

Billy was Mom's joy. The third year we were there, he maneuvered the latch on his cage door one afternoon while we were out, and flew directly into the small circular fabric ring that was used to pull one of the three roller shades down in the dining room. It may have looked to him like he could fly through it. Perhaps he was in rehearsals for his break on the *Sullivan* show. When we came home, Mom immedi-ately knew something was off, because we did not hear his "Hello!

Hello!" We found him hanging in the tassel ring like a pearl-hued decorative shade ornament, dead as a doornail.

Along three of the four lines marking the rectangular lot, the original owner had erected a split-rail fence and trellised it with honeysuckle when the house was built. By the time we moved to the house, the fence was all but invisible, crushed along some spans by the honeysuckle, which had grown to a hedge more than eight feet high; thick, redolent, and dense, impassable by anything larger than a field mouse or rock lizard.

At the same time the fence had been built and the trellises placed, sapling eucalyptus trees had been planted along the row, some twenty feet apart. When we arrived, they towered along the hedge line like quiet sentries, their pungent fragrance matched only by the sweet scent of the honeysuckle trumpets when they bloomed.

Above the leafy top of the hedge wall, you could just make out the slope and pitch of Bob and Dolores Hope's roofline. The Hopes' place was a large, sprawling compound, occupying two to three acres and with a personal one-hole golf range, on the corner of Moorpark and Ledge. They were quiet neighbors, unobtrusive and private. In the five years we lived next door, I personally saw and spoke to him on only three occasions, to two of their kids once (who were not really kids anymore), but I never once so much as laid eyes on Mrs. Hope. Had no idea what she looked like. For several of us in the neighborhood, she became somewhat of a mystery, prompting more than one attempted foray over, and several aborted penetrations through, the hedgerow separating our houses, in the hopes of gaining even one furtive, brief glimpse of the woman. Aside from the normal, petty mischief expected from neighborhood hooligans—good-natured and free of malicious intent though we were—I should in all honesty also admit that those incursions were fueled in part by the rumor (started, I still believe, by Chris Noonan, who claimed firsthand experience) that Mrs. Hope sunbathed and walked—walked *around*, according to Noonan—regularly in the nude.

For this gang of miscreants, the promise of such a vista, no matter how unsubstantiated the rumor, could not go unexplored. Great campaigns were planned in long strategy sessions in the fort—the same which later nearly burned down, if you recall. With all the deliberation and seriousness of a special forces unit, we sent out advance teams to recon the weak points in the hedge—the gaps of thinning vegetation that would give us not only relatively unobstructed passage through to the other side, but views of the uninhibited tableau that we hoped would greet us. Armed with a Brownie Instamatic that Kodak had given us as a gift following a photo spread they'd done at the house, we hoped also to capture that prurient image for posterity, as well as neighborhood fame. That Hope was rumored to have planted electrified lines just under the surface of the loamy ground along the fence—hot conduits that would fry our preadolescent guts to smoldering innards—deterred us for only the briefest time—long enough to send Brion through first, to see if it was true.

Finally the point of entry was selected. Arduous hours of painstakingly tedious pruning—by hand—was completed. We'd built a camouflaged tunnel, one nearly invisible to all but the trained eyes of a spy or a good gardener.

When the hour finally came, like true soldiers embarking on a mission of the greatest importance, it was determined we would draw straws to see who would go through and take the picture. Shortest straw wins. Had Dimitri Tiomkin or Henry Mancini been in the fort with us, they would have been scoring gut-wrenching musical interludes to accompany the tense, high drama unfolding in the playhouse. I mean, *fort*.

Sending Brion to the house with the ruse we were choosing sides for kickball, he came back with our housekeeper, Beatrice, who agreed, albeit reluctantly and hurriedly (she had a roast on, if memory serves me correctly) to appropriate the kitchen broom—for that was the source of our ballots—and hold the straws for the drawing. Obviously a professional at this, as she evidently was in many other endeavors, Beatrice positioned the five chaffs she'd cut expertly behind her palm, held in place by her thumb, the ends perfectly level and aligned just above the ridge of her long, bronzed and calloused index finger. Although it would have been next to impossible for any of us to have divined the lengths of the straws she held, she nevertheless added her own rule to the game, insisting that we turn our head when drawing so our choice would be made blind.

How such a short broom straw could have been so successfully aligned with the other three lengths without giving its size away, I can't say. Doubtless a skill Beatrice Smith took to her grave. Nor do I recall how that same straw ended up between my thumb and forefinger, but there it was. Beatrice wiped her hand on her apron, looking suspiciously at each of us like we were the Dead-End Kids.

"How are you going to play a fair game of kickball with *five* of you?" she asked. But before any of us had time to provide an answer that would allay the doubt furrowing her brow, her eyes shifted to take in the Brownie on the table in the corner, and then leveled on me. "And does Miz Ford know you've got that camera the commercial people gave you out here?" But again, before a suitable response could be formulated, her attention shifted a second time—to her watch. "Oh, Lord," was all she said, and then she was gone, striding at a long lope back to the house, and presumably to whatever was on the stove or in the oven. We were, evidently, saved.

With Beatrice gone, Mom shopping, and Dad on the back nine at Lakeside, the hour so long in planning had come. Muffled only slightly, we could hear laughter and splashing coming from the Hopes' pool. Clearly, it was now or never. Grabbing the Brownie, I slung the strap over my neck, and we made our way to the entry point. There, flanked by Thetford, Jedica, and Noonan (Brion bringing up the rear), I dropped to all fours and began removing the camouflaged greenery we'd replaced to disguise the tunnel. Once clear on our side, I said good-bye to my mates and began the crawl through the bore we'd cut through the hedge. Finally, I reached the outer wall. From ahead of me came a sound that could only be that of a body entering a pool. Surely this was her, I remember thinking. All that was left now was to carefully move the fewest of branches and vines, position the Brownie just so, and history would be mine. I pulled the last net of vinery away, and came face-to-face with—Bob Hope. On his hands and knees. Staring right at me.

"Let's see, you're Buck. The oldest. Right, young fella?"

Knees turning to oatmeal, hands rooting into the ground, where I expected jolts of electric current to shock me any second, my brain moved at a pace that astounded even me. As nonchalant as I could be, I took the Brownie off my neck and held it between my hands like a pro paparazzo.

"Can I take your picture, Mr. Hope?"

Somewhere, long since lost from those prized possessions of my youth, there exists a one-of-a-kind snapshot of the greatest profile in show business. Somewhat out of focus, if I remember correctly, but recognizable nonetheless; the vines draping over his one-and-only schnoz, the bright white honeysuckle trumpets dimmed by his brilliant smile.

Thanks for the memory, Bob. And for not telling Mom and Dad about the hedge.

Oh . . . and Mrs. Hope was wearing a one-piece. Another mystery of our youth dashed.

Within weeks after our move to North Hollywood, the rpm's on the Ernie Ford publicity engine were cranked to redline, and would burn at that speed continuously over five years. If *Life* magazine wasn't at the house doing a story, *Look* or *Saturday Evening Post* was. If Earl Wilson wasn't on the phone getting an exclusive granted by Dad's publicist, Mickey Freeman, then Army Archerd, John Crosby, Hedda Hopper, or one of several scores of other entertainment reporters was. If he wasn't shooting B-Roll for a new Ford spot, he was doing a spread for Dreft, or Alka-Seltzer, or Hi-C. If he wasn't in the studio cutting a new album, he was in the living room with Jack Fascinato working on the arrangements for it. If he wasn't in rehearsals for *The Ford Show*, he was running lines for his cameo on someone else's. And if he wasn't doing any of the above, it was summer, and he was rehearsing for the road.

Welcome to the Ernie Ford Family Show. Now appearing everywhere.

Early in November 1956, about a month before we moved to Toluca Lake, Ralph Edwards collaborated with Jim Loakes, Cliffie Stone, Mom, and—oh, hell, virtually everyone within an arm's reach of Dad—to produce the Ernie Ford installment of his hit series, *This Is Your Life*. In addition to that show, Edwards was a pioneering radio and television producer responsible for *Truth or Consequences*, *The Price Is Right*, *Name That Tune*, and, in more recent years, *The People's Court*.

This Is Your Life was a completely novel concept for television, in a time when virtually everything happening through the medium was novel to some degree. The genre was essentially documentary, but the format was videotape—kinescope, more precisely. Over a half hour, Edwards would act as a guide—a curator of sorts—and relive a star's life through old footage, stills, and the memories of friends and family secretly enlisted to appear on the show. All very tame, really. But what put teeth in the concept was that in all but a very few instances the celebrity guests didn't know they were the subject of that particular night's airing until they were informed by Edwards—some would claim ambushed—live, on-camera, at the beginning of the show. For many of us who remember the program, the opening sequence was, in many cases, the most dramatic moment of the show's next twenty-two minutes.

With the help of Loakes and his handpicked crew of coconspirators, Edwards engineered an elaborate plan that centered on re-creating Dad's home in Bristol on a soundstage in Hollywood—and it was ingenious. In the four weeks preceding the show, National Van Lines (one of the show's sponsors) loaded virtually every stick of furniture—sofas, tables, chairs, wall clocks, curtains, end tables, pictures, *everything*—from the living room in Clarence and Maude's home on Windsor Avenue in Bristol, and moved it to Hollywood. A decorator assigned to the crew located the same wallpaper pattern and bought enough to repaper an entire room. Clarence, Maude, and Dad's maternal grandmother, Nancy Long, were flown to Los Angeles and ensconced at the Hollywood Roosevelt Hotel across from Grauman's Chinese Theatre. At eighty-two years old, it was the first time Nancy Long had ever set foot in a plane, let alone flown in one. It was, I'm sure, also the first—and probably the last—time TWA has ever allowed a spit can for snuff in first class.

Three days after loading the furniture in Bristol, the moving van backed up to the loading docks of studio two at NBC—directly next door to studio three where *The Ford Show* was rehearsed and shot. Over four days, with the help of Clarence and Maude, set carpenters and dressers, production assistants and grips, painstakingly re-created their living room in every detail, down to the wallpaper and family pictures. Less than a hundred feet away, Dad never knew. Didn't have a clue. The night of the show, Edwards walked on the set of *The Ford Show*, where Dad and the Top Twenty were rehearsing, and ambushed him as the cameras rolled. When he led him back to studio two, Dad walked into the living room he'd remembered as a child. On the couch was his grandmother.

Clarence and Maude, Cliffie Stone, Briton Peter Ausden (author of Dad's first fan letter from overseas and lifelong friend), his voice-teacher from Bristol, Chuck Dermott—his training pilot from the Air Corps days at Victorville—Mom, Brion, and I were all paraded onto the set over the next twenty-two minutes.

I'm sure it was nothing more than a typical aversion some people have to showing affection in public, but—when each of the guests made their entrance—and I mean, *each* of the guests—they were embraced by Dad, and they returned the gesture, genuinely and tightly. When Mom came out, Dad threw his arms around her, but as he did, she pulled her elbows back, planted her hands on his forearms, and with a nervous smile and little laugh, pushed herself away from him. For the briefest of moments, fleetingly almost, a wistful, questioning look passes across his face. Unless you knew him, and knew him well, you probably wouldn't see it. But it was there. As quickly as it appears, though, it vanishes, and for the next fifteen minutes, sitting next to each other—Dad's hands noticeably, appropriately constrained—they are the two people I still most clearly remember them to be; ordinary souls who've awakened to find themselves travelers on an extraordinary journey, amazed by what they see happening to them. The cameras do not lie on this show. They show two people connected to one another, inseverable, coalescent, symbiotic. Two halves of one person. Root and branch, yin and yang. Coal and diamond. Glancing upward to those around them, and outward to the monitors displaying images of the past, then inward, privately to each other as if they were alone on the bus, they are like two tourists, seeing the world of their lives together for the first time. She is proud of him, and laughs at his asides. As I watch, I imagine it is the same way that she told me he made her laugh on the base at Victorville when they first met; easily, gently. Next to her, Dad basks in her radiance and evident affection, astonished that this is his—*their*—life.

Three short months later, on March 1, 1957, the house and grounds in Toluca Lake were transformed into a remote location by CBS and Edward R. Murrow, when Dad, Mom, Brion, and I became the sixty-fifth subjects of Murrow's seminal interview series, *Person to Person*.

Originally limited to fifteen-minute segments in its first few seasons, but expanded to half-hour shows from its third year on, *Person to Person* was the forerunner of generations of wannabe up-close-and-personal interview programs, none of which have ever come anywhere near the mark set by their predecessor.

From his studios in New York, Murrow sat in a comfortable easy chair, cigarette smoldering between two fingers, his head turned ever so slightly away from an oversized video screen on the wall to his left, giving the appearance that he was in his own private projection room. Smoke curling around his lapel, he addresses the camera and his audience. On the screen, an establishing exterior shot of the home or location of that night's interview can be seen. On the night of March 1, the establishing shot was of 10250 Moorpark.

As portrayed by David Strathairn in George Clooney's news-noir black-and-white homage, *Good Night, and Good Luck* one comes away with the distinct impression that Murrow despised doing *Person to Person*, that he would rather have been editing footage of bingo tournaments in Fargo than "interviewing" Lee Liberace, or, one would infer, Ernie Ford and family—that the show was somehow beneath him and true journalism. If that portrayal was indeed historically accurate, Murrow was as adept and talented an actor as he was a journalist, because the impression he gave us—one that still resonates with me these fifty years since—was one of genuine friendliness, interest, and affability.

Multiple cameras, nests of cables, and an entire crew filled nearly every room on the first floor. The driveway and garage became the base of operations for the production trucks and craft services, Mom's dressing room became makeup, and in the backyard, catty-corner from the lanai, a thirty-foot microwave relay tower was built the day before to beam the live line-of-sight transmission to CBS in New York, where Murrow intercepted the signal on monitors in his studio. And with the aid of cutting-edge audio and split-screen technology (which enhanced the show's success considerably), it was possible for us to not only hear Murrow's questions, but to see him, as well.

"Following" a subject through his home with a camera was impractical. Track was not laid down from room to room, and the steadicam harness had not yet been invented. To compensate, it was predetermined which rooms would be featured in the guest's home, in which order, and each would then be pre-equipped with camera, audio, and crew. In that way, the viewer could "follow" the guest as he gave Murrow and the audience a tour of his home.

Along with pre-blocking the tour, Murrow and his production team decided early in the show's gestation that it would be equally efficient if certain of his questions were made available to the guest in advance of the evening's interview. The answers, however, were completely ad lib. Nevertheless, certain members of the press corps who considered themselves journalistic "purists" raked Murrow, CBS, and the show over the coals for producing television programming they believed lacked substance, programming that was nothing more than "aimless armchair chatter," as columnist Harriet Van Horne termed it. Moreover, Van Horne and her ilk were aghast that such drivel would be produced by someone of Murrow's reputation and stature in television news.

For his part, Murrow defended the show and told Harriet Van Horne and the other purists where they could get off.

Our thirty minutes with Edward R. Murrow was vastly different from the half hour we spent with Ralph Edwards. Both shows were watched by some forty million people, but in the case of *Person to Person*, those forty million were guests in our home, as we were in theirs. There was no secret alliance contrived in advance by Murrow and CBS. There was no ruse, no stealthy collection of furnishings, and no shrouded re-creation of a corner of the house on a soundstage hidden from view. America was in our living room, our den, and the lanai. Forty million members of America, anyway.

As I watch the show today, nearly fifty years after its broadcast that March evening, I'm struck by the personality of Edward R. Murrow, and the effect that the personalities of Betty and Ernie Ford appear to have on him over the course of twenty-four minutes. As the show opens, his dour expression and grave delivery are immediately recognizable. Watching and hearing him deliver the opening biography of the man whose family he's visiting that night—chiseled features caressed by cigarette smoke curling from hand to head—one would think he's setting the stage for an in-depth interview with someone whose mere existence has changed the course of human history. That is, until the last line of that introduction, when, as he turns to the large screen—establishing shot of the house—and informs the audience that the house they're looking at is now home to "Ernie, his wife, Betty, their two sons, Buck, seven, and Brion, four, and Bubbles, their English bulldog. . . ." Fade to Dad in the lanai.

Hearing the world's most recognizable journalist introduce your bulldog, intoning the name Bubbles, may have contributed to those journalistic purists' conceited view that *Person to Person* was only so much drivel, but it made Edward R. Murrow way cool in my book.

Another huge point in Murrow's favor—while not taking anything away from Ralph Edwards—was that Brion and I got our own segment.

I mean, how many other kids can claim to have been interviewed by the world's most influential newsman at the age of seven? The same guy who skewered Joseph McCarthy wanted to see my electric trains, and wanted to know who my favorite singers were. Naturally, seasoned pro that I was (remember, I was a veteran of three—count 'em, *three*—Johnson's Baby Shampoo spots), I took the opportunity to plug Elvis, Tommy Sands, and . . . oh, right—"Tennessee Ernie Ford"—in that order. When asked the same question, Brion was far more paternally diplomatic: "I like my daddy and I like Mickey Mouse." As he paused for breath, pro that I was, I immediately covered for him, reminding Murrow and forty million visitors, "Well, I really like Elvis Presley."

Jesus, I gave my own dad second—no, third—billing on *Person to Person*.

The next mistake he makes is asking if Brion and I sing like Dad. By the time we finish our (well-rehearsed) a cappella rendition of "Ringo Rango Jimmy Joe Jango," the same grim-faced, humorless newsman that began this show is laughing along with the rest of the crew, whose mirth can be heard off-camera. He loosens up even more when Mom tells him the biggest problem she's had moving to the new house has been that "every time I hang the clothes out to dry, the tourist bus goes by." Then, with perfect Ernie Ford timing, Dad deadpans, "Actually, they're seeing the Hopes' laundry. Bob brings their clothes over every day for Betty to do."

Edward R. Murrow clearly hasn't laughed this much in years. You wonder what took him so long. George Clooney . . . David Strathairn—shame on you. This was a man with a sense of humor.

I realize full well that recounting the experience of these two shows may seem a bit artificial, pointless, and perhaps even cocky to some. I understand. But I recall them not to give myself credit or to ascribe any unwarranted self-importance, but because they have great value to me—because I treasure them more than my limited vocabulary can describe.

You see, I have cataloged literally hundreds of hours of moving images of Ernest Jennings Ford. I have codified years of recordings bearing the sound of his voice—talking and singing. I have lived all my life surrounded by transcriptions of my father.

But, aside from six cassette tapes she made late in her life—her own audio diary of a trip to Europe in 1981, and two tapes she recorded two years before her death on a night so saturated with vodka that she is at times unintelligible—aside from those six magnetic reels, two half-hour television shows from half a century ago are the only filmed records of Betty Ford that exist.

Hours upon hours of home movies taken by her father when she was young, miles of footage on reel after reel of Bell & Howell 8mm's shot by Dad and Loakes throughout our lives—all are gone—vanished sometime during that black hole of the last six months of Dad's life. That dark recess of diseased time when his mind was no longer his. When that illness manifested one of its more vile symptoms, and made him almost robotically susceptible to manipulation by those closest to him. When, in the throes of that illness, magnified by the bewildering loss of the one with whom he'd shared his life, he married Beverly Wood Smith, who claimed to have "placed all those old movies in storage," then claimed ignorance of their whereabouts. Who calmly took me into her confidence one evening backstage before Dad received the Minnie Pearl Award, believing me to be an ally in her usurpation, telling me, "Your mother's drinking killed your father." That "she never really loved him."

So, I am left with two fifty-year-old thirty-minute television shows containing some twenty minutes in all of Betty Ford. The only evidence I have of her grace and spirit, her laughter and poise. The way she moved. The way she looked into the eyes of her husband. The way she talked and breathed and, although only for a few brief, captured moments, the way she lived.

That is why I treasure them.

Commensurate with the quickening pace of his celebrity, Dad began to live and breathe for the golf course, the ranch, and the islands—not necessarily in that order. Mom began to live for whatever would take her mind off the fact that Dad was gone more often than not.

Keeping pace with his workload was quite simply impossible for her—after gamely filling in for Loakes and Cliffie Stone on his tour of England in 1953, she stopped trying. And although Beatrice took up great folds of slack at home, finding a commonality of interests besides traveling, dinner parties, and drinking was becoming more difficult by the minute. She tried golf, which lasted for about twenty minutes. By '59 she'd become physically unable to go to the ranch (another story—remind me to tell you later). She didn't hunt. She didn't fish. She wouldn't cut bait. That left Honolulu. And until they bought the penthouse at the Colony Surf in '61, the islands were an annual trip, no more frequently. All of that added up to Betty Ford with a lot of spare time. Not a good thing.

"After everything we'd been through to get your father where he was, here I was again, back in New Mexico, climbing on the proverbial windmill, waiting for him to come home. Beatrice had taken the bus back to Watts by five, and you boys were glued to the damned TV most of the time. Until I started painting, I listened to Judy Garland's records, read everything I could get my hands on, and drank. Christ, *after* I started painting, I listened to Judy Garland's records, read everything I could get my hands on, and drank. Which thrilled your father to no end."

On Thursday afternoons, Beatrice would pick us up at the end of the school day. At three o'clock sharp, she'd plant herself at the entrance, standing alongside the station wagon. Some days, she would dispatch our gardener, Johnny Valencia, to retrieve us when she was needed to commandeer the kitchen, or help the caterers prepare for a dinner party. Other days, she would enlist her husband, Fred, who would pick us up in his Super 88, wearing his do-rag over a freshly dipped pompadour. Our substitute Thursday chauffeurs were rare, though, and we looked forward to seeing Beatrice's stern smile at the end of the school day.

By the time we got home, Mom would already be in her dressing room, getting ready for the show that night. The scent of lilacs or gardenias would float down to the den or the kitchen from upstairs, mixed with the acrid odor of a burning Pall Mall, and the sweet tang of gin—an aroma I could identify and differentiate from other spirits by the time I was nine.

Beatrice would stay late on Thursdays to keep watch over Brion and me, and over her chicken potpies we'd wait expectantly for the sound of Mom's footfalls on the stairs, and the brush of her evening dress as she came through the foyer. Her entrance into the kitchen was cinematic; jet-black hair cut page-boy chic, cigarette gracefully resting between two fingers, the smoke curling up and around her wrist, then hugging the shape of her handbag, which she held with the aplomb and panache of Joan Crawford or Bette Davis—her two favorite actresses.

Her trajectory across the kitchen floor would tell us how much she'd had to drink that night. Steady for a step or two, then perhaps a slight weave as her hand sought the edge of the ashtray. If she made for the stove, Beatrice—her eyes riveted—would gently, laughingly intercede, heading off any possibility of a pan on the floor, a potpie on the dress. After the shortest of tenures, Beatrice Smith could read Betty Ford like a book. She was good.

Within minutes of her entrance into the kitchen, a taste of each of our potpies, and a sip or replenishing of her drink, like clockwork her ride to the studio would arrive, and with Beatrice's permission (always with Bea's permission, God help us otherwise), we'd dash from the table to the back door to be there when the car door opened.

Ken Thompson was officially Jim Loakes's assistant, but, like Loakes, his place in our lives was far too integral and familial to ever be regarded so unimportantly, or with such a mundane title. I'm sure, however, there were times, in the thirty years he was so integrally a part of us, that he wished an assistant was all he was.

Ken came up on the radar in 1955, when Dad was doing the daily series from the El Capitan in Hollywood. He'd been working for Ad-Libs, Barney McNulty's cue card company, running cards for Dad and other acts. Handsome, articulate, and seemingly possessed of way more answers than a cue card flipper should have any right to, his work ethic and easy charm endeared him to Dad, Jim, and Cliffie Stone instantly. When *The Ford Show* became a reality, almost simultaneously with the release of "Sixteen Tons," and the once-manageable life and career of Ernie Ford became bigger than anyone foresaw, Jim Loakes quickly realized dealing with things single-handedly was going to be impossible. By November of '56, Ken Thompson had become the newest member of BetFord Corporation, and an assistant to Jim Loakes.

Handling everything Loakes could throw his way, Ken, or K.T. as he was occasionally known, became indispensable virtually overnight. He knew Hollywood, he knew the business, he knew Dad's wardrobe, he knew where Brion and I were, he knew what Loakes and Cliffie ordered for lunch at Kosherama, he knew how many drinks Mom had put away by the time he picked her up at five thirty on Thursday nights to drive her to NBC, and he knew how to stay completely cool wading through all of it. He was unflappable. In thirty years, I never once heard him raise his voice or betray anger. His smile and laugh were infectious. As if all that weren't enough, he looked just like Clint Eastwood. Tall, chiseled, six-pack abs, and hair I would still kill for. When I tired of wanting to be Elvis, I wanted to be Ken Thompson.

For thirty years, he was the big brother I never had. In 1972, when Dad's career was showing signs of waning and business was beginning to decline, he and Loakes took K.T. to lunch in San Francisco and cut him loose. I felt as if I'd lost the best friend I'd ever had.

His natural cool probably factored heavily in his being assigned the duty of driving Mom to the studio every Thursday evening; ten-minute sojourns on DEFCON 3 that he remembers with the clarity of glass— as if they happened yesterday. "She'd start drinking early in the day, you know. By the time I got to the house, she was pretty well shot. But she . . . you know, she carried herself pretty well most nights. I could tell when it was going to be rough on your dad, though. Your mom could go from being just hilarious, you know—she was so funny—to . . . that sarcasm, you know—just pin somebody with it. I never knew, nobody knew when it was going to happen, you know— when she'd go from somebody you'd want to be around, to just . . . she'd say things that would just slam your dad. We were always on a sharp little edge with your mom. I had to be ready to kind of steer things away, you know. I loved her and your dad, so much."

The five years we lived in Toluca Lake radically changed our family, because the five years we lived there radically changed the relationship between Mom and Dad. As the tension became more palpable between them, Dad worked harder to keep Brion and I ignorant of the effect it was having on him and on all of us. He worked hard to hide the bad from us. He worked at protecting Mom from herself, and on some nights, when he knew what was happening and felt justified interceding, he worked at protecting Brion and I from Mom—from the belt in her hands—when she was too smashed to know that she was whipping us with the buckle end, and not the leather. More often than not, he would simply turn the belt around and hand it back to her, watching as the last few strokes fell. If the buckle hook had drawn blood, Mom would bring a bottle of Bactine from the medicine cabinet, and as we lay across our beds, crying, she would dab it on the cuts, reminding us to sleep on our stomachs so we didn't get blood on the sheets.

Dad worked hard at hiding these and other moments from memory. He worked hard at covering. He knew—like each of us, though Brion perhaps to a lesser degree—when Mom was most unpredictable and potentially volatile. What might have appeared rude—his answering questions put to her, interrupting and finishing stories she'd begun— were safety mechanisms, put into gear when the fear of what might actually come out of Betty Ford's mouth overruled otherwise normally observed amenities of courteous discourse. What even Dad failed to get, though—or if he did, filled him with even more trepidation—was that 99 percent of the time, Betty Ford knew exactly what she was saying, whom she was saying it to, and what the effect would likely be. She could stun someone into stupefaction as casually and pleasantly as she might answer the phone. Their forty-six years together are replete with examples, but two choice moments stand out, and stand out hilariously.

In July 1963, Dad combined his summer fair tour with our summer vacation. We crossed the country on the *Super Chief*, interspersing concert dates with trips to great corners of the country Mom and Dad wanted us to see as a family. Part of the itinerary that year was Jackson Hole, Wyoming, at the feet of the Grand Tetons. We were booked for two nights there, at the Wort, one of the West's great lodge hotels, and brought Mom's mother, Jesse, with us on the trip.

On our second day there, Mom and Jesse took Brion and me along as they shopped and Dad did an interview at the hotel. As word has a tendency to do, it got around very quickly that the one and only was in Jackson Hole. By the time he finished the interview, and stood with Jackson Hole's finest for a roll or two of film, some three hundred people had jammed the lobby, the restaurant, and the hotel's entry, hoping for a picture, an autograph, a gander. Accepting an invitation from the bootblack just outside the hotel's doorway, Dad led these hundreds to the sidewalk, climbed up on the bootblack's high chair, and while the spit shine was being popped on, he signed autographs for virtually everyone.

At what we have since deduced as being precisely the same moment Dad climbed onto the shine stool, surrounded by hundreds, Mom, Jesse, Brion, and I exited the town's department store, laden with boxes, on our way back to our hotel. We'd traveled all of about twenty feet when, directly in front of us, a man rounded the corner on foot, running as if his life depended on it, and slammed directly into Betty Ford and Jesse Heminger, nearly knocking Mom to the ground and scattering boxes everywhere. The guy is falling all over himself apologizing, but obviously still in a hurry.

"I'm sorry, but lady, do you know who's getting his shoes shined at the Wort—*right now?*"

"I don't have the foggiest," Mom lied. "Who?"

"*Tennessee Ernie Ford!*" And as he gathered up the last box from the sidewalk, Mom casually adjusted her girdle and, without making eye contact, said, "Oh. Him. Big Deal. I slept with him last night."

We left the poor man there on the sidewalk, agape; Jesse muttering what I think was the Lord's Prayer as we made our way back to the hotel.

Not long after, during his sold-out concert at the Central Canadian Exhibition in Ottawa, Mom happened back to the hotel room after an hour or so at the bar, and interrupted an interview Dad was doing with a lovely but rather prim society reporter from the Ottawa *Times*. "Are you Mrs. Ford?" the reported asked. Passing through the suite, Mom never missed a beat. "Oh, goodness no," she said with a laugh. "I'm his mistress. Mrs. Ford hates traveling." And then she was gone, leaving Dad to explain—or try to.

I've often been asked, and ask myself often, whether or not Mom "liked" what Dad did for a living. I have no idea. In thirty-some years, I heard her say one thing about one show—*The Mikado*—which she absolutely adored, and one thing about one album he cut in 1966. It was embarrassing, she said. She couldn't stand it. She gave that review during a particularly incendiary time in their marriage, a period I believe negatively impacted his artistry significantly, so I don't know and can't say that it was reflective of any opinion she might have held in the preceding years. The subject never came up. At least, not in any conversations *I* had with her.

I never caught her listening to one of Dad's records, or going out of her way to watch him guest on someone else's show. I never caught her humming one of his tunes, nor did I ever hear her compliment him on any of his work, save for *The Mikado*. In later years, however, toward the end, Dad told me a number of times that Mom "never cared about what I've done or what I do." By then he had long since given up covering, given up trying, and given himself to alcoholism as well, and that observation was almost always followed by what became a mantra, of sorts, one I expected whenever I would find the courage to talk to him about the two of them: "This is my lot in life. So be it."

In the good years, they were never hesitant to tell each other "I love you," to laugh at each other's jokes, or to say how handsome one or the other looked. But like their embraces, those were mostly private moments. Public displays of their affection for each other were inadvertent, usually catching them unawares when the juggernaut of publicity was in high gear, tearing breakneck through the house, the yard, our lives. I treasure those few shots, because they are rare, and reminders of better days.

And also in the good years, when they were both sober, and when we were all young, there was a bond—a band of light that encased us as a family. A sense that we were all on a great, mysterious, wonderful journey together. That we all belonged on the journey together, and that we needed one another to complete it, wherever it led. There were times that I truly, genuinely believed that Mom, and, although to a lesser extent, Dad, *needed* me on the journey with them.

When that bond was strongest, the band of light glowed brightest, and we were impenetrable as a family. Nothing and no one could enter unbidden. We drew our strength from one another, and sustained one another.

There was a time when the power, the rightness, the evidence of their love for each other was almost overpowering; it was intoxicating and addictive. When it began to crumble, to evaporate, the sense of loss sent me into a sort of mental delirium tremens, and I'm still going through withdrawal, still reaching back in time, trying with these words, these pages, these passages, to cop just one more jones, one more sense of that love, one more hit, one more feeling of what it was like when they were in love, when that golden band surrounded us. Before the light faded . . . before Mom pulled the darkness around her and didn't come out again.

I don't mean to imply that our lives together were one continuous thread of discontent and pressure, because they were anything but. I have crystalline memories of long spells of a joyous youth that sustain me now as I recall those darker times. The two balance each other, even though there are moments when the darker times can seem oppressive and consuming. They threaten to undermine the happiness I do recall, plunging me into depths of sadness over their loss of way, of love, of life. Yet I cling to both the good and the bad, and pray that all my memories will remain intact long enough to finish this manuscript, so that I may record the truth of their lives for my own children, and perhaps their children.

NINE

IN ONE'S LIFETIME, ten years doesn't seem like an especially long period of time. But all things are relative. In that span between 1955 and 1965, experiences that might otherwise cover many more years in another's lifetime were given to us. Were it not for Dad's Leica, Jim Loakes's Rollei, and the press, I would have only wistful, vague, fading memories of the events that now occupy so many of my waking hours. We were blessed beyond anything Brion or I could imagine, because we had no reference points from which to compare. We lived a life charmed with advantages and gifts we gave little or no thought to, and we were privileged beyond reckoning. So much was given to us. So much happened. So many stories . . .

As grueling as his schedule had become, network television and *The Ford Show* gave us something back besides privilege and advantage; it gave us our summers together—for the most part, anyway. It was common for MCA to book Dad on one or two concert dates between July and September, but the series had become a bigger sales tool for his Capitol releases than touring could ever match. So, summers became our escape valve, and we spent them traveling.

We crossed the country coast-to-coast on the *Super Chief*, the *Zephyr*, the *City of New Orleans*, and the *Lark*, the great passenger trains of our time. We saw the deserts, the plains, and the coastlines from the dome cars, and breakfasted with sterling in the dining cars. We drank Shirley Temples in the club car, playing Old Maid with new friends, while Mom, Dad, Loakes, Ken Thompson, and the rest of the crew played charades around endless rounds of drinks. We knew Union Station in Chicago, Nashville, Philadelphia, and Los Angeles, and Grand Central in New York, as well as we knew our own neighborhood in North Hollywood. Word flashed up the line, and depots from Denver to Salt Lake, Memphis to Moline would be packed with fans— hundreds-deep, waiting for a glimpse of Ernie Ford. From the coach steps or the club car deck, he'd step out, protected by Loakes and handpicked porters, and wade through the throngs, signing, pressing, posing, and hugging. At night we were rocked to sleep in our berths over the syncopated clip of the rails underneath us, carrying us away.

In private Pullman cars we railed into New Orleans, where suites awaited us at the Roosevelt on Baronne Street. We lunched with Sister Mary Phillips and the nuns of the Old Ursuline Convent on Chartres in the French Quarter, the oldest convent in New Orleans. She and the order had become fans in 1956, and on Christmas that year sent Dad and Mom a brace of hand-cut crystal aperitif glasses, monogrammed with their names on each. Sister Mary went straight to the A-list. On our first visit to the convent, great tables the length of telephone poles were set in the courtyard, just off the porte cochere. Around the tables were a score of sisters, all smiling, all robed, barely concealing a meal that covered virtually every inch of the boards. Creole shrimp, jambalaya, steaming gumbo, batter-fried chicken, fresh green okra and beans, and pones of hot yellow corn bread in cast-iron skillets flanked butter dishes that bloomed like sunflowers. Enormous tureens of lentil soup and étouffée floated like barges next to ears of corn stacked like cordwood. In the center, baskets of pralines, beignets, and corasse were dusted with powdered sugar. Pitchers of iced tea punctuated the tableau, sweating beads of moisture down their chilled, glassed sides. Under the warmth of the midday Bayou sun, in the shadow of the oldest church walls in New Orleans, we sat at God's table and broke bread with Sister Mary and her fellow nuns.

We dined privately at La Louisiane, guests of the notorious Diamond Jim Moran, onetime amateur boxer, ex-bodyguard for Huey

Long, and reputed associate of the Costello family. A legend in a city replete with legends, he bought La Louisiane in 1954, using funds most believe came through Frank Costello's hands, and promptly turned it into the best-known and most popular restaurant in New Orleans. Its opulence was matched only by Moran's own ostentatious and garish image. Never losing the fascination with diamonds that entranced him as a boy, he bought them like marbles and accessorized virtually everything he owned with them. As a fringe member of the Chicago families, he was regularly seen in the company of Costello and Lucky Luciano, both of whom he frequently took to church on Sundays when either was in town on "business." As a legit restaurateur, he cultivated a clientele that included everybody from Rocky Marciano and Jimmy Durante to Marilyn Monroe and Dwight Eisenhower. In the process, he created his own legend, and became one of the Big Easy's most visible symbols of excess and materialism. It didn't help that he was known to carefully secrete diamonds inside delicacies prepared for special guests. I remember our first of many evenings there as if it were a page from a Coppola or Altman script, relegated to the second disc in a DVD collector's set of lost scenes.

Stepping out of our limousine on Iberville, between Bourbon and Royal, we were greeted by a liveried doorman and hôtesse, who ushered us into arguably New Orleans' most famous and luxuriously appointed bistro, which was . . . empty. Not a soul in sight. Every table vacant, bare of all essentials—no napery, silver, porcelain, or glass. Every table but one. In the center of the main dining room—the Rothschild Suite—it sat, directly underneath a glowing, iridescent chandelier emanating a brilliance that threatened to enflame the room around it. And the table! A great, round diner, set with the most gracious of precision; the tines of the forks perfectly aligned, the napkins folded like oversized linen origami into the shapes of winged swans, nesting on gold-rimmed, intricately painted china. Under the illumined chandelier, the crystal goblets beside each plate reflected facets of light that danced across the walls behind the empty tables that surrounded this setting. At the far end of the room, a fire burned in the white iron foyer, casting shadows of flame that licked the ceiling. Other than the crackle of the hardwood burning there, the entire restaurant was completely silent. And other than the hostess, standing at sentry by the table, gesturing pleasantly for us to sit, it appeared we were completely alone. In the span of just a few hours, we'd gone from lunch with God in heaven to a Franco Fumagalli set from *The God-father*. The Mob had targeted Ernie Ford and we'd been lured here for our last meal. I was hoping for a Shirley Temple and Brion was asking Mom if he could order a hot dog, which was overheard by our hostess.

"You can have whatever you'd like, young man," she said. "Mr. Moran is looking forward to meeting you."

She'd no sooner finished than from the kitchen, through the bar, and past the fireplace came our host. Even these fifty years since, the image of his entrance is still vivid in my memory. He was dressed in a cream-white, three-piece suit and wore light gray spats. He carried an obsidian-black cane, its handle the head of a great black swan with diamond eyes. His glasses were black, too, and like his cane, his tie, his fingers and his cuff links, beset with brilliant diamonds. Diamonds were all over the man's body. He reminded me of a prism. A 280-pound beaming prism. He smiled, and I half expected his teeth to be made of the things.

Bowing, he took Mom's hand first and raised it to his lips. "Betty." He wrapped both his arms around Dad and hugged him like kin. "It's about time, Ernie!" Moving around to Jim (who was on Code Yellow), he held his hand out. "Mr. Loakes. My pleasure. Good to have you with us." Then he took his seat between Brion and me and put us both on his lap, one on each leg. He smelled like bourbon and raw fish. "You're Buck!" he said to me. "And this is Brion. You boys look just like your pictures." Smiling nervously, I looked away from him long enough to see Mom pulling Brion's hand away from Moran's tie clip, where he was ardently trying to pry a stone loose as a souvenir. Moran was unperturbed, and told Mom Brion was fine. "All the children love the things," he said. And then, placing me back in my chair, he scooched his seat away from the table, shifted Brion on his lap, and reached toward his crotch. "They love playing with this," he said, and folded over the lapel covering the zipper to his pants. Attached to the pull was a diamond the size of a garden pea. "Pull on that, young fella!"

Whether out of fear, outright disbelief, or numbing astonishment, I remember thinking then, and recall now, that I had never seen Dad, Mom, *and* Loakes all frozen with the same look of sheer incredulity all at once. For his part, Brion was blissfully unaware and giddy, playing with Diamond Jim Moran's zipper for the rest of dinner.

Over bluepoint oysters, bistro salad, and pork porterhouse—which Moran simply called "the pork chop"—we heard story after story of the legendary guests that had dined at La Louisiane. We heard about his days with Huey Long, and his short history as a heavyweight in the ring. We heard about our lunch at the Ursuline Convent earlier that afternoon with Sister Mary Phillips. "A kind, wonderful woman. Dear to all of us." None of us asked how he knew. We all chewed carefully but in the end disappointedly so, as no diamonds were hidden in our pork chops.

The *Zephyr* took us to Chicago where majordomo Doug Boone ensconced us in the presidential suite of the Sheraton Blackstone. Furnished with Louis XVI antiques, a Chippendale dining ensemble, and a Baldwin grand piano, it overlooked Michigan and Balbo, and seemed as big as our entire house. We were treated like royalty there, with personal attendants in waiting and private dining rooms downstairs, where we were always served personally by George Vasilakos, the Blackstone's resident maître d'hôtel.

On a bored afternoon one July, Brion and I decided to set off on our own. We left the lobby armed with our vacation allowance and walked across Balbo to the Rexall on the corner, where we selected a long string of fake costume pearls as a gift for Mom to wear at dinner that night. When we returned an hour or so later, the lobby had been cordoned off and was filled with Chicago police and FBI agents. Mom was crying hysterically, inconsolable, surrounded by brick-faced lawmen. We had walked into our own kidnapping investigation. The faux pearls helped, but barely. Mom loved them—so she said—and they saved us from the belt that night, and that was all that mattered.

On July 17, 1955, we rode through the gates of Disneyland on its opening day in Anaheim. We were Walt's guests at the Disneyland Hotel whenever we visited. At his invitation, we Halloween'd there every October, and had the run of the park as we tricked-and-treated our way from Tomorrowland to Fantasyland and up and down Main Street. On a clear Sunday morning in '58, we made our way to the front of the hotel where we were to be picked up for breakfast with Walt before we drove back home. We barely made it through the lobby once word made it to the crowd of patrons that Dad was among them. On the sidewalk outside the entrance we were surrounded, pressed in from all sides by fans clamoring for an autograph, a handshake, a word, a snapshot. Brion and I watched as Dad graciously and politely obliged all—an image I will always remember. The crowd slowly milled away, heading off to Adventureland or Cinderella's Castle, leaving a small knot of a few fans who'd waited patiently for the throng to thin. Kodak in hand, a woman stepped up shyly to Dad and asked if she could have her picture taken with him. As she did, a car pulled to the curb and a single passenger climbed out of the backseat. As Dad assured her he'd be happy to, she turned to find someone—anyone—who would snap the shot, and pressed the little camera into the hands of the man who'd just stepped out of the car waiting curbside. She barely acknowledged him as he kindly agreed to take the picture.

"Do you know how to work a camera?" she asked. His head down, face partially hidden, lining the frame up through the viewfinder, the man replied, "I think so." The shutter clicked and the man turned the camera in his hands as he advanced the film. "Honey," Dad said deadpan, "do you know who just took your picture?" As the stranger looked up, her mouth fell open. "I'd like you to meet Walt Disney," Dad said. Her mouth was still open when we climbed into the waiting car to take us to breakfast with Mr. Disney.

From the ports at Los Angeles and San Francisco, we sailed to Honolulu on the *Matsonia* and the *Lurline*, the great flagships of the *Matson Lines*. Five days at sea with glorious staterooms and lanais on the A decks, skeet shooting off the stern and dining at the captain's table. On the morning of the fifth day, bells would bring hundreds of us to the starboard rail to watch as daylight broke lazily over the islands and Diamond Head slowly came into view. Scores of outriggers would race to the side of the great ship, their oarsmen decked in leis, and we would fling quarters and half-dollar pieces into the sea beside their boats, watching expectantly as the kanaka would dive into the clear waters and retrieve the sparkling coins, layering them in their cheeks, waving for us to throw more. Catamarans and Chris-Craft cruisers brought service crews and bellmen from the hotels along Waikiki and set up reservation desks on the main decks as the big tugs pulled the liner to pier 10 under the Aloha Tower.

We began summering in Honolulu in 1956, staying for long weeks at the Hawaiian Village on Waikiki when it was owned by the legendary industrialist Henry J. Kaiser. We were there when the Village, the Ala Moana, and the Royal Hawaiian were *the* hotels, before the glut of construction ruined the beach. We were there when Michele's opened its doors at the Colony Surf in the shadow of Diamond Head, when Mom and Dad bought penthouse 9, eighteen floors above, and next door, the Outrigger Club was still the most exclusive address in Honolulu.

We flew in Aloha Air twin-props to Maui, and were there when the Sheraton and the Hilton were the only hotels on Ka'anapali—when you could walk an arced mile of pristine sand the color of freshly washed muslin, count the number of people you'd meet on one hand, and remember all their names. We were there when the ocean walkway on Front Street in Lahaina was a boardwalk, not concrete, and a windward breeze seemed to carry the scent of orchids from Molokai and Lanai across the inland waters.

We sang onstage with Don Ho, learned the ukulele at the hands of Alfred Apaka, and were taught to surf under the tutelage of Duke Kahanamoku and world champion—now state senator—Fred Hemmings. We were taken in by Kimo McVay, Hawaii's most irrepressible and flamboyant promoter, discoverer of Don Ho and owner of Duke's—Honolulu's most famous nightclub. We were introduced to the inner circle of his mother, Kinau Wilder McVay, great-granddaughter of the first missionaries to settle in Hawaii, estranged wife of Capt. Charles McVay—infamous, sacrificial skipper of the USS Indianapolis—and descendant-du-nom of High Princess Kinau, daughter of King Kamehameha the Great. Guesting at her ancestral home on the summit of Mount Tantalus, high above Honolulu, we sat enthralled as she regaled us with tales of ancient Hawaii and told us of sitting in the window ledge of the very library we were in and watching, transfixed, as the red-flagged Zeros careened "like birds of prey" through the canyons of Tantalus, down into the coastline below, and incinerated Pearl Harbor on the morning of December 7, 1941.

When Mom and Dad bought the penthouse at the Colony Surf, Honolulu became something of a second home. Brion and I were allowed our own room several floors below, and our stays there became longer, stretching on for weeks upon weeks. As the fifties snuck into the sixties, sailing from the mainland became impractical and we forsook the five days at sea on the Lurline, and began flying instead. We could not have known that our 1962 sail was the last voyage the Lurline would make to Hawaii and back to San Francisco. She was dry-docked at pier 35 in November of that year and never made the journey again—the last of the great luxury liners.

And now, in my mind's eye, hazy and glazed with a film of tears as I look back, I see us all on the deck of the great ship, rounding the bend at Diamond Head on Boat Day, our shoulders layered with tiered garlands of leis, heavy, damp, and soft, redolent with the scent of fresh orchids. I see Mom on the beach at the Hau Terrace, the pattern of her muumuu subdued only by the brilliance of her smile. I see Dad in his Outrigger trunks, browned and muscled, standing at the wheel of the *Kamahele*, the club's flagship catamaran, far out in Mamala Bay, off Kapiolani Point. The big twin hulls are slicing keenly through the blue waters, smooth and glass-like beyond the surf line, cresting in foaming ribbons between our boat and the shore. In her horn-rims and one-piece, Mom is on the forward deck with Brion and me—our faces in the wind, her arms around us both, her eyes on Dad. Westward, an amber-hued sun slowly, almost imperceptibly settles closer to the horizon, turning the sky the color of ripe mangoes and bathing us in a golden light as we tack leeward and head back to the dock. I hear the light wind pop the canvas on the masts above us, and the sound of Mom and Dad laughing together.

In those dream-like years every trip was an event, every arrival an appearance, every dinner reservation a story for the press. Every move was planned weeks in advance; every stage etched in stone on The Itinerary—the road bible, courtesy of Jim Loakes—a script one deviated from only at great risk. We didn't take family vacations; we took the Ford Show on the road: "*Ernie Ford, his lovely wife, Betty, their two sons, Buck (insert age here) and Brion (age again), manager Jim Loakes, associate Ken Thompson, and Cliffie Stone and his wife, Dorothy, arrived today . . .*"

As my fingers peck awkwardly across the keyboard now, I am filled with the memories of those trips and the reverie of a gilded youth. I can almost feel the palpable rush of excitement, the thrill of anticipation, and the giddy elation of knowing that wherever we were, we were the headliner, the magnum opus, the main attraction. Fame had given us the keys to the world and first-class seats to any destination we chose. All we had to do was promise to take Fame with us and book him a seat, make him a reservation, set a place for him at the table, and schlep his baggage—all of which Brion and I would have been happy to do for every trip we took for the remainder of our natural lives. Attention and privilege are powerful intoxicants, and Fame seemed to possess an unending supply of both. Traveling, living—without them, without Fame—would be . . . *normal*; a way of life I know now Dad yearned for and ardently began seeking, but a way of life that would never be his or Betty Jean's again. He may have known this, but I can't be certain. I believe *he* believed he could leave it all whenever he so chose, that he could trade lives, drop Fame off at a bus station somewhere. In the middle of the bowl in the salad days, at the zenith of his popularity and notoriety, he sought moments when he could get as close to anonymity as possible, when he could stop being Tennessee Ernie Ford, stop being someone everyone knew, someone everyone wanted to touch, someone everyone wanted to hear, someone everyone wanted to see—when he could just be Ernest Ford, husband of Betty Jean, father of Buck and Brion.

Nevertheless, he was not always granted those moments when he sought them; they eluded him, and with their elusiveness began to grow a distrust and disdain for the success and the business that should have given him the freedom he sought. Slaking that thirst meant escaping his success. And in escape, I remember the trips that mattered most to *him*; the journeys unplanned, when, in the dead of night, between the deep sleep of a child and near-wakefulness, I would feel myself being carried, cradled in Dad's or Mom's arms, still in pajamas, to the open hatch of the station wagon. Backseat folded up, blankets and sleeping bags padding the cargo bay. They're whispering, talking in hushed but excited tones, as they lay Brion and me next to each other and wrap us in the thick, warm comforters and bedding. Cocooned, I begin to feel the Country Squire moving, and, like the driving wheels of the *Super Chief*, the hum of the tires underneath me soon lulls me back to sleep. I smell suede and cigarette smoke. Hours of driving through the night later, I'm awakened by the same pitch and yaw of the road that put me to sleep earlier. I crawl out of the woolen envelope encasing me and raise my head slowly—sleepily—over the hub of the rear wheel-well. Country I've never seen is passing by. The morning sun is slanting through the redwoods. The Russian River is churning in a canyon below. Piñons stand sentry on the two-lane heading into the Sierras. Half Dome in Yosemite is just ahead. Waves are coursing up to the rocky shore along Bodega Bay. At the wheel, Dad is wearing his rough-outs, and beside him, Mom is in jeans and moccasins. We're alone, Mom, Dad, Brion, and me. There's no itinerary, no reservations. No police escort flanks us, no attendants are seeing to us. We're alone, and Fame is nowhere to be found.

More often than not, the road taken on those trips begun late in the night led to the one place Dad truly found peace and refuge—albeit for too brief a time—the ranch.

It was called Long Valley Ranch, and covered a handful more than five hundred acres of workable pasture ground, surrounded by low buttes and foothills thick with brush-pine, manzanita, eucalyptus, and oak, and was located a stone's throw northeast of Clearlake, which lay a little less than a hundred miles northeast of San Francisco.

A good half-day's drive from the Pacific Coast (in the fifties), the town of Clearlake and its nearest neighbor, Clearlake Oaks, were no bigger than wide places in the road, sitting squarely in the middle of Highway 20, a meandering stretch that cut southwest through the hill country outside Sacramento and ran along the shoreline of the lake that both burgs were named for. Aptly christened, Clear Lake is the largest natural freshwater lake in the state, and while some days it was more green than blue, its warm volcanic waters were clear and azure on most. The source of legends for hundreds of years, mainly from the fires and lodges of the Pomo Native Americans who were there long before us, it is said that Clear Lake may also be the oldest natural body of water in North America, watched over for centuries by the dormant volcano on its western cape, Mount Konocti. Under her cloud-wreathed summit, Dad and Brion and I spent our mornings fishing for bluegill and crappie in the brackish waters near the tules. The afternoons found Brion and me swimming out to the big pontoon raft just beyond the pier to watch and wave to Mom, Dad, and Jim as they skied past, kicking up rooster tails behind our sky-blue Evinrude outboard, the *Ski Bird*. Late in the day, we'd clean and eat our catch from the morning, or drive into town for dinner at Mae's before heading back to the cabins for the night.

Held for some seventy years by the Cross family, Dad found the ranch late in the summer of 1955 when he learned that its owners, May Cross and her son, Douglass, had made a decision to sell. Dad was ecstatic. It was everything he could have hoped for: good hay ground, abundant water from the natural artesian springs underneath it, fencing that was old but would do for now. The tack room, full barn, and original stone home, although all in need of shoring up, were standing. The price was right, and Mrs. Cross had only one condition before she'd close the deal: that she be allowed to be buried near the old rock fence she and her husband had built with the Pomo field hands after they were married. Two days later, her request was enumerated as a rider to the sales agreement, and Ernest J. Ford became the second owner of Long Valley Ranch.

Okay . . . jump ahead five years to 1961 for just a few minutes. This is so weird. We've moved to the Bay Area, and BetFord's offices are now located at 645 Larkin Street in San Francisco. The intercom rings in Jim's office, and Bea, his secretary, tells him that "a Douglass Cross is here to see you. No, he doesn't have an appointment, but says it's very important." Loakes picks up the story . . .

"Well, I tell Bea to send him in, and this guy comes into the office, introduces himself, tells me his mother was May Cross, she sold the Long Valley property to Ford, blah, blah, blah—and he says, 'And I'm a songwriter.' Well, I'm thinking, *Oh, Christ, I've let a goddamn songwriter in here . . . he'll* never *leave.* Well, he says, 'I'm a big fan and I've got a song I think would be just great'—they all think it would be just great, you know—'for Mr. Ford.' So he gives me the arrangement (which I don't even look at) and the next week, your Dad and Jack Fascinato are in town for a meeting and I bring this arrangement out. Cut to your Dad and Jack, who take it over to the piano, and noodle with it for a while, and they—we—all decided then and there that it just wasn't Ford's kind of song. We thought it was too much of a love song—a little too . . . I don't know, it just didn't feel like Ford. Well, I call Cross and pass, and of course, he's disappointed, you know, but the next night—I think that's right—he gets backstage at the Fairmont where Tony Bennett's headlining and gives him the same arrangement. Six weeks later, Tony cut it back in Hollywood, and it became his biggest record: "I Left My Heart in San Francisco." Of course, we all kicked ourselves, for Chrissakes, and your dad eventually recorded it in '66 on the *My Favorite Things* album. Who knew?"

Great story or what?

The public image of the man's man was big in Hollywood throughout the fifties, and Ernie Ford was not the only celebrity to project a largely illusory perception of rugged outdoorsman to counter that of the polished star of the silver screen, the stage, the long-playing high-fidelity record, or the TV set. Gable hunted with John Huston. Gary Cooper was an avid deep-sea fisherman, and John Wayne was, well . . . John Wayne. But for the biggest part, the idea of actually working a ranch was alien to most. Building fence and mucking out stalls was not something most people in show business aspired to do in their free time. But that was precisely what Ernie Ford looked forward to. This wasn't going to be some kind of retreat for a gentleman farmer. The thought nauseated him. This was going to be a working ranch from the ground up; one geared to raise purebred Herefords and putting up two, maybe three cuts of alfalfa. This was where he'd dreamed of retiring—which he was talking more and more about. This was where he wanted to *be*. This was where he wanted his family to be. This was his hedge against what he saw as an uncertain future in an unpredictable business. This was serious.

But as serious as he was, Long Valley Ranch was a long way from earning money, and an even longer way from paying for itself. Which meant that show business was still the family business, and would be for the foreseeable future. He needed help.

One morning during the daily NBC show from the El Capitan in Hollywood, he began talking about the ranch—rambling on about the land, the timber, the water, the hunting, the property's history, and he casually mentioned that the only drawback was he didn't have anybody to manage things. Before the week was out, more than five hundred letters came in from all over the country—ag students, field hands, cowboys, wives of cowboys, retired bronc riders—every one of them applying for the post. Loakes took it upon himself to winnow the letters down, finally selecting a handful of promising candidates. From that group, he and Dad selected Gene Cooper, a graduate of Pierce Agricultural College, herding cows for the Adohr Farms conglomerate in Camarillo. Three months later, he and his wife, Lorena, and their two children had moved into the old Cross stone house, and Long Valley Ranch was under new management.

For five or six years, the ranch held almost as much allure for Brion, Mom, and me as it did for Dad. One of my favorite pictures of Mom and Dad together was taken there; Dad at the wheel of the big Ford tractor, and Mom behind him, arms wrapped tight around his waist, her head pressed against his back. Smiles cover both their faces, and I can feel their happiness and love for each other in the texture of the old black-and-white shot.

We spent weekends there during our stays at Clearlake, bunking in the living room on rollaways and helping Gene. We built fence and strung wire. We dug irrigation ditches and learned how to shoot. We were taught how to curry a horse, how to cinch a saddle, how to care for tack, and how to ride. We gathered eggs from under dozing hens in the coop for breakfast and killed rattlers that found their way to the cool of the smooth, slick concrete porch in the heat of the day. We watched as this life seemed to transform Dad; to claim him, rouse him, peel the veneer from him, and strip him down to an elemental dad we'd never known him to be. We watched as he changed almost overnight—before our eyes, like time-lapse photography from a science film in school—and became someone else, talked like someone else, and acted like someone else. The ranch occupied his every waking hour. In time, it became less of a place than a state of mind for him. He was closer now—closer to making the break from the life that he was becoming more weary of, almost by the day, very nearly by the hour. Every break on tour, every hiatus from the series, every spare or free weekend out of the studio, he was off to Long Valley. And by the time he'd thrown his duffel bag in the station wagon and climbed behind the wheel, the change to Rancher Dad was well under way.

Dad was not unusual in this way; spiriting away from the grind lightens everyone's load who works for a living, no matter what you do. In that regard, Ernie Ford was no different from anyone else. Whenever he was cut loose, wherever he fled to—Honolulu, Palm Springs, or Clearlake—the break from the tedium and pressure and schedules was healing and brought out the best in him. But with the ranch, it was different. Being there, talking about going there, on his way there, wholly altered him, recasting him in a role he seemed to be in continual preparation for. Like an Actors Studio method student under Strasberg, we would watch as he climbed into the skin of this character, taking on his mannerisms, his gait, his inflections, and his appearance, very nearly completely transforming himself in the process. Underneath, Brion and I saw occasional glimpses of the other Dad we knew was in there, but over time, he became harder to find, harder to identify and discern. He would fall into character at dinner parties, on the golf course, in the market, on the beach. He talked glowingly of plans to groom (no pun intended) Brion and me to one day run the spread when he was gone. To enroll us in 4-H, and send us to ag school, like Gene Cooper. To get us out of Hollywood and set our feet on paths that would lead us to become real men, sons he could be proud of. Sons who saw the flippancy of show business for what it was, who shared his growing disdain for it and the "squirrels" who worked in it, who would gladly follow their father out the belly of this unforgiving beast of a job and into the great wide-open world of real work, honest work, work that put sweat on your brow and calluses on your hands.

At nine, ten, and eleven years old, Brion and I were happy to oblige. By then, we'd grown accustomed to the new Dad, and his ability to change personas apparently at will. Early on, it was only mildly confusing that he would wax philosophically about his rural dreams for us while he was backstage waiting to hear his introduction, or to reporters in a break from recording, or on the set of *The Ford Show* during his monologue. And although I can't speak for Brion, I will admit that my dreams of succeeding Elvis or Link Wray or Johnny Burnette were way more palatable than the thought of four years of college studying bovine reproduction systems.

But both of us wanted one thing above all. To make him proud of us, a desire that was at times—in my case—overpowering. And this apparent duality, this ability to be both rugged man of the land and cool entertainer, became my mantra, my blueprint for success. If Dad could do it, I could learn, and I could be just like him. I watched and copied, absorbed and reflected. I could be all these people. I learned to brand steers and clean fish. I learned how to caddy and how to swing a nine-iron. I learned how to deliver lines from old scripts Jim would secretly bring home from the studio. I learned how to hunt and snake logs. I learned how to play a twelve-string and pose just like Ricky Nelson. I could do all this—I could change at will, just like Dad.

Then one night on the ranch, in the big living room not long after everyone had gone to their beds, a change of another sort began happening—to Mom. From under the covers on the rollaway, I could hear her and Dad behind the door to their room, at the far corner of the house. Something had awakened them and they were arguing heatedly, but in guttural whispers, vainly trying not to wake anyone. It was apparently working in Brion's case. He was dead to the world under the blankets next to me. But I had no sooner shifted my eyes away from regarding his peaceful countenance when the door to Mom and Dad's room opened, and she walked haltingly into the living room, her hand on her chest, her body bent. Her mouth was open in an O and she was arching her body backward, then pitching forward, then backward—mouth wide open—as if she was trying to suck something in the air into her body. Behind her, Dad was feebly patting on her back, speaking in low murmurs, telling her she was going to be all right. "Take a deep breath. You're going to be all right." Pat, pat. "You're going to be okay, Bet. Just take a . . . ," and that was about as far as he got. Damning the embarrassment of waking the house, she straightened up as much as she could and wheeled on him, gasping. "*Goddamnit*, Ford! Are you *deaf*? I . . . can't . . . breathe!"

Throwing my covers off, I ran to Mom's side, earning a gentle but firm rebuke from Dad and a wheezing attempt at the same from Mom. Within a few minutes the attack seemed to subside, and her breath, though labored, began to return to more natural and smooth cycles, allowing her body to straighten up, and alleviating the fear that had propelled me from bed to her arms.

The next day we drove back to the house on Clearlake, and a few days later, we packed the Ford and drove back home. Mom was fine until, unpacking Dad's duffel and shaking his ranch clothes out before laundering, she was stricken again by the very same attack that had assailed and awakened her that night at Long Valley.

In time it was determined—though I do not know how—that Mom had become allergic to horses. But not just to the animal itself—to anything and everything that had anything whatsoever to do with horses. Horsehair, horse trailers, horse blankets, horse hooves, horse stalls, horse lovers, and horseshit. For a year or so, the attacks were relatively rare, but grew worse as time went on. They became more pronounced, fierce in their onslaughts—many unexpected and in the most unlikely of places—and were unforgiving in their severity; robbing her of the air she so badly craved, and the dignity she prided herself on. Each attack seemed worse than its predecessor, and with each, her body seemed to shrink—from the effects of the strike and from the world Dad had found so much happiness in.

It was the last time she would ever go back to Long Valley Ranch, and save for one brief visit, she never set foot on the Nevada properties that came later. The ranches and their lives became his, not theirs, leaving Mom to seek other avenues and other corners of refuge for herself.

TEN

I've just finished watching Gene Kelly's daughter, Kerry, interview on her dad's segment of the *American Masters* series on PBS. She was commenting on how, growing up in Hollywood, "every adult she knew" was seeing a therapist. Every adult except for her father. I can relate. Ernie Ford thought psychiatrists and psychologists were a big part of what was wrong in the world. He couldn't understand how they functioned or why they were so vital, it seemed, in people's lives. Especially people in show business. And he was scared shitless of continuing in a business—in a town—where Mom, Pop, and all the kids had their own analysts.

But familial psychotherapy was, as he saw it, only one of the warped by-products of raising a family in Hollywood. The town *did something* to people. The business did something to people. It changed them. People sacrificed everything: marriages, families, children, and sanity, for a shot, a cameo, a break, a discovery. The well-adjusted, family-tied star, producer, or director was a rarity; they were few in number and far between. Dad sought out those who were like him, but they were hard to find. You had to peel back the veneer of makeup and gloss, and that was too painful for too many. You just didn't reveal who you really were. Publicity departments did that for you. Granted, sometimes they performed that service with a bit more creativity than necessary, but they knew best; it was important that the studio, the network, the label be comfortable with the image their star was pro-

jecting. You played the game, you got used to it over time, and, eventually, you became a reflection of someone whom someone else had created. You became a commodity, a product, an asset—but with a finite worth only as good as your last picture, the last ratings, your last record.

It was a viciously impersonal cycle, trading in people, dreams, and fantasies. Timothy Hutton described its vagaries and ouroborean appetite beautifully in an interview some years ago. *Timothy who? Get me Timothy Hutton. Get me a Timothy Hutton type. Get me a young Timothy Hutton. Timothy who?"*

Dad saw these darker aspects of Hollywood clearly and early on in his career, and he knew they were necessary evils; something he needed to work with, work through, and, for a time, work in. But for the biggest part, he did so completely on his own terms. From the beginning, he refused to conform completely to what Hollywood expected of its stars. He rejected every mold, every preconceived notion, and every press angle. He was an anomaly, an oddity. There was nothing fabricated, nothing produced or synthetic about him. What you saw was what you got, and neither Hollywood nor Madison Avenue had the slightest idea what they had.

He didn't care. For forty years, he performed and lived by a work ethic that hadn't changed: "I don't perform for executives in L.A. and New York," he said many times. "I play all the houses in between."

I don't want to suggest that Dad did not love his work; he did. No one worked harder at loving show business. He loved rehearsing, he loved the people he worked with, he loved the excitement and unpredictability of a live show, the scripts, the lights, the curtain—he loved it all. And I would be misleading you if I told you he didn't love the attention and applause, because he did. In show business, you're paid twice—if you're lucky. You take the money to the bank, but you become *invested* with the applause. It's intoxicating, invigorating, addictive—no matter who you are. It's what a performer lives for, and in that regard, Ernie Ford was a pure professional: He loved the applause.

But here's what separated him from so many others in the business: He left it in the studio, he left it on the stage, he left it on the road. He worked just as hard to avoid bringing it home as he did to earn it. What he did was not what he was, and he worked tirelessly—obsessively—to maintain that difference. Most people in the business didn't.

Success in show business, stardom in Hollywood—they were means to an end, not the be-all and end-all. He admired but felt sorry for show people—many of whom were dear friends—who dreamed of dying in the wings in greasepaint; their lives one-dimensional one-acts, lost and rudderless outside the confines of the industry they toiled in.

My God, I'm psychoanalyzing him. If he were still alive, he'd kill me.

Dad first began talking openly about getting out of Hollywood in 1958. He was careful in interviews to express his gratitude for the success the business had brought him, but he became more emphatic and vocal about the damaging effects he saw being wrought upon his family— primarily upon Brion and me. In fact he never bemoaned any ill effects being wrought upon him or Mom. Just Brion and me. In scores upon scores of press releases, magazine leads, and front-page stories, he lamented that his two sons were not leading what he thought were normal lives, and rued what he saw as an impending eviction and subsequent vacancy of values from our lives. All of which he laid at the feet of show business in general and on Hollywood's doorstep in particular. Of course, nobody ever asked Brion or me—and we didn't know from vacancies. We were having a blast, for God's sake. Bob Hope lived next door, Chris Noonan's dad was a Hanna-Barbera artist who was always giving neighborhood kids sketches out of his book, the Warner Brothers lot was just a few blocks up the street, Bill Thetford's dad got us into movie theaters he managed for free. You could ride your bike to the Hot Dog Show and Lakeside Pharmacy; there was no telling who'd show up at the NBC parties in the backyard . . . life was great. *We* were fine.

There was something happening to Mom, though, and ergo, to Dad; something that was changing the dynamic between them, stretching the bond between them. Even at eight and nine years old, I began to sense it. It was not always visible, not always readable, but I sensed it; like a current of cold water you'd have to add to a tub that was too hot; invisible, but you felt it, like a thread of cold rope, snaking through the tub and coiling briefly around your body before being absorbed and equalized in the warmer water. The comfort level changed immediately, and your skin prickled. She grew increasingly quick to anger, seemed to lose patience with Dad over trivial, mundane things, honed her sarcasm to a serrated edge, unafraid of whom she might cut, and they argued more often than I remembered. Then the cold current would disappear as quickly as it had come in, and the love, the warmth, the symbiotic *thing* that emanated from them would reappear, binding them, joining them, erasing the memory of the cold thing that snaked through me only hours, minutes, maybe days before.

I know now that these abrupt changes in her personality were due mainly to an unchecked dependency on drink and an unwillingness, or inability, on the part of anyone close to her to rein it in. One took her glass away at one's own peril, and hell had no fury like that of Betty Ford without a drink. Compounding the situation was the fact that Dad and Mom—and virtually all the satellites that orbited around them—lived, moved through, and reveled in a culture of drink. It was as much a part of their lives as eating and breathing. Granted, in those early years of the salad days, post time came at five o'clock, rarely earlier. The Bloody-Mary-for-breakfast-era was still a good six years off, but in our house, you could set your watch by cocktail time.

I remember clearly a *People* magazine interview in the seventies with Bernie Taupin, Elton John's lyricist. The press was clamoring because he'd changed clothes, or some damn thing, and during the interview he was asked if he'd given thought to curtailing his well-publicized coke habit. "Never," he replied. "It's too much a part of the lifestyle."

Substitute *vodka, scotch,* or *gin* for *coke,* and the interview could have been conducted with Mom or Dad. They simply didn't know any better, and other than the occasional embarrassing evening, saw no real danger in the habit, a habit that, had Brion or I been sickly, would surely have been acquired by one or both of us far earlier in our own lives.

In the Betty Ford "clinic" *we* checked into, our common colds, earaches, flu, or sore throats were all treated with the same elixir: three tablespoons of bourbon with a pinch of sugar. Go ahead, laugh. The treatment worked wonders for both patient and physician. Three big, sweet spoonfuls of Jack Daniel's and neither of us cared whether we were sick or not. We were out cold by the time Mom was back in her room, and she was free from our stuffy, feverish complaints for the rest of the night. While the same treatment today would raise eyebrows at the very least, and possibly invite Child Protective Services over for a visit, the knowledge we have today of inheriting the traits of substance abuse simply didn't exist then. No one knew enough psychology to connect the dots between Mom's grandfather, her older brother, her older sister, and herself. Betty just needed to be watched, managed, and monitored. She'd be fine.

Right.

By the end of our first year in North Hollywood, her volatility and unpredictability after a few rounds of drinks were putting everyone in the circle on the defensive, especially Dad. In October 1956, on the night of *The Ford Show*'s premiere at NBC in Burbank, she could barely walk a straight line as she and Dad made their entrance into the studios. He was quietly furious, she was flightily happy, besotted with glee and intent on infecting everyone in the room. Dale Sheets, one of Dad's agents at MCA, remembered Dad smilingly excusing the two of them, pulling Mom behind the set walls, and threatening, pleading, begging her to pull herself together. Of course, in Mom's opinion, she was together. This was who she was. Screw anybody who didn't like it. Smoothing the skirt of her Chanel fall ensemble, she made her way back to the reception, charmed everyone completely, and was the talk of the evening.

As Dad's fame grew and our lives in Hollywood became more . . . Hollywood, Mom began to slowly move out from under the shadow that Dad's fame was casting. Like a rare orchid, dormant for years, unseen, undetected, hidden in the folds of some giant banyan tree's trunk, or in the shade of an arboreal canopy shielding it from the wilting effect of light, she slowly began to unfold. She blossomed at parties, entertained effortlessly, held court at dinner parties and captivated guests. She could discuss anything with anyone—from art and politics to fashion and literature. She absorbed books like a sponge, dabbled in poetry, began painting and collecting art.

It is said that timing is everything, and I believe it was at this juncture that the timing of their lives together began to ring dissonantly. As her horizons were expanding, Dad was resolutely trying to bring his—and, therefore, the family's—horizons down to a smaller, more manageable size; a little ranch, a few weeks on the road, a couple of network specials, and one or two sessions a year. As he was becoming more disenchanted with Hollywood, she was finding herself more comfortable in its environs. As he was feeling the pull of escape, she was finding her own place in it. Just as he was beginning to hate it, she was falling in love with it. She didn't pursue a Hollywood lifestyle; she *was* a Hollywood lifestyle—all by herself.

Artistically and intellectually, she was growing beyond the simple man she'd married, and beyond the simple girl she'd once been. And at that same time, I believe a small seed of jealousy began to germinate in Dad; a fear, almost, not only that she was capable of eclipsing him, but also that she was aligning herself with the very thing and the very people he was trying to free himself from.

Many years later, the note I found when she took her own life would bear that out. I kept it secret, though, and never betrayed its existence to Dad.

Initially, no one believed Dad was serious about leaving. *Variety*, *TV Guide*, *Hollywood Reporter*, Hedda Hopper, and Earl Wilson all called it brilliant publicity. Ernie Ford the Common Man. Ernie Ford the Gentleman Farmer. Ernie Ford the Shrewd Businessman. Retire? Move away from the lights, the camera, the action? It was completely unthinkable to some, and laughable to others. For five or six years running, Bob Hope's Christmas card had a five-dollar bill inside, for Dad's "retirement fund."

Any concern that he might be serious about leaving was quelled in 1959. But only for a brief moment.

At the end of the '58–'59 season, *The Ford Show* was the number one show in its time slot. It owned Thursday nights, and had so for two years. It was broadcasting into more than thirty million homes every week, the overnight ratings were off the radar, the mail was coming into NBC and the Sunset and Vine offices by the truckful, and Fairlane 500's were almost flying off the showroom floors. In just three years, from the series' debut on October 4, 1956, Ernie Ford had become one of the most popular stars on prime-time television and one of the most visible and powerful salesmen in Hollywood.

At the time, Dad was represented by Berle Adams, Sonny Werblin, and Dale Sheets at MCA, the agency headed by the (even then) legendary Lew Wasserman. MCA had been handling him and our family company since 1954 and were known as the shrewdest, toughest agents in the business. They set the tone for that representation late in '54, when they demanded NBC give Dad complete creative control for his first network series, *The Tennessee Ernie Ford Show*, his daily half-hour variety show shot and broadcast from the El Capitan Theater in Hollywood from January 1955 to June 1957.

NBC was incredulous and indignant. Responding to MCA's demands in a blistering memo to Dad dated December of '54, NBC's West Coast head, Tom Sarnoff (the youngest son of General David Sarnoff, founder of RCA), made it very clear that the network had no intention of ceding creative control to the host of an untested, unproven, sponsorless, sustaining half-hour show. Nothing remotely like that had ever been done by the National Broadcasting Company before, and they were certainly not going to start now.

Within four months it was the number one show in its time period, Ford Motor Company was in talks with MCA for Dad to host its debut into prime-time television, and his single "The Ballad of Davy Crockett," the theme from the Walt Disney film, was on virtually every station on the radio dial. When MCA submitted a revised contract to Tom Sarnoff, again demanding creative control *and* more money, the network gladly, almost giddily reversed itself, and signed off on the raise.

Once Ford Motor Company knew they'd found their host for *The Ford Show* in Dad, MCA's negotiations with Ford's advertising agency, J. Walter Thompson, proved far more acerbic, lengthy, and ultimately profitable for all. Under a three-year-long current of sometimes bitter, sometimes mutually congratulatory, sometimes outright hostile arbitration between the two camps, everyone was generally happy. Until the end of the third season.

Four weeks before the last show of the season, J. Walter Thompson notified MCA that they were exercising the option to renew for two more seasons—'59–'60 and '60–'61—and would likely exercise their prerogative to sign for a sixth and a seventh season. Profits were up, ratings were off the charts, the show was firmly ensconced in the Nielsen Top Five, and it was holding to the number one position in its time slot for the third year running. Business was good. Ford had a bona fide star in the stable and was looking forward to another record year.

It was two weeks before MCA sent the first salvo across J. Walter Thompson's bow; Ernie was thinking seriously of quitting. The grind was taking its toll, he was losing time with his family, and the show was beginning to feel tired. The material was used, he was exhausted, and . . . he was giving a lot of thought to leaving Hollywood. He was in for the '59–'60 and '60–'61 seasons, but there were going to have to be some very substantive changes in the deal.

The substantive changes were subsequently transmitted to J. Walter

Thompson in a memo that would set the stage for one of the most bitter battles never recorded in show-business history.

The bottom line: MCA was demanding $5.5 million for the fourth and fifth seasons; more money than any sponsor had ever paid for any program on prime-time television to date. Bottom-*bottom* line: Ford and J. Walter Thompson refused.

This made life very difficult for Dad's agents at MCA. He was only one act, to be sure, and *The Ford Show* was only one of the twenty or so shows they repped and packaged to the networks. But even in the most popular of those shows, they saw finite possibilities, limited lifetimes on the air. In Ernie Ford, they saw something else altogether: a personality uncannily aware of his audience, a star with marquee power beyond the television screen, a man who could sell Frigidaires to frigging Eskimos. He and Ford Motor Company were an act and an account they couldn't afford to lose.

So Berle Adams told J. Walter Thompson that he would do everything in his power to convince Dad to agree to the sixth season, and would work on him for the seventh as and when the time was right. On the strength of that commitment, Ford anted up five and half million dollars for the fourth and fifth seasons each, making Ernie Ford the highest paid prime-time television star in the business.

At the end of the fourth season, the second salvo was fired. Dad announced publicly that the 1960–1961 season was his last. He was leaving Hollywood, leaving weekly television, leaving the grind, and moving north.

The shock wave reverberated from Burbank to Madison Avenue at about a 7.5 on the Richter scale. Memos flew back and forth from coast to coast like ICBMs, crossing each other in the ether that was then Western Union's domain. Accusations were leveled, hands were raised, phone calls placed, demands made, lawsuits threatened. The press pounced on the story for all it was worth, covering each week's developments like its own ongoing soap opera: *Ernie Ford Retiring— Says Good-bye to Hollywood. Ernie Ford to Leave Network TV. Ford Motor Company and Ford Split. Ford Tries to Woo Its Star Back.* In May 1961, Danny Seymour, Farlon Myers, and Tom De Paolo—J. Walter Thompson's most powerful media trio—met Dad and MCA's top brass at the NBC studio in Burbank to watch the live feed to New York for the May 11 show with Cliff Arquette. After the show, it was a cordial, pleasant enough dinner along with Jim Loakes, Ken Thompson, and Cliffie Stone at China Trader, a quick "so long" to Cliff Arquette in the parking lot, and then back to the house for drinks and to watch the West Coast airing at 9:30.

After the show, Mom made a quick drink and said good night, gamely making it upstairs with help from Beatrice, our maid.

There was an uncomfortable silence in the living room, broken only by the clink of ice into fresh glasses for everyone as Jim mixed drinks for all. Over his scotch, Danny Seymour got right to the point.

"Okay, Ernie. Let's *talk*. This whole thing is still workable. Just tell us what you want. Tell us what you've got to have—we're ready to pay you whatever you want."

Dad did not blink. The most powerful men in the biggest advertising agency in the world were sitting in his living room, offering him anything he wanted, if he'd only stay in the game. He took a long pull from his Cutty and branch, leaned back in his chair, crossed his legs, and leveled his eyes at Seymour.

"You don't have enough money, Danny. And you don't understand. It isn't about the money. I'm leaving. I'm building a house in the Bay Area, you know? I'm done. I'm through."

And just like that, it was over. They shook hands, smiled, and everyone wished everyone good luck, but within a week, press releases were being issued saying that Ford Motor Company had dropped Dad.

He was unperturbed. In a *Variety* story that ran some two weeks later, he was characteristically honest and brief: "We've had fun, it's been a ball . . . but we've taken this about as far as it can go . . . and we're beginning to milk it. I want to go out at the top of the game, before the audience begins to feel the same way."

In truth, Dad had left the show months before, and it was telling. His heart hadn't been in it for nearly the full season. It had lost its magic for him, lost its brilliance, lost the fun. It had become work. On June 29, 1961, the curtain came down for the last time. Ford never sought a replacement host, and the show was never revived.

That same month, honorary Mayor Johnny Grant and a host of show-business royalty unveiled the completed Hollywood Walk of Fame, where 1,558 stars, directors, writers, producers, arrangers, and announcers were immortalized forever along what would become the world's most famous promenade. But among that group, 175 stood out; 175 honored with not one, or two, but three stars. And included in the roster of that rarified fraternity was the name Tennessee Ernie Ford.

* * *

We moved to the Bay Area in July 1961, within weeks of *The Ford Show*'s last night on the air. And while preparations, packing, and leaving Toluca Lake took their toll on Brion, Mom, and me, Dad couldn't leave fast enough. Stressful as it was for Mom, though, she was not resistant to leaving. In truth, she was probably just as excited as Dad, but in typical Betty Ford fashion, she restrained herself, putting her energies instead into ramrodding the movers, cracking the whip behind Brion and me, and demanding that Dad do something constructive besides packing his gun collection, his own duffel bag, and his golf clubs. By the time the Bekins trucks were out the driveway and on the road, she was spent, and as ready to leave as she could be. The residence at 10250 Moorpark was just an empty house now. Our home was six hours away and 352 miles north.

Moving to the San Francisco area was something Mom and Dad put on the planning board—what there was of it—in the early fifties, when we first began vacationing in Clearlake. The drive from the L.A. basin to the lake passed through the Bay Area and San Fran, and Mom's older sister, Vayle, had moved there with her husband in the late forties. Mom and Dad both loved the romance and élan of the city, and the expansiveness of the Bay Area, and began talking about moving there long before it became a reality for them.

The property, totaling fifteen acres in all, was located in an area south of the city called Westridge, a semirural subdivision some ten minutes from Palo Alto. They bought the property in 1958, two years after Dad bought the ranch outside Clearlake. While the ranch got volumes of press attention on a regular basis, the purchase of the Peninsula property was kept under a cloak until 1960, when he announced he was leaving Hollywood, *The Ford Show*, and NBC. By then, the network, Ford Motor Company, and J. Walter Thompson were all under the impression he was going to retire. "*Ernie Ford and his lovely wife, Betty, are building their dream home just ninety minutes from Ernie's dream ranch.*" He'd work a few weeks every year, record every once in a while, and spend way more time with the family and way more time on the ranch.

Of course, nothing even remotely like that ever came close to happening. And when those powers that be—that *were*—learned he'd signed with ABC for a daily series from KGO in San Francisco, they publicly castigated him for committing, as the Dallas *Tribune* called it, "career suicide." Ernie Ford had stuck it to the man—the men—and they were pissed. ABC, on the other hand, was ecstatic. After months of secret negotiations with Dad's agents at MCA, ABC and its ebullient CEO Tom Moore celebrated pulling off a network television coup of front-page proportions, and handed Dad and BetFord the single biggest, most lucrative contract they had ever extended to anyone.

When the move became a reality, it generated a lot of press and a lot of attention, both North and South. Burbank bemoaned Dad's flight, and the Peninsula prepared for the arrival of a third wave of show-business royalty; Bing Crosby and his brood had been living in Atherton for several years, and Shirley Temple Black and her husband had called Redwood City home for some time.

While other forces strained, shook, and stirred Mom and Dad's relationship, planning the move and building the house strengthened it. For two years they reviewed bids and plans, read blueprints and commissioned renderings, eventually settling on a design from San Francisco architect-wunderkind Eric Clough, a controversial, forward-thinking designer who later became best known for designing nudist colonies and for his highly publicized experimental drafting sessions conducted while under the influence of LSD and mescaline. His associates on the build were contractors John Hadley and George Patterson, business and domestic partners who went on to open the Drogstore Café in Haight-Ashbury, a classic Victorian pharmacy that became one of the Haight's anchor establishments and a well-known coffeehouse hangout for the Grateful Dead, Jefferson Airplane, Boz Scaggs, Janis Joplin, and the city's burgeoning bohemian contingent. It was temporarily shut down a few weeks after the Summer of Love when it was discovered that coffee wasn't the only Colombian product you could buy there. Hadley became one of the city's best-known restaurateurs, and Patterson earned his own unique, albeit sad footnote by becoming one of the first people in the country to die of AIDS.

That's right, folks—the Bay Area Ford estate was designed by an acidhead who was into nudism and built by a couple of closet stoners swinging for the other team.

Today, if one is contemplating building or remodeling in the city or the Bay Area, the chances are good your contractor or architect and designer have had experiences in both mind expansion and/or lifestyle experimentation—no biggie, there. But in 1960, both sorts of activities were conducted well under the radar, with great discretion and no small degree of caution. If you had it, you were about four to five years away from flaunting it. And you definitely didn't flaunt, or even so much as suggest it to Ernie Ford, who believed for all the world that in moving north he had escaped and pulled his family from the very jaws of lubricity and saved us from the den of iniquity he believed Hollywood had become.

Of course, Clough, Hadley, and Patterson were only on the fringes of those later cultural exploits when they collaborated on 255 Mapache Drive, but the inspiration of free-flowing form that would become the signature of that era was evident in the floor plan and layout of the house.

Built on the crown of a hill that rose from the center of the property's fifteen acres, the house was a single-story, five-thousand-square-foot horseshoe, its facade a blend of planked redwood siding stained a sagebrush green, balanced against hand-turned, natural-tinted adobe bricking, all capped by a roof of shiplapped thick cedar shakes.

The open U at the rear of the house framed a rectangular pool and aggregate deck, accented with a Vermont black-slate, stepped patio that ran the length of the slate-floored hallway just inside the plate-glass windows and sliding doors. Besides the adobe and redwood, glass was very nearly the main component of the house, plating entire wall lines in places and affording an almost unencumbered vista of the Stanford hills to the east and the Skyline range to the west, redwood-laden mountains that stood quietly vigilant along the Pacific Coast Highway and Half-Moon Bay.

At the far end of the house, the master bedroom and Mom's dressing room anchored the northwest corner, flanked by Dad's office and private bath on one side, the guest room, and boys' bedroom on the other. At the south end lay the maid's room, the kitchen, the den, and the dining room. At the very center, joining both wings, was a massive sunken living room with an eighteen-foot ceiling, supported by sixteen exposed oak beams the same color as the adobe walls accenting the house. At the north end of the living room, a natural, moss-flecked, Sierra rock wall spanned the entire width of the room and reached from floor to ceiling, framing a fireplace and black-slate hearth.

Climbing southward out of the living room, the dining room faced you, and the bamboo accordion door to your left opened into the kitchen, which was nearly as big as the living room, and was the room in which most of our lives there were spent.

The acreage that came with the property was probably more important to Dad than Mom—we fenced the lower twelve and built a three-stall barn and adjoining bunkhouse the year we moved in—but the privacy and seclusion it afforded us was a draw for both. Fifteen acres guaranteed nobody would be building next door anytime soon—a guarantee ensured by the subdivision's required minimum purchase of five acres before a permit to build would be issued—and the "backyard" was two hundred acres of protected land owned by Stanford University. Rolling hills and streams, shaded horse trails and thick woods. Wildlife was everywhere; deer roamed freely alongside the hill below the house, bobcats tiptoed around the perimeter and hunted by the creek below the barn, and, until encroachment eventually drove them out, rattlesnakes were damned near as common as the deer. Ditto the gopher snakes and king snakes, both natural enemies of the rattler. Summers brought them right into the garage, occasionally into the pool, and usually under the shaded corners and eaves of the house. Dad and Brion and I carried snakebite kits when we went to the barn, cut timber on the property, or helped Jack, our gardener, in his landscaping chores around the house. We learned not to walk barefoot at night in the summer months, and to freeze when you heard the buzz of a rattler's tail buttons.

All of those precautions came to naught, though, when I was bitten in 1963.

The barn had three stalls—two for our horses, Jody Brown and Jody White—and a third to store hay bales for their fall, winter, and supplemental feed. The bales filled most of the stall, but gave you enough room to buck a bale down from the top, cut the baler's twine or wire, and carry the flakes out to the corral for the stock. Most bales will flake open effortlessly, but if hay has been baled wet, the flakes will stick together over time, and you have to kick them apart, or, as I did that afternoon, plunge your hands into the center of the bale and break it apart.

When I did just that and felt the stab of pain on my left hand, I initially thought I'd been poked by the end of a piece of baling wire. Jesus, was I in for a surprise.

Although I reacted typically by jerking back, my hand—or my sleeve, I couldn't tell which—seemed to be hung up on something I assumed to be the wire. It was not. With my other hand, I spread the bale apart. Hanging on to the meat of my left hand was a California diamondback about as big around and as long as my arm. As I lifted my arm, she pulled out her fangs and dropped back into the broken bale, which was covered with scores of tiny, pink newborn rattlers, swarming around her as she coiled and prepared to strike again. I backed up quickly, opened the stall door with my good hand, and eased out, my left hand throbbing seriously now and my heart pounding. My snakebite kit was in the kitchen, in the house, which was an uphill climb and about two hundred yards away. With my right hand I undid my belt, cinched it as tightly as I could around my forearm, and slowly walked to the house. By the time I opened the door from the garage to the service pantry, I was light-headed and my left hand was turning black.

Had it been a scant few hours later, I doubt Mom would have been able to move as fast or as sure-witted as she did that afternoon. She was like a military nurse on a battlefield. Bite kit out and open. Tourniquet out, wrapped, tied off. Razor knife out, incision. Hand held down, squeezed tightly, venom released. Patient's hand is swollen grotesquely, mother breaks speed limit carrying him to the doctor. Boy survives.

Unlike North Hollywood and Toluca Lake, our nearest neighbor was a few yards less than a quarter mile away, and the closest town was Portola Valley, a sleepy bend in the road with a public school, a post office, two churches—one Episcopalian and one Catholic—and a town center with one small restaurant that served about fifteen. Next door, a smaller neighborhood grocery and a Mobil station anchored the lot.

Groves of redwoods, stands of eucalyptus, and massive California live oaks grew in patterns that shadowed, shaded, and shielded the fruit farms, stables, and homes that parceled the valley floor. This was Peninsula exclusivity at its most desirable—a mini-ranch gated community with no gates, old-money enclaves of Stanford and Palo Alto just over the hills, and a short, thirty-minute drive along the Bay to the Golden Gate, Fisherman's Wharf, and the world's most beautiful city.

For the first few months it was like an extended vacation, moving to this new place. Our family had extended as well, with Jim Loakes and Ken Thompson making the move with us, bunking in the maid's room until they found their own places and organized the new offices

A work in progress—North Hollywood

In the dome car on the *Zephyr*

Dressed for dinner on the *Lurline*

Boat Day on the deck of the *Lurline*

With Jim Loakes and Ken Thompson

With *The Ford Show's* Top Twenty

With *The Ford Show's* director Bud Yorkin

On tour under Jim Loakes' watchful eyes

On the Warner's back lot with Andy Griffith

Arriving in New York

Guesting on the *Perry Como Show* with Ginger Rogers in New York

Dad with T.C. and Maude

At Henry Kaiser's Hawaiian Village

Brion and me on the *Matsonia*, 1959

In the surf off the Outrigger Club

On the deck of the *Kamahele* off Kapiolani Point

Hollywood, 1960

Taking direction from Lee J. Cobb on NBC's *Connecticut Yankee* special

With Elvis on the set of *G.I. Blues*

Refuge and solitude

On the starboard deck of the *Matsonia*

Portola Valley, 1965

The calm before the storm in Indiana

A break from rehearsing his first NBC special

At Penthouse 9 with Jim Nabors

On the town with Ethel Waters and Jackie Cooper

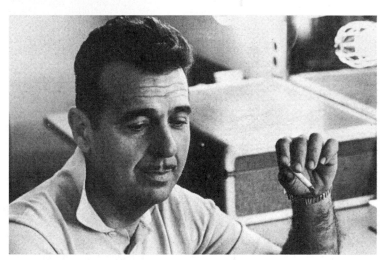

In the dressing room at KGO in San Francisco, 1963

Hosting Robert Kennedy

With singers Dean Kay, Hank Jones, and Dick Noel at KGO in San Fran

At the Crosby with Hope

San Francisco

With jazz great Keely Smith

Listening to playback at the Capitol studios

Conducting the Nashville Symphony

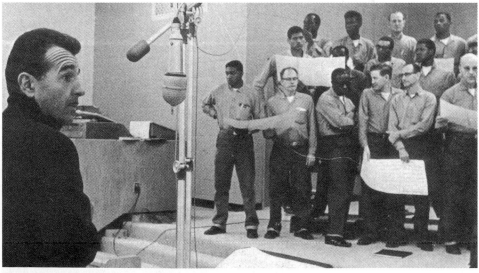

Recording at San Quentin

On stage in Ottawa with the Back Porch Majority

Giving pal Dean Martin a big hand

With old friend Jack Benny

Vacationing in Tahoe

Backstage at Harrah's

Gate City, Virginia

With Danny Thomas and the Smothers Brothers

At the Danny Thomas St. Jude's
benefit with Wayne Newton
and Sammy Davis Jr

In Nashville

Receiving the Medal of Freedom from President Ronald Reagan

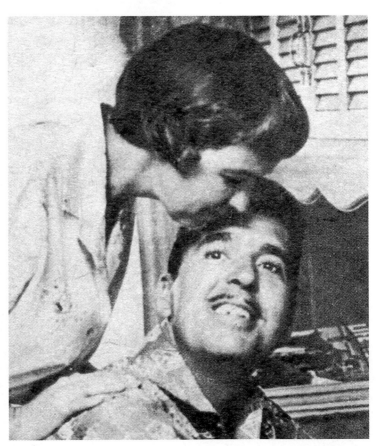

Last kiss

downtown. Our days were filled and happy, our nights sleepless with the anticipation of what the next day would bring.

The change seemed to work a kind of magic on all of us, especially Mom and Dad. They laughed with each other more often, went out together more often, and, for a time, argued less often. San Francisco and Peninsula society welcomed them with open arms, and it was only a matter of time before they were the toast of both. They seemed to revel in these new environs, in our new home, and in this new life— this new life that Dad had dreamed of for so long now. In his dream, he'd freed himself from the responsibilities that had become chains to him. He'd found a way of getting Brion and me, and especially Mom, out from under the glare of the spotlights and into a life he believed he could control, a life that would save the lives of his sons and the woman he still loved.

The problem was, leaving Hollywood did not dim the lights. If anything, they became brighter because now, he was an enigma, the fabled star who had turned his back on Hollywood, stardom, and everything he'd come to despise about both. Now he'd become an even bigger story because of not wanting to be the story anymore.

I think it's possible Dad recognized, or was convinced by others, that it would be futile to expect he could completely shut the machine down, pull the light plug, and put one of the most celebrated careers in the business—along with his family and the employees who depended on him—in the dark. He was prepping for another network series, for Christ's sake. He was packing for concert appearances in Ottawa and New York within months of our first night in the new house. As disappointing or discouraging as it may have been to him, the truth was he needed to work, and he needed to work in the business that had given him the freedom and the independence he *did* have. I believe he instinctively knew the same and resigned himself to the fact, albeit grudgingly. And while he had never been actively involved in the crafting of his image in the past, believing it a vain pursuit, leaving such work to his press agent, Mickey Freeman, he now took a very different view. If he could not shut the machine down, he would use it and manipulate it to what he thought would be his advantage.

If the press wanted to see, write about, comment on, review, and interview Ernie Ford, they would see the Ernie Ford he wanted them to see—the Ernie Ford he wanted to be seen as. The Ernie Ford he wanted to be. And for the first six months or so, that's precisely what they got. Save for the occasional story that slipped through the cracks, an entire image campaign was geared around this new version of Ernie Ford: Ernie the Rancher. Ernie in his jeans, Levi's jacket, boots, and hat. Ernie feeding the horses. Ol' Ern, the father of two boys in 4-H. Ernie cleaning tack down at the barn. Ernie in the saddle. Ernie at a livestock show. Ernie with a newborn calf. Ernie the pensive, simple, quietly reflective, show-business renegade man of the land.

The images themselves cast Dad in kind of a cowboy light for Brion and me, and that was cool. The press that came with the images, however, was infuriatingly ignorant, myopic, culturally insulting, and way over the top embarrassing for two boys trying to fit in at their new school. *"There's a Pea picker in the Peninsula!"* *"Hadley Builds a Hillbilly's Haven."* *"How Ya Gonna Keep 'Im Down on the Farm?"* One Sunday morning entertainment supplement from a major-city paper actually had a front-page caricature of Dad using a guitar to paddle himself across the San Francisco Bay in a goddamn pea pod. Open the front page, and here's a three-column black-and-white of him cleaning caked manure from a horse's hoof.

Paddling in a *pea pod*, for Christ's sake.

I can't even begin to tell you how much this whole new image thrilled Betty Ford. Not to mention the fact that within a year of developing an allergic reaction to horse hair that sapped her of oxygen, threw her into spasms of retching that doubled her over, made Medihalers her third most requested item—behind Pall Malls and Smirnoff—and effectively prevented her from ever being able to go to the ranch again—ever—what does Dad do? He trucks not one, but *two* horses from the ranch to the new house in Portola Valley. Horses in that part of the Peninsula were not unusual; more people had stables than didn't, and the surrounding hills were ribboned with riding trails. But, as far as I can recall, none of those lucky souls were deathly allergic to the animals. Mom, on the other hand, *was*. At least we all believed she was. Earth to Ern . . . what were you thinking?

What none of the wonderfully insightful articles I mentioned above covered was the fact that before Rancher Ern could set so much as one foot in the new house, where his lovely wife, Betty, was waiting, he had to strip off every stitch of clothing, including socks, leave everything in the garage, and scrub himself down with an industrial lather before he could come anywhere near her. For that matter, until we were eventually sent to boarding school in Carmel, the same held true for Brion and me; we both rode, and Mom being allergic to horses was something we dealt with every day. One hair could set her off, and we inspected each other like orangutans before we went back in the house after a ride.

Dad downplayed Mom's allergy, not insensitively so (around Brion and me, anyway), but in the balance, he placed our chores around the horses on a higher priority level than her condition. I believe now that he believed it was psychosomatic, a self-induced reaction to a life and lifestyle that he dreamed of but she wanted no part of. And as I look back, and bend my memory to those years and the events that marked them, I find myself considering that he may have been right. She loved her husband, she loved the life they'd been given, she'd loved Holly-wood, and she adored San Francisco. She worked hard at being who she was, and worked harder to make her husband all he could be. She was a writer, a painter, a lover of fashion and art and literature. Against all the odds that had been arrayed against her in her life, she'd mar-ried a man who'd brought her to a city where all of those appetites could be pursued and indulged, where she could invest her sons' lives and intellect with the same, and experience all of it on the arm of her husband. And now, he was ready to forswear all of it and raise cows. She loved her husband—he still made her laugh—and she loved her family, but shoveling manure, joining the horse set, and living on a quasi-ranch was not what she'd signed on for. Been there, done that.

In time, her allergy—real or not—became so overwhelmingly oppressive that Dad ultimately relented, and our mare and gelding, Jody White and Jody Brown, were loaded into a tandem trailer and trucked to a friend's ranch up on the eastern face of the Skyline range, where they pastured out peacefully for the rest of their days. The barn's stalls and garage were used for storage, and the bunkhouse became a hangout for Brion and me when friends came for a sleepover. Bottom-land winds eventually carried the last strand of horsehair out with the breeze, and while her Medihaler was still a necessity in the area, she breathed easier and we didn't have to strip in the garage anymore.

With the horses' departure and the barn's relegation to other uses, Dad eventually came to grips with the fact that he was going to have to practice controlled schizophrenia. He was going to have to be Rancher Ern when he was on the ranch, and Ernie Ford while at home. And in time, it appeared he was adapting well enough. Moreover, the glow that seemed to illuminate the space between them when we first moved was sparking again, intermittently and occasionally misfiring, but sparking nonetheless.

They both joined Sharon Heights—Palo Alto's A-list golf and country club. They went to shows at the Fairmont, dined with the mayor, were on a first-name basis with the maître d's at Alioto's and Ernie's (no attachment), and jumped feetfirst into the Bay Area's social, charity, and (though not as visibly or energetically) political scenes.

It might have been the city, perhaps the advice of cooler heads around him, possibly Mom's insistence, maybe realizing that "*when in Rome . . .*"—or conceivably a combination of all the above, but, Dad began to morph again. The Stetson was replaced by a city fedora from Bullock & Jones. His Levi's jacket by a topcoat from Cable Car Clothiers, and his rough-outs traded for a pair of Amedeo Testoni oxfords. The image of Rancher Ern all but evaporated. In his place was a sophisticated man of the Bay Area. Guest of honor at the city council. Host of his own Pro-Am golf tournament. Box-seat holder at the Giants games in Candlestick and the 49ers games in the city. Dominoes partner with the Peninsula's upper crust, and urbane gentleman of the stage and (small) screen. Ernie Ford and his lovely wife, Betty, were on everybody's short list, and they became *the* couple to invite and *the* couple to be invited by.

Underneath the silk, though, lay a sow's ear, and while Mom would have been furious, he would have been proud, not embarrassed, if there'd been a smidgen of horseshit packed between the heels and soles of his wing tips. In his mind, shoveling a little manure was something everyone ought to experience at least once in their lives. By the end of that first year, he'd become a full-fledged San Franciscan, but if you got close enough, you caught the faint scent of manzanita, suede, and creek water. His duffel bag, boots, hat, and Bohlin saddle were not far away. They hung in the storage room in the garage, within arm's reach when it was time to change back.

ELEVEN

WHEN THE ABC DAILY SHOW launched in April 1962 from the studios at KGO in San Francisco, it was heralded as the first network television series to originate from the city. Movers and shakers from one end of town to the other were tripping over themselves to finagle some kind of attachment to *The Tennessee Ernie Ford Show*, Dad, or both, and sponsors were lining up like shoppers outside Wal-Mart on the day after Thanksgiving.

Like the first NBC series from the El Capitan Theater in Hollywood, this show also featured a small, regular supporting cast. Bay Area radio personality Jim Lange, who would earn fame later as the host of *The Dating Game* and then *Name That Tune*, made the transition to television as the show's announcer and second banana. Local quasi-folk duo Hank Jones and Dean Kay brought the "youth" demographic to the table, and singers Dick Noel and Anita Gordon balanced things out with mainstream pop and standards. Just before the close of the second season, guitarist and singer Billy Strange joined the cast, staying for a tumultuous year in which he was fired and rehired twice—in both cases by the show's director, Bill Burch, a veteran who'd earned his stripes producing George Gobel, Jack Benny, and other greats.

As was the case with *The Ford Show*, the ABC series was a Bet-Ford Production, covered below and above the line by the family company, then licensed to the network for broadcast. The series itself, though, was only part of the overall deal between BetFord and the network. The agreement also included a development deal, partnering BetFord with Revue Studios in Hollywood to create television properties exclusively for ABC or its fledgling syndication outlets.

In addition to his daily gig directing the series, Bill Burch was the key player in this part of the deal; a highly creative mind, constantly evolving, he threw himself into the task alongside Bill Martin, the series' associate producer. Nevertheless, between 1962 and 1965, only two of the twelve shows they pitched were picked up for development: a word-game show called *Perquackey*, which never made it past the pilot, and *Channing*, a drama starring Jason Evers as a college professor, set on the fictitious campus of Channing University. As episodic dramas went, this was excellent television for its day; provocative, insightful, strong writing—so naturally, it lasted only one season's worth of twenty-three episodes. Memos among Revue, BetFord, and the network reflected some general disappointment in the progress of the development deal, but that sentiment was overshadowed by the attention ABC and BetFord gave to Dad's series.

For the first season, the show was met with good-to-great reviews, and ratings were more than respectable. Dad looked great, he was in good voice, the *feel* between him and the cast was a natural fit, and the buzz from the network was particularly strong. The press was rife with front-page stories trumpeting Dad's return to television, and the public was primed to welcome him back. The high points for the notices and the numbers for that first season, however, had little to do with any of those factors. They came in the wake of two guests: Bobby Kennedy (during his tenure as attorney general) and Russian cosmonaut Gherman Titov, the second man to orbit the earth in a manned satellite and the youngest astronaut in history.

Visiting San Francisco as part of a goodwill tour of the United States, his invitation to come on the show was a spur-of-the-moment decision—a lark, almost—extended by KGO's general manager, Dave Sacks, who'd been involved in planning Titov's visit to the city.

Nobody was more surprised than Ernie Ford when the Secret Service, the KGB, the mayor, and Titov and his wife, Tamara, enthusiastically accepted the invitation.

Given the tense and tenuous posture that existed between the Kremlin and Washington in 1962, Dad was determined not to allow that tension or even that mind-set to manifest itself on the set or on the show. "Politics was not on the agenda, or on the table," he told the *New York Time*'s. "We talked about things common to all people—subjects I felt the three of us could relate to, regardless of where we lived." Indeed. Over the course of twenty minutes, with the aid of an interpreter, the Titovs and Ernie Ford discussed, and laughed about, marriage, sports, food, and other mundane matters, with any and all cultural and political differences evaporating in the process. Mrs. Titov promised to send Mom a recipe for Siberian venison, and Dad gave the couple a basket of cornbread mix, black-eyed peas, and hushpuppy batter at the close of the show.

It was vintage Ernie Ford, and it was a public relations and television coup of immeasurable proportions. Press from coast to coast jumped on the story, celebrating a crack in the iron curtain and giving Dad big props for what many in the press—and elsewhere—thought was a skillfully maneuvered diplomatic stratagem, implying Dad himself had been maneuvered—that he'd been under the covert direction of someone other than Bill Burch up in the booth. The implication was both annoying and laughable to Dad, but Washington took note nevertheless, and took the conversation with Gherman Titov into account when he was invited to headline the first major country music tour of the Soviet Union twelve years later.

The format of this series was a relaxed, laid-back, talk-variety sort, though it was heavier on the talk than on the variety. A short monologue, a number from one of the cast, introduce the guest, yak, a number from the guest (if the guest was a performer), yak some more, another number from one of the cast, yak ad infinitum, the closing hymn, and out. Filling the holes was a regimen of commercials and live spots for sponsors that seemed to come out of the woodwork overnight. By the end of the second season, everybody in the cast was pitching in; pitching dog food, dish detergent, toothpaste, Rice-A-Roni, or any of a score of other products. Dick Noel, in fact, would go on to become one of the most successful jingle singers in the business.

Television shows rely on sponsors and the life-sustaining flow of advertising dollars. In the case of the ABC series, however, their pro-liferation was largely held responsible for the show's eventual steep decline in ratings. The same columnists who were panting with antic-ipation in the weeks and days before its premiere were foaming at the mouth by the end of the second season, rabidly ripping the show for being, as the Chicago *Tribune* called it, "a twenty-minute soap com-mercial between two two-minute songs."

Bobby Kennedy and Gherman Titov were not the only bright spots of the ABC series—the guest roster was impressive and varied and included personalities ranging from Willie Mays to Andy Williams—and there were other brief, fleeting moments that made it fun, even for Dad.

Two segments he developed himself stood out; once a week he opened a telephone book from somewhere in the country, ran his fin-ger down the page, and dialed the number he stopped on. The audi-ence loved it, the person on the other end never forgot it, and the network ate it up; they had instant awareness results coast-to-coast. At the start of the second season, with the blessings of his good friend, golfing partner, and creator of *Peanuts*, the inimitable Charles Schulz, Dad kicked off a nationwide search for Snoopy's look-alike. Tens of thousands of snapshots of dogs from one end of the country to the other flooded the studio. Dad had fun, the network had another poll they didn't have to pay for, and a woman and her beagle mix in Terre Haute had fifteen minutes of fame, along with a six-month supply of Purina Dog Chow.

A few bright moments of good television notwithstanding, the series was but a thin shade of the shadow Dad had cast in the medium, and as the last season came to a close, it was evident why. His heart simply wasn't in it. Daily, even weekly, television was something he felt like he'd done, taken as far as he cared to, and had no desire to pursue or stay involved in. When the initial three-year deal came to an end, so did Ernie Ford's place in network television. The last show aired on March 26, 1965. When the set lights shut down, Dad never returned to series television again.

Some in the industry congratulated themselves for accurately fore-casting the failure that they said would come about in the wake of his flight from Hollywood. They obviously had not been listening; he never intended on continuing network television after ABC. It was a decision he'd looked forward to, planned for, and anticipated eagerly for three years. But it was a decision he'd been strongly advised against making; a decision that set ill with some on the BetFord payroll—one in particular; one who was gambling the family's futures with BetFord money, Ernie Ford's sweat, and the dreams closest to his heart. Gambles that set in motion events that would eventually threaten not only the family's financial future, but the family itself.

In 1962, BetFord Corporation began expanding its holdings under the advice of accountant Peter Brown, only son of Charles Brown, who'd been the company's financial adviser since its formation in '55.

Like his father, Peter was decisive, persuasive, domineering, and intimidating. He stepped into his father's shoes with the blessing of everyone in BetFord, taking the financial reins of both the company and the family firmly in his hands. If it had anything to do with money, it went through Pete. He controlled the spending, the investments, the payroll, the plane tickets, the insurance, and the taxes. Everything. Anything whatsoever that had anything to do with every dollar that came into or out of BetFord, and, therefore, Betty Ford's and Ernie Ford's pockets, had Peter Brown's fingerprint and signature on it. The tutelage he received under his father, coupled with his strong showing in business school, had given him a keen and astute awareness of the machinations of banking and financing, an awareness matched only by his knowledge of the power of perception, the art of deception, the signs of gullibility, and the weight of a name. In this case, the name was Ernest Jennings Ford.

Between 1962 and 1975, Brown engineered deals, loans, and notes worth more than ten million dollars, all but two resulting in losses, and all with the notes being held solely by Ernest J. and Betty Jean Ford. The two that did not result in losses were the only two deals Mom approved: the penthouse in Honolulu and a condominium she picked out in Palm Springs in '73. She was all but shut out of the decision-making process for everything else.

Starting with a land-lease and apartment complex deal in Orange County in 1962, Brown convinced Dad to sell Long Valley Ranch in Clearlake and put himself, BetFord, and its new subsidiary, Eagle Banner Corporation, on the line for a succession of four vast ranches; two spread across the northern border of California, one in Oregon, and one in Nevada; the latter covering nearly 30,000 deeded acres, 250,000 leased acres, and more than 6,000 head of purebred Hereford cattle. In the mid-seventies, he added a one-million-dollar interest in a Santa Gertrudis breeding operation in Mississippi to the portfolio. The year before, almost as an afterthought, he signed off on the condominium in Palm Springs at Mom's request, but put the family and the company on the line for nearly four million in a failed development just outside Reno—a deal that would result in the federal government's collection agency, the Resolution Trust Corporation, filing a claim against Dad's estate after his death.

Successful entertainers (or plumbers, or grocers, or developers) will tell you that the two most important people in their organizations are their attorneys and their accountants. The trust placed in each is critical to the success of the relationship between employer and adviser, but the employer who blindly trusts either is both fool and victim. Ernie Ford qualified as both. He was never a businessman. He simply had no head for the numbers involved. He had no concept of balancing a checkbook or reviewing accounts, those tasks having been handled exclusively by Mom from their earliest days together. But as his fame grew, commensurate with her dependence on lubrication, the simple, basic trust he'd placed in her to keep their heads above water began to erode, aided by the whisperings and advice of others within the inner circle. As Ernie Ford the Man became Ernie Ford the Enterprise, he was slowly but resolutely convinced that putting Betty Ford in any decision-making capacity involving money would amount to little more than folly, and surely bring about their ruin. The complexities of investment banking and intricacies of financial speculation were best left to those with the knowledge and aptitude for such matters. Certainly not Betty. God *almighty*, Ford . . . *not* Betty.

Within the organization, one person quietly, though not regularly, questioned Brown's choices and arrangements, always giving a patient ear to Mom, and always seeking to guide Dad in a conservative and balanced fashion, the family's long-suffering attorney, Frank Martin.

One of Chicago's most accomplished network radio announcers in the forties, Frank left the lights for the law early in 1950, and left Chicago for Los Angeles at the same time to focus on entertainment law. His partnership, Martin and McCarthy, was already one of the industry's preeminent firms when he was hired to do reviews of Dad's contract with Capitol in 1955. Two years later his dedication, honesty, and diligence earned him an invitation to go on retainer full-time as

BetFord's legal adviser. He accepted without hesitation or reservation, and remained at the post until his abrupt removal by Dad's second wife six months before he died.

I believe that Frank was aware of the tenuous nature of many of the deals Brown put together. And while he was a capable and knowledgeable counselor in many matters related to show business, his purview did not extend as far in real estate, banking, or accounting. He'd been a close friend of Brown's father, Charles, had known Brown since his youth, and, like Dad, was impressed with his rapid rise and persuasive skills. Moreover, Frank was keenly aware of the trust and belief Dad placed in Brown, and was, perhaps wrongly so, hesitant to pour cold water on his client's dreams—dreams that were being fueled by Peter Brown, and dreams that Frank, also, had been led to believe were viable and would eventually pay out. His hesitancy, though, was a mistake, and in the months after Mom passed away, he privately admitted as much to me. By then, though, it was too late.

It's doubtful I will ever forget sitting next to Frank's wife, Maude Lee, on the evening of the day of Dad's funeral, tissue in one of her hands, a drink in the other, dabbing tears away from her eyes and gently patting my shoulder. "You know"—dab—"Frank had nothing to do with any of the ranches." Dab. "That was all Peter." Of course, nothing anyone said registered clearly with me that night—and both Frank and Peter were in the other room—but her words would come back in echoes in the years of legal entanglement that followed Dad's death.

The simple dream Dad had nurtured for so many years, the dream he saw come true when he bought Long Valley Ranch, had grown into something beyond even his ken. What began as 540 acres of ground he actually owned had mutated into holdings of nearly half a million acres spread across four states. Holdings he poured millions of dollars into, but from which he never saw one dime of return. Holdings he would eventually have to sell to cover the losses that seemed to be growing beyond his control. He would not learn until the year before his death that many of those holdings had been largely worthless, that he'd been duped into believing he owned a controlling interest in those vast spreads, that his dream of being a rancher had been usurped by a man he trusted, a man who used that trust for his own benefit, leaving him, Mom, and after their deaths, their children and grand-children holding the proverbial bag.

Generating the deals that Brown put together, however, took more than the power and weight of the name Ernest Ford. The deals took money, great sums of money. From Peter's mouth to Dad's ear, each deal was necessary, each note crucial, because it brought Dad one step closer to his dream of being able to retire and take one last bow. Until then, he needed to work. He needed to work because the note was due on the Alturas deal, the Modoc deal needed cash, the Eagleville part-ners were ready to sign the expansion agreement, the Carson City bankers were waiting on the loan papers, the Coarsegold and Madera properties would eventually turn a profit. . . .

All the promises he'd made to himself, all his dreams, all his hopes, designs, and plans—doing a couple of shows here, a special or two there, recording once or twice a year; "spending much more time on the golf course, at home, and on the ranch; spending much more time with Betty and the boys . . ."—all of that went to hell in a hand bas-ket. Now, he *needed* to work more than he'd ever worked before. He was making more money than he'd ever made before, but now, he needed it more than he ever had before. People's jobs depended on him; people's paychecks depended on him. People's lives depended on him. He wasn't working in show business any longer. He was working *for* show business, and for the business that he had become.

In the early sixties Dad left MCA and signed with Norman Brokaw at William Morris. It was a keynote decision—one that would set the stage for the next decade. From 1964 through the early seventies, he toured more than he had in his entire career. He filled grandstands in state fairs covering virtually every state in the union and Canada. He sold out *the* showrooms in Tahoe and Vegas. He broke records in the-aters everywhere from Phoenix to south San Francisco. When he wasn't touring, he was booked in L.A., doing guest spots on the shows of Andy Williams, Jim Nabors, Andy Griffith, Dinah Shore, Dean Martin, Joey Bishop, Mike Douglas, Carson, or *Hollywood Palace*. When he wasn't guesting, he was hosting. Leaving series television opened the opportunity to sign a multimillion-dollar deal with NBC and CBS for a series of specials that put him back in the Nielsen Top Five every time. His recording schedule with Capitol was ramped up, putting him in the studio when he wasn't on the road or on the set, and turning out a handful of LPs that ranked among the best of his career. His golf game virtually became a second tour schedule, booking him on the Crosby, the Bob Hope Desert Classic, performing at or MCing the Masters, and kicking off his own celebrity Pro-Am, covered by ABC.

Contrary to everything he'd planned and envisioned, leaving Hollywood had resulted in Ernie Ford becoming a bigger star than ever, in spite of himself.

Between the mid-fifties and the late sixties, you could count on one hand the number of touring acts as big or bigger than Ernie Ford and still have a couple of fingers left. The impact he generated when we arrived in Chicago, or Allentown, or Kansas City was seismic. Cadres of state troopers would meet us at the Union Station and motorcade us presidentially to the hotel or the showroom. Press conferences were chaotic, matched only by the zeal of the fans. Ticket sales for sixty-thousand-seat arenas or grandstands rarely lasted longer than an hour. He was as big as you get. Period.

Nowhere was that impact felt more than in Indianapolis, at the Indiana State Fair. If for no other reason, Indianapolis was particularly important in Dad's career because it was the location of the first major concert in which he performed "Sixteen Tons"—before it was recorded—at his first appearance at the fair in 1955. That date galvanized Ernie Ford into the Hoosier psyche and embedded him there. His four return engagements over the next five years were always the high point for him of each season's tour.

In '63 I made the first of several trips to Indy for the show. I was officially a teenager, and although my music world was pretty much orbiting around the Ronettes, the Surfaris, and the Four Seasons, I was pretty sure I wouldn't be scoring backstage passes to their shows anytime soon. On the other hand, Rick Nelson (actually, he was still being billed as Ricky then) was on this bill, and what impressionable thirteen-year-old who knew every verse and chorus of "Travelin' Man" wouldn't jump at the chance to meet Ozzie and Harriet's favorite son? When I did, I was knocked out to discover that he thought *Dad* was cool. Holy shit . . . Ricky Nelson—the guy whose hair I'd been trying to form on my own head, the guy who looked almost as tough as Elvis and sounded far tougher than Johnny Burnette—thought Ernie Ford was *cool. Well, damn,* I remember thinking, *maybe I should pay attention here*. For the rest of the date, in the wings backstage, I did just that—paid attention and watched every show—standing next to Rick Nelson, who was singing harmony with every song Dad performed.

But the show was not the only thing I paid attention to. I watched the people. Tens of thousands, on their feet after every song, crowding the skirt of the stage, reaching for him as he drifted forward, flashbulbs firing like a wave of white lasers from the floor and the balconies. They were screaming his name, crying with laughter, and moved to complete silence. Seeing one's own father creating that kind of effect—that degree of impact on a stadium filled with people in the throes of adulation—is a powerful thing, and an image I have never forgotten.

After the show, the dressing room resembled a war room. Teams of police and troopers surrounded the entrance and stood at posts within. As Dad dressed down, Loakes, Thompson, Jack Fascinato, Eldred Stacy (Dad's agent), fair organizers, and security hunkered over a table, planning what I overheard to sound like an escape. Bags in hand, briefcases locked, gear stowed, the troopers took their hats off, perched them on our heads, and surrounded our team like a phalanx of soldiers. In that formation, we moved through the loading bays at the rear of the stadium and out the back doors.

The troopers had parked their cruisers only a few feet from the big metal doorways, but those few feet were carved through a human gauntlet; hundreds upon hundreds of fans walling a thin passage to the cars, a passage held fast by additional officers, straining to hold back the press of bodies. As the doors flew open, the people began screaming, pressing forward, reaching through the arm-linked troopers—reaching to touch the hand, the arm, the shoulder, the elbow, the head of Ernest Jennings Ford.

From behind, the troopers pushed us hard, driving us into the waiting cruisers, slamming the doors, and fighting their way to the driver's side. Encased now, the engines were started, blue lights engaged, and sirens turned on. But with the cars unprotected, the fans swarmed them like locusts, enveloping each cruiser, some laying across the hoods and trunks, fighting for a view through the windshield or the windows, autograph books and Instamatics clutched in their hands. Then, like flakes of skin being shed in layers, they began peeling off the patrol cars as each vehicle slowly inched its way through the thinning mass of fans, the din of their shouts gradually fading in the night.

* * *

It was rare for Mom to join Dad on tour. The pace was not her thing, and the schedule was simply too demanding for her. And while she was proud of her husband and of the work he did, traipsing off to an arena or fairgrounds for a matinee or evening show was about as exciting to Betty Ford as watching paint dry. It wasn't that she didn't care—she just didn't care. It was also rare for Dad—or anyone else in the entourage—to encourage her accompaniment. Her unpredictability after five o'clock or, in some cases, earlier, added a layer of tension to the trip that Dad didn't need, before, during, or after a show. When she did make a trip, however, it usually dovetailed with a vacation for all of us, or included a city she wanted to see or shop in. Indianapolis, Missoula, and Columbus were definitely not on the Betty Ford itinerary of exciting cities to visit, but in 1965, Ottawa was.

Dad had been booked for a return engagement to the Central Canadian Exhibition, the country's premier performance and arts festival in Ottawa. His first date there broke every attendance mark since the event's inauguration in, like, 1800 or something, and the advance notices for this gig were giving every indication that he was poised to break his own record. He did. In fact, attendance for the entire festival peaked in the week we were there, then dropped off dramatically just afterward. The lion's share of attendees were coming in the gate to see the Ernie Ford Show, and he did not disappoint them. Six shows in all, every seat sold out, ecstatic fans and encore after encore.

Mom dragged herself to the festival to watch one show and make her expected appearance, but otherwise shopped, saw sights, lounged, or lunched with the wives of the exhibition's kahunas in the suite at our hotel, the downtown Château Laurier. As usual, she captivated most of the city, and—unintentionally—drew almost as much press coverage as Dad. Canadian politicos, Ottawa society, TV, radio, and newspaper people were falling over themselves to meet and spend even a few brief moments with Ernie's lovely wife, Betty. Parties in the suite were like receiving lines at Buckingham; formal, oh so polite, and glittering. For the first few of those, Betty Ford was brilliant, effervescent, beautiful, and utterly fascinating. At the close of the week, the night before the finale, that changed.

I had seen nearly every show, toured the entire festival, ridden every ride, and seen the opening acts ad nauseam. We had one more night in the city, with a major party to be held after the show, so I elected to hang at the Laurier with Mom, looking forward to room service and maybe a movie on TV before she'd have to get dressed and meet Dad in the hotel's ballroom later that night. Kicking back was not on Mom's agenda, however, and she asked me if I'd like to join her for dinner in the hotel's steakhouse and an early show by the local act, Barry Green, in the lounge afterward. "We'll go on a date just by ourselves," she said. "You can be my escort."

At six sharp, I rode the elevator from my floor to the penthouse and met Mom at the door to the suite. She'd chosen a blue silk Capri pantsuit, trimmed in Chinese brocade and pearl buttons. Around her neck was the strand of faux pearls Brion and I had bought for her in Chicago several years earlier. She was beautiful. She smelled like orchids and vodka, and I knew as soon as she opened the door that she was halfway in the bag. The ever-so-slight buoyant weave in her walk to the elevator was the giveaway. Putting the growing sense of dread out of my mind, I held out my arm, as I knew a gentleman should, and took her hand as we made our way through the lobby and up to the maître d's station at Wilfrid's, the Laurier's four-star restaurant.

Throughout an elegant dinner, attended by an almost overzealous staff, I felt as if I had somehow transcended adolescence and become a man. With a wink from the waiter and an approving smile from Mom, I was allowed a small, tinted glass of wine, which coursed through my fifteen-year-old bloodstream and certified my pending adulthood. We talked of all manner of things, our conversation peppered with her laughter and her keen interest in my opinions on everything from Peter, Paul and Mary to Brion's immaturity, Dad's best songs, and sightseeing in Canada. Guests from other tables stopped to genuflect and heap compliments upon Dad, but she deflected them, and instead directed them to me, introducing me as her oldest son, "and my gentleman escort for the evening."

After the wine, which left me somewhat hazy, my Coke refills were matched glass for glass by Mom's vodka martini rounds. By the time we left Wilfrid's—Mom chatting up everyone and waving gaily at anyone she thought deserving—she was looped, and ready for Barry Green's lounge act at Zoe's in the hotel's west wing.

Barry was mod, did all the latest hits with a little five-piece band backing him up, and worked the room with all the flair and panache of a . . . lounge act. He was a pro. He was also in for a surprise when he made the mistake of introducing Mom and I about midway through his second set. From then on, Barry Green took a backseat, and "The Betty Ford Show" took center stage.

"Ladies and gentlemen. Please welcome Tennessee Ernie Ford's lovely wife, Betty—and her son Bob." I smiled, cringing as a powder-blue spotlight danced across the club's tables and found us. Mom waved—graciously, with her best Princess Anne—gestured for me to do the same, then placed her napkin on the table as Barry gestured for us to stand. As we did, I noticed a distinct change in the volume of the sizable crowd's polite applause, and an equally obvious change in their overall demeanor. In fact, I watched as many of the smiles around us began to morph into looks that landed somewhere between disbelief and incredulity, interchanging on their faces as they followed Mom's trajectory across the dance-floor stage to Barry Green's side. As she did, the reason for the crowd's transformation became embarrassingly obvious to me.

Smashed for a couple of hours now, Mom had lost control of her bladder sometime since our arrival in the lounge. She was either unaware or didn't care, but in any case, blissfully stoned. Standing next to Mr. Mod, her beautiful mandarin pantsuit was ruined, soaked, the blue silk legs and seat of the pants having turned a deep azure-black. Giddy, aware only that all eyes were upon her, she did two minutes of compliments on Barry's act and his wardrobe before she introduced me to him, correcting his earlier misnomer. By then I was at her side, my sport coat off and draped around her as best I could, gamely leading her off the floor, waving to the now completely shocked crowd, out of the lounge, through the lobby, into an empty elevator, and up to the penthouse.

By the time we arrived at the suite, she was aware of the state of her dress, and that she'd had an accident, but was completely unaware that we'd been to dinner together. It made no difference. What had happened, happened, and, like always, she found a reason to laugh about it, thanking God that it had been me with her, "and not your father, who is now expecting me to make a goddamn appearance in the ballroom and make nice to all the mucky-mucks in town."

Fifteen minutes later her bedroom door opened and she emerged, fresh, dry, beautifully dressed, and ready for me to escort her to the cast party downstairs. I had no desire to go anywhere but back to my room, but I was nevertheless looking forward to walking into the ballroom, Mom on my arm, her earlier savior. Dad would eventually learn of the incident, of my quick thinking, and be proud of me for coming to Mom's rescue. Making an entrance into the ballroom would definitely enhance that pride and secure his approval; both of which I was ardently seeking then, as I stood on the threshold of adulthood, still a little queasy from the red wine earlier.

Perhaps it had been the wine or my anticipation of approval; my pride, or fear—possibly a combination of all of the above—but at the door to the ballroom, I became immediately protective of Mom. Scores of guests and hangers-on were jamming the doorway and the alcove just outside the entrance, reaching for her, handing her drinks, and pawing. Suddenly, she was being pulled away from me through the swarm of people, and I lunged for her, grasping her hand, and pulling her back toward me. "I'm supposed to be your escort, Mom. Remember?" Pressed from all sides, she wheeled around, grabbed my elbow, thrust me out into the hallway, and slapped me—hard—the underside of her opal ring digging a small divot out of my jaw.

"Don't ever—*ever*—embarrass me in front of your father's employers again!" she said. It was almost a whisper; the words pushed through clenched teeth and tightened jaw. "I'll beat you within an inch of your life if you ever—*ever*—try a stunt like that again. Go up to your room now. Your father will hear about this later."

And then she was gone, breezing through the crowd, smiling, greeting the bartender, and deftly taking a fresh martini from a proffered silver tray.

Against Dad's better judgment, but with his reluctant blessing, my baptism into the business came during those years, my proselytism, as it were, under the tutelage of Jim Loakes and Ken Thompson. When I wasn't in school I was on the road, schlepping bags and road arrangements, coordinating itineraries, learning the lighting cues, running audio checks, helping the grips strike the sets, and hanging out with the opening acts. Learning the back side of the business, as opposed to being groomed as a performer, was Dad's trade-off. He had great respect for the people and crews behind the scenes, the people who were not in the spotlight. They did honest, hard work, work that wasn't likely to lead them into some kind of show-business neurosis. A performer was at the mercy of fickle taste, and lasted only as long as his flavor was in style. A grip, a gaffer, an audio tech, a boom operator—even trained musicians—were working-class in his eyes and could always find gainful employment. If I was going to go into the business—and as much as it may have nauseated him, he must have known instinctively that I would—better that I learn from the ground up, from behind the curtain, than risk addiction, rejection, and the likelihood of needing my own analyst.

Ernest Ford logic at its most fundamental.

I ate this up. I loved every minute of every trip, every setup, every teardown, every rehearsal, every opening cue, and every stage. I watched, listened, paid attention, and remembered. I memorized the show note-for-note, cue-for-cue. I knew his every move, every take, every story, every song, and every punch line. By the time I was sixteen, I could do twenty minutes of Ernie Ford better than Ernie Ford. Loakes and K.T. loved it. Dad, on the other hand, needed a couple of drinks afterward.

My tenure as a roadie had a short life span, however. Once Dad saw how quickly I was taking to the business of the business, he took me out of the loop, off the road, and put me to work on the Carson City ranch. I was fresh out of my junior year in high school, scanning the itinerary for that summer's tour, when he gave me the news. It would be good for me, he said. I'd learn new skills and be ready for ag school when I graduated, he said. Ag school would groom me for taking over and managing the ranch after I finished my education. My agricultural education. And if I still wanted to go into show business, I'd have something to fall back on, he said.

Even at the age of sixteen, when there's nothing about which a teenager doesn't already know everything there is to know, the "fall back on" logic made sense, in a kind of weird way. But at the same time, the earlier logic of "learning the back side of the business because you'll always find gainful employment" wasn't in his playbook any longer. In fact, his entire outlook on my having anything whatsoever to do with show business, including working for him, changed almost overnight. To be sure, he'd never been wholeheartedly supportive of my following in—or anywhere near—his footsteps, but where he'd been grudgingly willing at one time to help guide me into a nonperforming area of the business, he was now adamantly opposed to even that.

Publicly, I saw a father who gave every indication, and sent a clear, unambiguous impression, that he reveled in the work he did, a dad who appeared to love his profession and the rewards and acceptance that his talent earned him. When the press queried him about Brion or me joining the family business, he stuck to the script and gave his stock answer. "I'm not shoving it down their throats. I want to see them finish college, and then, if this is the career they want to pursue, I'll do whatever their old man can."

This was complete bullshit. Privately, he decried any such choice we might make and did everything he could to dissuade us from the same. What he *did* shove down our throats was the regular, stern reminder that going into any line of work other than show business was the only thing he would approve of, give us paternal succor toward, and the only choice that would make him proud. If he wasn't priming me for managing one of the ranches (properties that would become the financial bane of the family before ten years had expired), he was extolling the virtues of taking the Civil Service Exam and making a career in the post office, as both his father and Mom's father had done.

Naturally, the more he tried to steer us away from show business, the more we gravitated toward it. In 1966 that gravitational pull was strong indeed. The business was changing, the music was changing, the concept of performing was changing, and the lifestyle was changing. As myopic as Ernie Ford could be, he could see that those changes were affecting me. Changing me. And therein lay the rub.

This radical change of outlook about the business was not solely a fatherly effort to broaden the possibilities for our futures, or simply make us aware of the need to have something to fall back on . . . a "day job." Those instincts and lessons were, and remain, valid and practical, regardless of what career one's child wants to pursue. Indeed, I find myself taking the same tact with my own children today.

No, this change was made out of fear. It was a change reflective of and made in the face of a greater, much more extreme change that was scaring the living hell out of parents just like Ernie Ford, and it was washing across the country like a tsunami. A tsunami with an electric guitar sound track.

TWELVE

WHEN I ENROLLED at the University of Denver, it appeared I was on my way to accomplishing something neither Mom nor Dad had achieved: earning a college degree. In fairness, Dad attended the Cincinnati Conservatory of Music briefly in 1939, where he hoped to study voice, and when he passed the airman's exam in January of '41, it gave him two college credits, allowing him to apply for pilot candidacy in the Air Corps. And Mom did attend the National Youth Administration School in 1940, after she'd graduated from San Bernardino High, but neither the NYA nor the Conservatory was a fully accredited college or university, and neither Clarence and Maude nor Charlie and Jesse could afford the tuition for a complete higher-education ticket. Thus, I became the favored first son to achieve what the parents had not.

I lasted roughly three months at DU before I consciously—and on some days, semiconsciously—began the process of dropping out, a process that had actually begun two years earlier.

I had graduated in 1968 from Robert Louis Stevenson School for Boys in Pebble Beach, lettering in varsity water polo and coming out with a low B average. It didn't matter that it was on the low end, the fact that I graduated was all that mattered to Mom and Dad. Their dreams for me were, by all appearances, coming true, and the college fund they'd begun some years earlier was earning respectable interest at Wells Fargo.

Stevenson was an exclusive boarding academy designed to prepare the minds, hearts, and bodies of young men for college. And for the decades it had been active before I was shipped there in 1964, it accomplished that mandate diligently. Located on the Seventeen Mile Drive in the Del Monte Forest just outside Carmel, it boarded the scions of the rich, famous, and powerful, from the sons of the president of Dow Chemical to the sons of the secretary of defense, preparing each for university life and then for the task of accepting the standards of their family names and the positions of power, wealth, and, in some cases, fame, that awaited them.

Many of my classmates did indeed follow that path, excelling academically, socially, and politically, earning the admiration of faculty and family and going on to great things. But in 1964, seeking that path of conservatism also earned them the suspicion and derision of many of their peers.

What many of their parents did not realize was that the island of collegiate preparation they believed Stevenson to be sat squarely in the middle of the ocean of cultural upheaval that was California in that decade. Thanks to Bill Graham, the Fillmore, and Haight-Ashbury, there were many who believed that center to be San Francisco, and, in all fairness, waves of social change did wash over and flow out from there. But in truth, those waves were but the crests of the groundswells that rose from the real epicenter located south of the City by the Bay in the artists' colony that was Carmel. And Carmel was a mere three miles from the beloved school of the favored that was Stevenson.

By 1965 Carmel had grown beyond its early reputation as an avant-gardish art colony, and had become a focal point of countercultural life, music, and, to a lesser degree, social politics. While it still held the romance of having been home to Robinson Jeffers, Doris Day, Clint Eastwood, and Jack London, it was now a refuge for Bob Dylan, Mimi and Richard Farina, a young Stephen Stills, and Joan Baez, who built her Institute for the Study of Nonviolence not far from Stevenson itself.

The influx and influence of these new forces of poetry, music, intellect, and social change threatened the very fabric of the philosophy of Stevenson and the mothers and fathers who sent their young men there. But by the time they were aware of the changes being wrought upon the minds of their sons, it was too late. The damage had already been done.

That was the view, anyway, if you looked upon those changes as damaging. There were those of us, of course, who held an altogether different view.

I was sent there to get me away from radical ideas—they flourished in Carmel. I was sent there to separate—isolate—me from influences contrary to the establishment. Those same influences were gestating there at about the same rate as mushrooms on a wet night. And not all of them were popping up at the Arcade on Ocean Avenue. Many that resonated most compellingly with me—and with others like me—came into being in the classrooms of Stevenson itself.

The first time I was introduced to Bob Dylan was in English teacher Steven Brooks's sophomore class. Third period. I walked into his room after biology, we stood by our desks until seated, and he put a portable RCA turntable on his desk. He took an LP out of his brief-case; on its cover was a strange-looking little guy in a corduroy cap holding a guitar.

"Put all your books on the floor and listen. This man will change your life."

We listened to Dylan's first album for the remainder of the class, and I came to realize that even English teachers might actually be instructive in things that mattered. He was right, of course. The record did change my life.

As did Arthur Eikenberry, who arrived my junior year to take over the biology and the applied sciences program. He accompanied all his classroom dissections with music from Ravi Shankar and his own man-dalic lectures. *"The frog is not dying. There is no death, really. . . ."*

And there was Jerome Fenton, English II, who had come to RLS a fugitive from the Office of the General Counsel under Eisenhower, and then the legal advisory team of Pan Am Airways—a sixty-year-old towering figure of a man, face chiseled like Lincoln, or Gregory Peck, long white hair cascading down to his shoulders, demanding we pur-sue literature and art with the same fervor and devotion as Ahab. "Melville *matters*, for God's sake, gentlemen . . . little else in life does!"

These ideas were coming from within the sanctum sanctorum of *classrooms* at the very school I'd been enrolled in, in the vain hope that I'd be shielded from just such ideas. Ideas our parents, or, in my case at least, Dad, were working overtime to stifle and stem.

It did not help his cause that Betty Ford was, albeit gradually and tentatively, also exploring similar ideas. Unfortunately her exploration was somewhat diluted through a cocktail glass, but the artist in her sensed these new ideas and tried to flow with them nonetheless. Granted, a little unsteadily on her feet at times, but flowing as best she could. While she did hold fast to many of the values and social mores she'd been raised under and taught to observe, she, unlike Dad, was intrigued by the freedom of thought and flowering of artistic expression pervading so much of society. On Christmas morning, 1965, she presented me with a coffee-table book of the late photographer Anne Brigman's nudes in black and white. Nudes in trees, nudes on the beach. Nude on a roof. I think Dad gave me an ascot. I don't remember what Brion got that morning, but after I'd opened Brigman's book, I don't think *he* remembered, either. To this day, I think she did it solely to get a rise out of Dad. No . . . not that kind of rise. She did it to anger him, to declare herself, to connect to a culture and a sensibility that she saw on the horizon, ahead of me, but saw Dad moving away from.

It worked, and made Christmas incredibly fun for the rest of the day.

"Jesus Christ—it's *art* for God's sake, Ford!"

"They're *naked*, Betty!"

Other than variations on that theme, they spoke very little for the rest of the day—to each other, anyway. When we came back from dinner later that evening, the book was gone, and I knew better than to ask. I never saw it again, nor was it ever mentioned.

Two weeks later, as I was packing for the drive with Dad back to Stevenson for the winter semester, Mom gave me her old copy of Grace Metalious's novel *Peyton Place* for my sixteenth birthday. Ten years after it was published, it was still *the forbidden book*. "For God's sake put it in your duffel bag. Your father probably won't know from Grace Metalious, but put it away, anyway. When you're ready to talk about girls, call me. God only knows what he'll tell you."

When Mom wasn't expanding my pulp-fiction awareness of sex, she dabbled in transcendental meditation, explored yoga, paid attention to the poetry of folk lyrics, and poured herself—on some nights, literally—into the art she'd begun seriously in North Hollywood, which was oil on canvas and charcoal portraiture.

Her early work was most influenced by the David Immerman school, but her tastes in other artists tended toward the eclectic, ranging from the stylized portraits of close friends Margaret and Walter Keane to David Hockney's realism and the abstract impressionism of

John Donegan. Over the years, the collection she acquired reflected this broad brushstroke of her taste and filled the walls in our home with great splashes of color and quiet, contemplative studies in anatomy. No wall was untouched. Actually, save for a couple of gold records, a few framed photos, and a marlin he'd caught off the coast of Kona, the walls in Dad's office were pretty much untouched—by art, anyway.

As the fifties gave way to the sixties and we relocated to the Bay Area, Mom's tentative explorations into the emerging culture began to noticeably affect her art, as did her reliance on vodka and gin, which was increasing in frequency of intake and volume commensurate with the conflict and division that the emerging culture was inflicting on the canvas of our family. The faces and features of the subjects she painted were becoming Dorian Gray–like; beautiful on the surface, but holding some terrible secret under their skin that would materialize if you looked too long at them. That sense of underlying conflict was most evident in two 1965 self-portraits done in charcoal, a portrait of herself as a Hindu bride done in oil and completed in 1966, and a fourth work in charcoal that may have been her best and was certainly her most dramatic work.

Home from Stevenson for an extended weekend in 1966, I wandered into the kitchen early one morning to find her asleep in her chair, her knees tucked fetally into her chest. Curled up between the armrests of the big leather club, she looked like a child swallowed by an oversized prop from a movie. On the end table, the ice had long since melted in her drink, which, from the milky red tint, I guessed had been a Bloody Mary. In an ashtray next to her glass was a long, gray ash, devoid of any paper, draped like a lazy cat's tail over the rim of the ashtray, the last remnant of what had been a Pall Mall sometime during the night, forgotten and left to slowly burn away. On the easel in front of her chair was a portrait of what appeared to be a man. Next to the easel, she'd opened one of the TV trays from the den, her oils and brushes neatly—meticulously—arrayed on a towel she'd draped over its surface. Next to these, a second ashtray and a second long, gray ash, but at its end, the barely recognizable hint of cigarette paper, stenciled red with the pattern of her lipstick.

Leaving Mom to sleep, my eyes drifted to the portrait. It was indeed a man, but in the half-light of the kitchen, the sun's rays slicing patterns through the big venetian blinds, his features were mottled and undefined. I didn't recognize him. And as I moved closer to the easel, I didn't hear Mom stirring in the club chair.

"What do you think?" she asked.

As I turned she was sitting up—slowly—reaching for her cocktail glass with one hand and her pack of Pall Malls with the other. It was 6:15 in the morning.

"It's John the Baptist," she said.

Apparently having second thoughts about the drink, she put the glass back on the coaster and tapped a Pall Mall out of the opened end of its long, red pack. She was sitting now, but not erect—both her elbows resting on her knees. Bleary-eyed. There was a brief silence, broken before I could answer by her racking cough, a cough that seemed to be coming from her feet—long, heavy, then thin and gasping. In a moment, the diffused light in the kitchen was graying with trails of the smoke that pumped from her nostrils and mouth, in perfect tempo with the rhythm of her coughing.

I put my hand on her back and gently tapped to loosen the tension.

"Jesus—*hack*—Christ—*cough*—I'm—hack *again*—gagging. And your father's bound to get up . . ." This thought brought a bitter laugh, which turned into a syncopated wheeze, and then another full-blown fifteen seconds of coughing. Finally, her breath returned. With the care of a museum curator, she slowly brought the smoldering Pall Mall to the ashtray and gently tapped the ash, which, over the past few minutes, had burned dangerously close to her fingers.

"It's John the Baptist," she said again.

"I know, Mom, you told me. I heard you." But I wasn't looking at the painting. I was fixed on her, preparing for another round of hacking. She'd actually broken ribs because of her coughing in the past, and I was keyed on her, not her art. She sensed that, and it angered her.

"I'm fine, Buck. Open the goddamn blinds, so I can see what I did."

I was hesitant to leave her side, even if it was just to cross the room, but more hesitant to not do what she asked. An angry Betty Ford at this hour trumped a half-bagged, emphysemic Betty Ford any day, and I didn't like the odds. So I moved to the big picture windows looking out on the aggregate pool deck and opened each of the long bamboo-slat shades. I kept one eye on her, though, and when I rolled the last of the three up, I decided, *Light is a good thing*, crossed to the other side of the room, and turned on the overhead. Through the entire process, Mom had remained immobile, her eyes fixed on the easel and her work from the night before.

Now, in the revealing and clarifying light of the room, I was able to fully focus on the portrait.

His hair was long and jet-black. His eyes a dark sapphire blue, recessed into deep pockets that made him instantly penetrating and hopelessly sad. I was immediately drawn to them. But it was the other features of his face that took my attention and breath away. His cheekbones, the bridge of his nose, his chin and forehead. At first glance, he looked to be covered with blemishes, leprosy-like lesions that appeared to disfigure him.

"Do you see them?" Mom asked. I leaned closer and began to see the blemishes clearer, and I saw that they were not lesions at all, but faces. Three faces: one of a man, and those of two women. Together, she had crafted and integrated them so that they formed the visage of John the Baptist. And it was *these* faces that were disfigured. Misshapen and deformed, they appeared stricken with agony and despair, giving John's countenance the anguish I sensed at first look.

She had painted his portrait with the faces of Herod, Herodias, and Salome—his persecutors and killers.

For a moment it felt like the air had been sucked out of the room. There was a vacuum that had removed all sense of place, time, and reality. The walls beyond the kitchen disappeared into a void, and I was alone with Mom in a world she'd created somewhere inside herself. For a moment—one that seemed to stretch time interminably—the only sound I heard was the raspy rattling of her breath.

"Help me take this back to my bathroom," she said, breaking the spell. "If your father sees this, he'll think I'm nuts."

Some time later, she did a second portrait of John. Both disappeared, and I never saw them again.

Early in 1964, at about the same time Mom was beginning to show interest in yoga and openly declaring her crush on Yul Brynner, Dad became a member of the Bohemian Club in San Francisco. Google "Bohemian Club" or its annual retreat, "Bohemian Grove," and you'll have at least an hour or more of wonderful fun exploring several dozen sites, all purporting to have exposed or infiltrated the most closely guarded private men's club in American history. Think Priory of Scion meets the Klan, meets the Hasty Pudding Review, and you've got a pretty good idea of the image the Bohemian Club conveys to many people.

Started in the late 1800s by a group of bored businessmen in San Francisco who lamented the lack of culture in the then semiwild, Barbary Coast city, the club grew in size, notoriety, stature, and desirability over the years, attracting membership from virtually every Republican president since 1923, the heads of nearly every major oil company, corporate CEOs who could buy and sell half the Bay Area on a lunch bet, political and industrial advisers who fashioned the policies of fledgling nation-states in their spare time, and several noted members of the film, music, and entertainment worlds.

Every July, the club's members gathered in Monte Rio, a small community in northern California bordered by redwoods and coastal hills, and for two weeks celebrated their power, their wealth, their freedom to pee in the woods, their penchant for behavior that would probably have them jailed anywhere else, and their ability to drink like fraternity initiates from dawn until . . . dawn. Decisions affecting the shape of the world were made during the retreat's famous Lakeside Talks, including the first meetings of General Leslie Groves and Robert Oppenheimer when they were formulating the Manhattan Project in 1942. ·

Today it's not unusual to read about people as diverse as Jimmy Buffett, Danny Glover, and even members of the old Grateful Dead either visiting as guests or joining as new members. In 1964, however, when Dad was accepted, somebody from the Dead would have stood a better chance of being shot at the front gate.

The Bohemian Club was, in those years of upheaval, *the* epicentral think tank for conservatism, and bastion of the Establishment. And as much as I wanted to envision otherwise, Dad sought, promoted, and defended the politics and social power promulgated from within that establishment, believing, ultimately, that the growing counterculture was going to be the ruin of America, its youth, its faith, and its power. By '68 he was lacing his concerts and press conferences with opinion, both political and social, and booking opening acts he felt conveyed that posture: the Young Americans, the Doodletown Pipers, Up with People; boy/girl acts in uniform, "mod-like" outfits, sanguine and saccharine, well-groomed, Stepford groups, singing nonthreatening watered-down folk/pop. They were booked not necessarily for their talent, but because their very appearance was in direct opposition—visually and musically—to the plethora of rock and folk acts Dad thought were contributing to the downfall of the society. For a time, Randy Sparks's group, the Back Porch Majority, toured with him, but they were a bit too hard-core folk and went somewhat against the grain. I thought they were great. They didn't last. They were replaced by the Kids Next Door. It was his way of fighting back a tide he ultimately saw washing over him.

Betty Ford thought the Bohemian Club was idiotic, and she told him so. Regularly. For that matter, she told anybody within earshot—whether she felt they were listening or not. Her commentary at dinner parties on the club and related subjects made for wonderfully dramatic moments at the table or in the living room over drinks, moments simply pregnant with tension.

The more she drank, the louder and more insulting of Dad and his new friends she became. The louder she became, the more animated she became, which on more than one night, required that Dad, one of the guests, or on special nights when we were allowed in the living room, Brion or me, to pick her up. Literally. By that time, whatever remaining guests there were who weren't hunting for a door—any door—had been relegated to a corner of one of the long sofas at the other end of the room; tense, rigid, embarrassed, laughing nervously. From our bedroom, Brion and I would dial the intercom for whatever room the party had moved to that night, and follow the show, scene by scene.

But through each episode—through it all, even in her most stuporous condition—she remained this magnetic pole, gifted, insightful, drawing people to her like a magnet. Completely literate and, by all accounts, completely aware of what she was saying and doing. She was like a hypnotic, black hole that those around her could not resist gravitating toward, and were eventually sucked into. A beautiful, chic train wreck with a lost husband as its only passenger—a zephyr, gleaming, silver, and sleek—hurtling through life, unable to brake, unable to stop, and unable now to change the course of their lives together.

Dad had found his way into circles orbiting presidents, but he was losing his way as an artist and the free soul I remembered him being. He became someone I no longer recognized as the man I'd looked up to heroically all my life. His politics turned him further right, and his outlook on society began to turn with him. Golf games, real estate deals, and dominoes at the club with power brokers began to mean more to him than picking a great song or rehearsing for a show. He was steadily losing his interest and his passion for show business, and by the end of the decade, he was making a concerted effort to distance himself from the very thing that had given him the freedom to live as he wanted.

Concurrently, he began losing touch with Mom, who began to drift deeper into herself, slowly but steadily adding Valium, Mepergan, and other tranquilizers to her diet of smoke and drink, gradually withdrawing from him and the separate life he was increasingly involving himself in.

There were periods when the distance between them appeared to close; moments when the Sturm und Drang seemed to abate and recede, and the light that had bound them together, drawn them together, and held them together, was rekindled, renewed, and replenished. But now those moments were few and very far between. Nevertheless, I relished them when they occurred, and basked in the love that I believed—hoped—they still had for each other.

In the last months of 1966, Mom stopped drifting and crashed, locking herself in her dressing room and overdosing on a prescription cocktail of Darvon and Demerol. Somehow the maid, Bonnie Mae, was able to get the door open, resuscitate her, and induce vomiting before she called 911, saving Mom's life that day. Dad got the call at Sharon Heights in the middle of drinks and interrupting a game of dominoes.

For a brief moment they clung to each other, each fearful of what their lives would be like without the other. Mom appeared penitent and alarmed at how close she'd come to checking out. Dad appeared stricken and genuinely troubled at the depth of Mom's pain.

But appearances are largely superficial; they can evaporate, dissipate, and be overlooked. And with the help of a screwdriver for breakfast and a Valium for lunch, one can completely forget that those darned old appearances ever existed. Within weeks of the incident, that's exactly what happened. Betty Ford's inaugural suicide attempt was by all accounts forgotten and never spoken of again. Everything went back to normal, and life in the Ford house went on. Until July 1967.

Ken Thompson remembered taking the call backstage at the New

Mexico State Fair in Albuquerque just before the start of that day's matinee. An urgent call for Dad from home. From Mom. For ten minutes, in an office behind closed doors, he spoke quietly, too quietly for Ken or Jim to hear. When he emerged, he told them both he was canceling the remainder of the gig. He had to fly home immediately.

The call had come from Mom's dressing room. Bonnie Mae was gone. She was alone. She was at the end of her rope. She was through. She was tired. She'd been to the doctor for the biopsy results. It was terminal. She was calling to say good-bye. Don't come home. She wouldn't be there.

Leaving Jim and Ken to tie things up, Dad jumped on a loaned Gulfstream G150 and made the flight home; racked, afraid, needing a drink and unable to raise anybody or any help on the in-flight phone. As it turned out, help—at least the sort Dad believed might be necessary—was not required.

When he rushed into the house late that afternoon, he arrived to find Mom in her lounge chair in the kitchen, halfway through a Mary Stewart novel and a Bloody Mary. She seemed surprised to see Dad, but more surprised that he'd believed her telephone call.

Whether she intentionally fabricated the report of terminal cancer, or in a drug-and-drink-induced state had hallucinated it, none of what she'd told him on the phone had happened. There'd been no biopsy and there was no cancer—that they knew of. A call to David Shields, the family doctor, confirmed the same. It had all been a lie.

In his anger, however, Dad did not, would not, could not see or hear that it was also a cry, a plea, an act of sodden and pharmaceutical desperation. The only act she felt, believed, or calculated she could get his attention with. But when she knew she'd succeeded, seeing him standing there in the kitchen, pale and livid, she berated him for being angry with her and cursed him for his carelessness.

The bitterness that flowed through the house in the months that followed was palpable, tangible, and acrid. They argued incessantly over paltry, inconsequential things, with the slightest mistake or misspoken word enough for ignition. The tension drove Dad from the house for hours on end, whiling his time away in trivial pursuits over Cutty and dominoes, or over small talk at the hardware store. For her part, Mom spent those separate hours directing the maid, drinking and cooking, and entertaining well-intentioned but annoying neighbors and friends, covertly enlisted by Dad to check up on her.

She found solace in the kitchen, and her skill as a chef had earned her a culinary reputation that put her recipes on the menus of more than one four-star restaurant, including the Pub in Palo Alto and Michele's in Honolulu, who listed Betty Ford's Chicken Gumbo as one of their featured entrées. In those years, most of the work she did in the kitchen was done far into the night, well after everyone else had retired, and her best work was done when she was completely smashed. Go figure.

At two and three in the morning, she'd be into preparing a complete French meal for four, a vat of stoup (her stew and soup) substantial enough for a legion of Marine recruits, or a casserole for the gardener's family. Meal upon meal upon meal—night after night after night. Completed, she'd package, bag, or Tupperware the entire repast, label it, and stock it in the freezer. The big Amana in the service pantry held literally hundreds of them. Alone, the house quiet, she'd finish her drink, have one last cigarette, and then slowly shuffle back to her bedroom.

She'd be up by ten—Dad long since gone—pour a cup of coffee, suck down three or four Pall Malls, and by noon she was on her first screwdriver. By two she'd dropped her first Valium, scared the living hell out of the housekeeper, and by three she was finding one reason or another to damn Dad to hell.

Eventually the darkness overtook her again, and on a night I was home from Stevenson on break, a violent argument between her and Dad concluded our dinner together. Cursing him—and me—she stormed from the kitchen with a butcher knife in her hand and locked herself in her dressing room, threatening to kill herself.

The drama was a rerun both of us had seen before, and so, had become desensitized to. When we finally moved from the table, it wasn't to rush back and save her, it was to clear the table, put the dishes in the dishwasher, and turn on *Bonanza* in the den.

Had we acted more instinctively, we might have prevented the overdose, but our instincts also told us "been there; seen that"; she'd come out after an hour or so, make another drink, curse us both again, open her book, and brood in the kitchen. When Dad finally went back to check on her, the door to her dressing room was ajar, her body crumpled on the floor behind it. Had she been her normal body weight, we might have had a far more difficult time opening the door, but as light as she was, the swing of the door rolled her away easily, allowing Dad and me to move to her side. In one hand—her thin, frail fingers curled weakly around the handle—was the knife. By her other hand was the Valium bottle, empty.

The initial shock quickly gave way to relief when we realized she was breathing, albeit barely. And then our relief—though unspoken—quickly gave way to euphoria when she found enough air to damn Dad to hell.

The emergency room stay was short; her stomach pumped and a bit of soup piped in intravenously. The amount of valium she'd taken was dangerous, but not necessarily enough to end her life, a shortcoming that infuriated her when she regained strength enough to reflect on what her intent had been and why she'd failed. Par for the course, it was Dad's fault.

Unlike her first overdose, the emotional wake from this incident did not bring them closer together—did not plea for the reunion of their bond. Instead, the space that had been growing between them widened. Dad took the bed in the maid's room, and Mom rarely left hers. They orbited around each other like cold planets, aware of each other but distant, lest they collide and damage themselves. And the great house, once filled with the light and shades and tones of a family in love, had turned empty, silent, and funereal, filled only with wisps of echoes of the life they'd once shared, the life that had brought them here.

It was that world I walked into when I returned home after dropping out of Denver University in '68.

I'd enrolled in DU after graduating from Stevenson, not because of any strong academic lure, but because I was enamored of the prospect of living near the mountains of Colorado. It was also the only school that overlooked many of my scholastic shortcomings at Stevenson and welcomed me nevertheless. While Dad had hoped I'd see the wisdom of his dreams for me and go for an ag school degree in animal husbandry, or shoot for the Air Force Academy, he was grudgingly proud of my settling on DU, and with Jim Loakes in tow, proudly accompanied me to orientation at the start of the first semester. Stepping off the plane at Stapleton, we were met by a salesman from one of the local Ford dealerships who handed me the keys to a new, white F-150 pickup; Dad's way of congratulating me for becoming a man of higher education and the first in the family to attend college.

In retrospect, I began dropping out mentally by the time my first-quarter class schedule was handed to me. Like my contemporaries, I made a valiant initial effort to focus on academia, the pursuit of a degree, and all things collegiate. But that focus quickly changed, and within a month I was cutting classes. Modern Dance . . . out—I hated the tights. Western Civ . . . gone—way too complicated. Theater 1 . . . sorry (a class I should have seen the promise in, but . . . no). English Lit . . . nope—too boring.

University life was simply not going to happen for me. I was, however, well on my way to receiving a higher education; I was getting high in the morning, high in the afternoon, and way higher after dark. Recoiling from the culture of alcoholism that Mom and Dad had been swimming in for decades, I dived headfirst into the culture of drugs, a pool I first dipped my feet in along the Seventeen Mile Drive during my junior year at Stevenson.

Like many of my colleagues, I began the affair with marijuana, quickly developing a discriminating taste for the more potent and expensive strains and cuts. Without so much as a pause for breath, and with a stupidity matched only by my recklessness, I moved with equal speed to LSD and mescaline before the end of the second month at DU. By the time I was looking at my failed grades for the first quarter, I was living illegally on campus, deceiving my professors, my friends, and Mom and Dad, and although I would not realize it for many years, myself.

It seems completely self-serving to cop the "I never did the hard stuff" plea, but it's true nevertheless. My experimentation was limited to the psychedelic category, but in hindsight, hell, they're *all* hard drugs. Anyone who tries to tell you different is lying, stoned, stupid, or all three. And regardless of my earlier reference to recoiling from the culture of alcoholism, I won't pretend to lay my own addiction at the doorstep or feet of Ernie and Betty Ford. The fact is, I was weak and looking for acceptance among a growing coterie I sought entrée into, believing that membership was predicated on being a stoner. Moreover, I loved it. I loved getting and being high, loved the lifestyle and loved the sensation of complete detachment from reality.

The art, music, dance, sex, and community of the new culture revolved around expanding one's mind, and the tools for that expansion were rolled, smoked, dropped, or chewed. You didn't *get* Donovan unless you were stoned. You couldn't hear the undertones in Hendrix's solos without a hit of acid. You had to be wrecked to appreciate the Fill-more's poster art. And God knows, sex when you were high was . . . oh, man . . . it was . . . actually, I don't remember.

While I won't itemize the haze of those years on their account ledger, I believed that every joint, every blotter, every mushroom was my passage out, my ticket to a life away from Portola Valley, from the Bohemian Club, from the nights of bitterness and reproach, from divi-sion and separation, and from the blackness of depression and threats of suicide that had become the common threads running through the fabric of our family. In my ignorance, my selfishness, and my own ine-briated state, I failed to see that I was not escaping at all, but rather, simply adding a new warp to the weave.

My story was I'd just missed the registration deadline for the quar-ter then in progress. I'd be coming home for a couple of months at most, file an early registration for the following quarter—which was already paid in full—and be back on campus by spring. I was lying, of course, but telling them the truth was the furthest thing from my mind.

"Mom? Dad? I've lost all interest in anything but drugs and rock and roll; I'm doing acid twice a week—at least—and learning how to make bongs from old pipe fittings and plumbing parts. I took my last class about two weeks ago, and they won't let me live in the dorm any-more. I thought I'd come home for a while until I figure out what I'm going to do for the rest of my life. 'K?"

Hair to my shoulders, crowned by a gray wide-brimmed hat, in faded and threadbare cords, I was wearing a Navy pea jacket and muk-luks when Dad met me at the Greyhound station; my duffel bag in one hand and my guitar case in the other. For the briefest of moments, I had the distinct impression he was embarrassed to be seen with me. Both hands full, I raised my guitar case and swung it back and forth in a kind of wave. He nodded, turned his back, and walked out to the parking lot, where he waited at the rear of the station wagon. The ten-sion manifesting itself on his face was severe enough to literally pull his hairline back, and he looked at me as I came out of the depot with an expression that bordered on revulsion, then spiked with what I can only describe as fear when I gave him a big hug and stowed my gear in the back.

I wish I could adequately convey the depth of silence that filled the interior of the car as we rode home. It was like riding in a sensory dep-rivation chamber on wheels. In the twenty minutes it took to go from

Greyhound to Mapache Drive, some fifteen to twenty words were exchanged between us, though not wholly willingly. Each utterance was forced, pushed from thought to voice, requiring every ounce of effort from both of us. Every mile or so he'd rotate his head, regard my appearance silently but angrily, gripping the steering wheel so tightly his knuckles were turning white. I pretended not to notice, keeping my eyes on the road or averting them altogether, turning toward the passenger window. Had I been riding with anyone else, being the free, countercultural cat that I'd become, I'd have turned and flashed them the peace sign. Instinct told me I'd need splints for my fingers if I offered the same gesture now. I was relieved when we reached the driveway but had I known what waited inside, I'd have begged Dad to take me back to the bus station.

In the kitchen Mom was at the table, a cigarette burning in an ashtray to her right, a cocktail glass with a fresh drink on her left. In front of her was an IBM Selectric, the keys of which she was intently striking. She did not look up as I came in. Her lips were pursed, and her visage reflected the tone of the entire space around her: bleak, dark, and hardened. I could feel her eyes on me, however, as I turned to set my duffel and guitar down.

"Your father is heartbroken."

"Mom, I don't . . ."

"And he's taking it out on me."

"Mom, I'm not . . ."

"He's at the end of his rope. And if you think you're getting one dime from us, you're sadly mistaken. When are you leaving?"

Jesus, I just got here. "As soon as spring semester starts. And I don't want . . ."

"Take that goddamn guitar back to your room. And take that goddamn duffel bag with you."

At "*with you*" she was up, ripping whatever she'd been typing out of the IBM's carriage, and, with it, her drink, and her cigarettes in hand, she turned away and walked down the slate hallway back to her room. Dad had disappeared; he wasn't in the den or the bar, but caution told me not to go looking for him. I picked up the guitar and duffel, and in Mom's wake, made my way to the rear of the house and my old room.

Over the next few days, their temperaments changed slightly, and they warmed somewhat to my being back home. If one had placed a thermometer in the house, however, the warming would barely have registered—Fahrenheit *or* Celsius. For the life of me, I could not imagine that they knew the truth. I could not imagine that my ruse had not fooled them. I could not imagine that they might have actually communicated with someone at DU who told them what had actually happened. I was that dense, that stupid. That blind.

As the days turned into weeks, it became clear to me that I could not remain there. My room did not feel like my room any longer, and the house was no longer a home to me, or for me. That I was making no effort toward registering for the spring semester was surely evident to them, and I knew that I could not keep the charade up or put off telling them the truth much longer. Telling the truth, however, would have required that I face my fears and take responsibility for my actions. And if I rose to that challenge, I'd be expected to be appropriately contrite, atone for my sins, resume the life they'd hoped for, saved for, and planned for me, and probably cut my hair.

That, or create another lie, avoid responsibility, and leave under the cover of darkness.

There really never was a choice. I began planning to escape immediately. I knew that leaving might mean never seeing them again or, at the least, for a long, long time, and the thought was wrenching. But the thought of continuing my life under their dominion was far more daunting, and not a future I wanted to be a part of. I longed for the road, for the freedom that Kerouac and Dylan wrote about. I needed to be my own man, create my own world, and live my own life. I needed to get out.

I also needed money, and I needed it quickly. Rifling Dad's wallet and Mom's purse would have required skills of theft I didn't possess, and if those faculties had been among my repertoire, it was doubtful that purse or wallet either one would have yielded enough cash to make the risk worthwhile. I paid no attention to the morality of the act I was pondering, only the practicality—and there was little to no upside there. That left one avenue, one I was loath to pursue, but necessity demanded it. I would sell my guitar. A Martin D12-20 twelve-string with a hard-shell case sold new for six hundred and change. Two years old, good condition—I could pull down a couple of large easy. Enough for bus fare back to Denver. I'd get a job doing something, save enough for a basic six-string, and never miss the twelve. Good plan.

Needing a diversion to ensure the success of the deception, I borrowed the station wagon one morning under the lie of taking the Martin to a music store in Palo Alto to be restrung "and have the bridge shaved to lower the action." They wouldn't know from bridges or action, and it sounded just plausible enough to be true. Plus, they had no reason to doubt the story. So far, so good. Next step: unload the twelve-string without crying, pocket a few hundred, and I'd be back by midday.

Three hours and four music stores later, the highest offer I'd had was $150. I couldn't believe this. A Martin-D-frigging-12-20, and the best quote was under two hundred dollars. Four music stores, four idiots. The last one had the nerve to suggest it might be hot.

Undaunted, I pressed forward with the plan to leave anyway. Yes, I needed money, but I'd find some way to make it work. I had a thumb, and my guitar would be my ticket. I'd be like Woody or Bob, play on street corners if I had to, pass the hat. I could live on next to nothing out in the world—but I could not live here, under the roof of my father's house, any longer. The time had come. I would leave that night after they'd retired and call them from somewhere down the road—maybe.

That night, after a short dinner, I slipped back to my room, quietly packed my duffel, adding a few pairs of jeans, a couple of sweaters, and two or three T-shirts from my bureau. I'd need every stitch—it was going to be cold in Denver, and colder still on the road between home and there. From the bookshelf I took my old, worn copy of *The Prophet* and wedged it between my clothes. It, too, would serve me well in the days ahead. "*Man cannot live*" . . . and all that.

Finished, I secreted my packed gear behind my bed, lest it be seen from the hallway, and made my way back to the den. Dad was in his rocker, feet up on the ottoman, watching *The Big Valley*. As I sat on the couch, he rose and stepped to the bar, swirling the ice in his empty glass as he crossed the floor, his eyes straight ahead, not so much as acknowledging I was even in the room. From behind me, I could hear the sounds I'd learned to identify as clearly as the sounds of their voices; the clink of ice, a bottle cap unscrewing, the short pour of Cutty (an aroma as familiar as the smell of pot roast), a splash of water, and his finger slowly stirring the cocktail.

Back in his chair, we silently watched Barbara Stanwyck rule her California ranch kingdom—both of us aware of but neither of us regarding the other. In the quiet that filled the gulf between us, I began to feel the first pangs of regret, of doubt; that perhaps I was being rash, perhaps I needed to rethink things—to reconsider other options; that maybe I was making a mistake. My pangs were short-lived, however, interrupted by another sound I'd grown accustomed to over the years: the *slap-slap-slap* of the folding partition from hall to kitchen—opening and then closing—the padding of moccasins on the linoleum floor, and the angry, tired voice of Betty Ford.

"Buck!" My name sounded like a word, not my name, and it had the power to pin me to the couch and nail my mouth shut. From the corner of my eye, I watched as Dad took a long pull from his Cutty and branch. His eyes did not move from the TV. Barbara Stanwyck was splitting wood, wiping sweat from her brow, and scolding Lee Majors.

"Buck!" Louder now. "Get in here. Now!"

Seated at the kitchen table in her usual place, the ash of a Pall Mall burning perilously close to her fingers, a thinning screwdriver in an iceless glass on a damp coaster perilously close to the edge of the table, Mom was gripping a prescription bottle of Seconal in her right hand, unscrewing the safety cap with her other, causing the ash from her cigarette to fall on the place mat in front of her.

"Sit. Down," she said. And as I did, two things happened. Dad appeared in the den doorway behind me, and she slammed the prescription bottle down on the table, scattering the Seconal across its surface; little two-toned, gray-and-white capsules dancing across the table and falling to the floor. She didn't move.

"This is what you've done to me," she said. She waved her hand across the surface of the table. "This is what you've done to your mother." I did not look at her. "Is this what you wanted?" She was nearly screaming now. "Look at me, goddamnit!" I turned to Dad. As I did, she slammed the palm of her hand on the table, nearly upending her drink, and jarring her cigarette out of the ashtray. "Look. At. Me! Is this what you wanted? For me to kill myself?! Because that's *exactly* what you've done to me."

From behind me, Dad was moving around the table to her rear. "Betty," he said, "this isn't the right way . . . Let's put the pills away."

Isn't the right way to what, I'm thinking, *threaten suicide? Open a bottle of Seconal?* He was behind her now, trying to ease her up and out of her chair. Her eyes burning through me, she was angrily brushing his hands off her arms.

"Let go of me, Ford."

"Come on, Bet." She was up now, and Dad was trying his best to encircle his arms around her, but unsuccessful as her arms flailed against him, all the while, her eyes locked on me.

"Goddamn you to hell . . . let go of me! I can't take this anymore, goddamnit! I hate you . . . I hate both of you. Let *go* of me!"

Somehow, she'd untangled herself from Dad's arms, and now she spun herself away from both of us, nearly pirouetting to the floor, barely stopping her fall on the corner of the table. Dad's arms around her again, he began to slowly walk her out of the kitchen, Mom struggling to free herself with each step, cursing him and me, her voice fading as they fought down the long hall to her bedroom.

Rooted to my chair, I had not moved. And now, I was ashamed that I'd not spoken, not tried to help. Pushing my chair away from the table, I took the empty bottle of Seconal and began picking up the capsules from the floor, the place mats, under the chairs, and in the ashtray, putting them one by one back in the container. I was screwing the top back on when Dad returned. With the briefest of glances my way, he walked stoop-shouldered into the den, retrieved his drink, came slowly back into the kitchen, and stood at the edge of the table, surveying its surface, like a man lost in his own home. His eyes did not lift from their downward cast.

"Your mother is tired, son. She loves you and your brother, you know. She doesn't hate you—or me—I don't think. She's tired."

Before I could answer, the partition slapped open again, and Mom walked back in the room, swaying unsteadily on her feet as she navigated to her place at the table. On the place mat in front of her she fanned a small pile of bills; twenties, tens, and fives.

"Sit down, Buck." The untrained ear might not have understood those three words. I did. After nearly all day and half the night spent drinking—compounded with the Valium or whatever drug she was doing to take the edge off—she seemed to lose the use of her mouth when she spoke. The words just sort of sounded themselves from inside her, like a ventriloquist, but a ventriloquist who could not keep her eyes open, or—now—hold a cigarette between her fingers. Twice she made the effort to bring it to her lips and twice she failed. Finally, she gave up and then tried to simply place it in the ashtray next to her. It fell out, rolled to the edge of the table and on to the floor. I picked it up, ground it out in the ashtray, and sat down across from her. By now,

Dad had seated himself in his chair at the table's head. As if they were made of iron, heavy and dense, she slowly pushed the fanned bills toward me.

"This is for the bus." Her body seemed to shrink as she spoke. "This is so you don't have to run away. This is for the bus." To my right, Dad was silent, his head cocked downwards chin on chest.

I was stunned, unable to move or call up even enough courage to look at them. How could they have divined my plan; how could they not only have known that I was going to leave, but apparently known that I was planning on doing so furtively? How could they have known . . . and now, how could I find the strength to tell them the truth—a truth they obviously already knew?

When I broke down, I was embarrassed that I could not seem to stem the tide of tears that were coursing down my face; ashamed of my inability to control my emotions and my failure to speak to them as a man. In halting, broken sentences, I confessed all; dropping out, trying to sell the guitar, the plan to leave—to hitchhike back to Denver . . . everything. I loved them, but I had to leave, I had to go. I had to get out. I had to make them understand . . . I had to leave them and find my own way in the world. I'd get work, it would be hard, but I'd be all right. I *had* to go.

The room was silent. I'd finally stopped crying, gathering strength with each intake of breath and strengthening my will with each exhale. But as I felt myself regaining control, I felt my will to go forward wavering. In the very same moment of believing I had convinced them of the rightness of my leaving, I found myself wanting to stay forever, to never say good-bye to them, to never leave them—never leave them alone. My will returned not because of any reservoir I'd plumbed, any great grasp of resolve on my part, but through the words I heard from the chair to my right—from Dad.

"You'll find work?"

"Yes, sir."

"And you'll call us every once in a while?"

"Yes."

"We love you, boy. Don't forget your mom and me . . . okay?"

At that moment, it took every ounce of everything I had to not rescind all and give myself and my life up to them completely. But in the next few minutes, the plans were laid and designs for the morrow put in motion. Dad would fix me breakfast, help me pack if I needed it, take me to the bus station in Redwood City, and I would be gone. I would be gone with their blessing, and I would be gone in the light of day, buoyed by and guided with, but not anchored by, their love.

Later, alone in the darkness of my bedroom, I lay awash in tears, hardening myself as best I could for the road ahead; steeling myself against the emotions that pulled at me, rewinding the memories of years long gone, cursing myself for the decisions I'd made and the pain I'd brought to our home. *I have to be strong, I kept telling myself. I'm a man now . . . I'm going to be on my own. I'll see them again—I'll be the man they've always hoped I'd become, and I'll make them proud of me again.*

Exhausted but resolved, sleep finally began to take me. But as I slowly drifted off, I could hear Mom calling me from her dressing room, which was situated catty-corner from my connected bath. Filtered through the walls that separated us, her voice sounded weak but insistent; a sound I'd heard hundreds of times, beckoning Brion or me to her side where, smashed, stoned, or both, she'd sit us down on the thick, plush carpet, run brushes through our hair, and talk ramblingly about having a daughter. Possessed, inspired, she'd tow us into her closet and pull out outfit after outfit, dresses, pantsuits, furs . . . hold each up to her, and ask if we had a girlfriend who might want the clothes. Back to her settee, Brion and me in tow, she'd sit us down, brush our hair, finish her drink, and send us to bed.

In the past, any other night, I'd get up without thinking and answer her bidding obediently. But now I shut my eyes to those memories, and tried to shut the sound of her voice from my ears. I would not go in tonight. I would not go in again. *I will not go in, Mom. Not tonight.*

But as I lay there, cutting the umbilical memory and silently refusing to respond to her call, I heard the sound of her bedroom door opening and her moccasins pad their way to my door. Then, the unmistakable sound of her kicking the bottom of the door. Twice. Not hard enough to cause damage—God knows she didn't have the strength—but hard enough to slightly rattle the frame and reverberate through the hollow casing. Twice. Followed by an abrupt silence, then the sound of her voice from the other side of the door, her words paced, clear, and intelligible.

"Buck. I don't want to die now."

Then I heard her turn, and without waiting for an answer pad back to her bedroom. I didn't hear the door open or close.

Jesus, I thought. *I'm never going to free myself from this. It's never going to end. I will never leave this place. Okay, Mom,* I said to myself, *once more; one more time . . . one more night. One last time.*

I pulled on my jeans and buttoned them, threw a loose cinch in my belt, slipped my feet into my boots, stepped into the hallway outside the bedroom and slipped, nearly falling. My first thought was Mom had spilled her drink, which explained why she'd kicked the door instead of opening it. I was wrong, but I didn't give it any further thought. I regained my footing and traced the steps I'd taken to her corner of the house so many nights before. The door to her bedroom was open, the room dark. To my right, a thin band of light escaped from the crack in the doorway to her dressing room. I stood at the threshold and spoke her name. From the other side, she repeated what she'd said outside my bedroom earlier—"I don't want to die now"—and I opened the door.

She was sitting at her vanity, blood pumping from both wrists, a Pall Mall between her index and middle finger, the ash not quite an inch long, hanging delicately off the burning paper. She was quite calm, actually, but weak. Too weak to raise the Bloody Mary to her lips, which she was in the process of trying to do as I opened her door. Save for one difference, it all seemed perfectly normal; a tableau I'd seen hundreds of times growing up. Mom on the seat at her makeup table, a drink in one hand, cigarette in the other. Prescription bottles arranged like a collection of tiny vases to the right of the sink, bottles of Smirnoff and cans of Snap-e-Tom balancing the whole feng-shui thing on the left. The only thing different, the only thing that made this scenario unlike any before, was the blood. It was everywhere. Flowing out of her arms as she turned to me, laving the countertop and rolling down the walls of the sink in thick, dark red rivulets. Turning calmly but fearfully to me, she laughed, then coughed. "Don't tell your father," she said. "He'll kill me."

I tore the belt off my jeans and wrapped it around both her arms, cinching it as tightly as I could, and covered her wrists with an embroidered hand towel next to her sink. Her head was beginning to loll to her chest—she was losing consciousness. Laying her on the floor, I told her to be still, and exploded from her room, running down the long hallway, screaming for Dad as I ran. By the time I reached the kitchen, he was out of the den.

"Mom's cut her wrists!" I shouted. "I've put my belt on her, but . . . Oh, Jesus, Dad!"

He was carrying her when he came from the bedroom, running as best he could, gathering speed as he came down the hall.

"Start the car, son—now!" he shouted. I already had. I climbed in the backseat and he laid her next to me, her head on my lap. Stroking her hair as Dad sped to Stanford, I could feel the flow of her blood soak my jeans, warm and thickening. She had stopped moving, but was feebly trying to speak . . . though I could not make out the words she was saying.

At the hospital Dad and I sat quietly just outside the ER, as a team of doctors stanched the flow, stitched up her wrists, and replaced the blood she'd lost. We had arrived just in time. Another few minutes, and she would have been gone. Throughout everything, neither of us had spoken to the other. He seemed resigned sitting there, stoic and unmoved. Behind his eyes, though, I could see wells of sadness, and in his lap, his hands were opening and closing, opening and closing, opening and closing. When he spoke, he did not look at me, but kept his eyes on the doorway leading to the room Mom was in.

"If anyone asks—ever—your mom cut her hands when she broke a casserole dish. Okay?"

I felt sick now, covered in her blood, seeing her at her vanity in my mind's eye. That Dad was already thinking about a cover story didn't really register—I only remember thinking, *Yes, that sounds like a good idea . . . She broke a casserole dish, the blood was pumping out of her arms, and she didn't want to die.*

I stayed at home for the next few days, until she was released from the hospital. I believed that Dad needed me, needed me to be with him until she came back, until she was home again. But over the few days, he showed little to no emotion, and we never spoke about that night ever again.

Mom recovered quickly, but naturally she remained in a somewhat weakened state for a while following her return home. After a week had passed, I came in the den one evening after dinner and sat down next to Dad. I did not need to tell him why I'd joined him.

"I guess you're probably ready to go, son. Your mom will be okay . . . She's just tired. But she loves you and your brother. You know that, don't you, boy?"

The next morning he fixed breakfast for both of us, the kitchen quiet and close. We ate without speaking. Afterward, I tiptoed back to Mom's bedroom to say good-bye. She was sleeping on her stomach, her mouth squinched up on her pillow, breathing deeply and quietly. I leaned down and kissed her softly on her cheek, not wanting to wake her. She turned her head, and I started for the door but was stopped by her voice from the bed.

"Buck. I love you. Write your father and me, and for God's sake don't get anybody pregnant. Now go on." I said I loved her, too, that I would write, and not to worry. "Go on, son. You're a man, now. Go on." In a salty, thick stream, tears silently flowed down my face and neck as I turned away and quietly closed her door.

I got my ticket at the terminal counter, stowed my duffel in the baggage bay, and waited with Dad in the parking lot for the bus to board. We didn't say much; we talked about the ranch, about Brion, about how we knew Mom would be okay soon, about where I thought I might end up. I was heading east, I told him—probably back to Denver, but I might look for ranch work up north in Carson City first . . . I wasn't sure. My first stop was Reno. After that . . . but I didn't get the chance to finish. The depot's loudspeaker announced my bus number and called for boarding. I pulled my peacoat on and grabbed my guitar, gratified that I still had it with me, feeling some of the sadness fall away. But as I started to say good-bye to Dad, he handed me a small package; a plain, brown manila envelope, folded twice and wrapped with a thick rubber band. "This is something I want you to have, son. Open it up after you're on the road a few miles." I took the package and as I slipped it into the deep pocket of my coat, he slipped both arms around me. "We love you, son. Promise me you'll give us a call . . . for your mom."

"I will, Dad. I promise." The boarding call sounded again and I climbed into the cab, racking my guitar in the bin above my seat. From the window I could see Dad waiting by the station wagon in the parking lot, hands deep in his pockets, his eyes looking off into space— looking everywhere but at the bus. I waved, but if he saw me, he didn't—maybe couldn't or wasn't going to—wave back. As the engines revved up and the bus pulled away from the terminal, I covered my eyes with my hand, as if shading them from a sun too bright, unwilling for any of the souls traveling with me to know I wasn't the man I appeared, that I was nothing more than a child in the guise of a man. A child unable to stop crying.

As we left the city limits and the billboards began to give way to redwoods, I took my peacoat off, intending to toss it up above with my guitar. But as I threw a fold in it, the package Dad had given me fell out of the pocket. Inside was a small Bible, bound in wood and leather, with gold trim on the edges of the pages. Behind the hand-tooled wooden cover, on the frontispiece, was a single line, written in pen, in Dad's unmistakable hand. *To Buck—with my deep love—Dad.* I shut my eyes and held it tight. I love you, too, Dad. And you, Mom . . .

Finally, I fell asleep; the dull roar of the engines like a droning lullaby. All the sadness faded, and I let myself be rocked away by the roll of the big Greyhound.

THIRTEEN

IT SEEMS AN ALMOST UNIVERSAL GIVEN that anybody who actually lived through the seventies either can't, won't, or pretends not to remember much. I should be so lucky.

For a while I lived on the western slope of Colorado, doing ranch work, and then made a halfhearted stab at the folk scene out of Denver, touring as a solo act, and with a small, three-piece group on the college coffeehouse-and-club circuit. *Halfhearted* may not be entirely accurate; I toured from New York to the West Coast, and Green Bay to Texas six or seven times, playing every university and college town on the map that would hire me. The work was steady if not profitable, and I used the road to hone what passable craft I had, developing a folk-blues style that earned more than a few decent reviews and a handful of follow-up gigs that actually paid. It was cool while it lasted, but as a performer I was admittedly one-dimensional, and as a guitar player . . . *minus* one-dimensional. My best dates were my best because of the players I coerced to tour with me: Mary Flower and Katy Moffatt—who sang harmonies like sirens from Texas. Randy Handley—a blues pianist who influenced Lowell George and sounded like Dr. John; and bassist Lon Ephraim—an Orthodox, Hasidic cat who looked just like Rasputin and could play any instrument ever created by man. They were all artists. I was not. I was, in retrospect, more interested in the lifestyle than in actually becoming an accomplished musician and performer, and that dog wouldn't hunt for long, no matter how much time you spend on your attractiveness. By '77 my career as a singer-songwriter was all but done.

I returned home several times in that hazy span of years—unannounced, to Mom and Dad's surprise and confused dismay—the last time with Mary Flower and Lon Ephraim in tow, on the way to a gig in L.A. I halfway expected them to welcome me with open arms; prodigal son, troubadour home from the long road . . . along with his bass player, Rasputin. Dad was evasive, largely uncommunicative, and Mom was not impressed. We stayed for two days, I bummed some much-needed cash for the group, and I was gone again—leaving them confused, disappointed, and uncertain. Again.

Over the same period, Mom and Dad journeyed to Colorado together twice—Dad, four or five times. Each of those trips they undertook to the mountains was an occasion I made a concerted effort to completely wipe from my memory banks within minutes after they'd said good-bye, and, in one case, within minutes after I'd said hello. The chasm that separated us then had widened to a span and depth approaching that of the Grand Canyon, and bridging it wasn't even considered. Even when we were in the same room, we were shouting across a cultural, linguistic, artistic, and social divide so enormous, communication was simply a formality, not a reality.

That division reached a breaking point with Dad late in 1970, when I was arrested in Breckenridge for possession of marijuana. My lineage made me a poster boy, of sorts, and the presiding judge milked it for all it was worth, hinging the sentencing for my first-time offense on an appearance by Dad—in chambers. The story in the Summit County paper was timed to coincide precisely with countywide elections, and the judge counted on his power to summon an international celebrity to court, duly impress everyone in the process, and thereby guarantee his seat on the bench for another term.

He did *not* count on Ernie Ford and his errant son both being picked up for disturbing the peace the night before the hearing, nor did he count on Betty Ford coming to town with her husband, and the memorable send-off she'd give His Honor, and His Honor's fair city.

I'm actually surprised that Dad didn't throttle me that night. He came close, and if Loakes hadn't jumped in front of him and Mom hadn't jumped on his back (honest to God), he probably would have. I had become the antithesis of everything he held dear, and our fight that night was a microcosm of the generational conflict dividing families all over the country. The conversation began politically, Dad wanting to know whether I "bought" what the hard-hats had done in New York. (In May of that year, four days after the Kent State shootings, some two hundred construction workers employed on the World Trade Center site attacked a group of antiwar demonstrators from NYU and Pace University, bludgeoning and brutally beating scores of students. Nixon publicly thanked them for their patriotic support of his policies in Vietnam.)

Separated by Mom and Loakes, seemingly cooled down with a couple of drinks in him, he suggested he and I take a walk together. I agreed. We'd gone about two blocks when his anger returned and his voice began carrying, garnering the unintended attention of more than one citizen. Embarrassed, and amazed that my own father was threatening me in public, I had decided to leave him on the street, return to the hotel, and remove my things, when he started throwing punches. Nonviolent, peace-loving mountain hippie that I was, I thanked God less for Gandhi at that moment than for Cutty Sark, because if he'd been sober and connected with my jaw, I'd have been prone on Main Street. He was as surprised as I was, however, when a cruiser pulled to the curb, blue lights flashing, and carried us both back to the hotel like petty street thugs. I can't even begin to tell you how pleased Mom was.

She was almost as pleased as the judge was the next morning. His grand visions of judicial stardom and a second term shot to hell over a street fight, he proceeded to instruct both of us on our public behavior, which thrilled Mom even more than the events from the night before. Within minutes, though, she'd seen through him, and when he suggested a picture with him and Dad before we left the building, she knew the real purpose behind his summons and their attendance. She was furious, her anger quietly boiling just under the surface of her skin, requiring every ounce of civility she'd ever acquired or practiced to be put into play.

My sentence levied (probation and a stern talking-to), we were excused from chambers, Dad courteously declining the photo-op when Mom began feigning nausea. On the steps outside the courthouse, Betty Ford emerged from her cocoon, and as we looked up to the second floor at the image of the judge smiling from his chambers window, she hitched her bag to her shoulder, jerked her arm from Dad's supportive hand, turned toward the beatific magistrate above, and flipped him the bird. Not once but three times, thrusting the obscene gesture in the air like a digital lance; at the judge, the courthouse, and the fair town of Breckenridge.

I can't begin to tell you how pleased Dad was.

Outside the story in the Summit County paper, and a one-paragraph blurb in *Variety*, there was scant press about the Breckenridge incident, which made it easier for Dad to ignore, if not forget. Not so with Mom. She delighted in telling the story, embellishing it over the years with layer upon layer of rich fiction until it bore little to no resemblance whatsoever to what actually happened. Eventually, the story was that she had actually been arrested and jailed *with* me; mother and son potheads busted together. It infuriated Dad and embarrassed him, which, while that may not have been the intent, was a by-product of the tale she did not regret causing every so often.

In the same vein, the fact that the public had never learned anything about Mom's attempts to end her life made it easier for almost everyone in the family to ignore, if not forget what she'd done. But unlike her dramatic retelling of the Breckenridge affair, she never discussed, laughed about, cried over, or confided in anyone—that I know of—concerning any of those desperate, grim adventures. Sworn to secrecy that night in the waiting room at Stanford's emergency center, Dad's hands trembling ever so slightly—a sight I had never seen—I agreed to a lie and vowed solemnly to live by it. The power of such a vow made by a son to a father is not easily resisted, contested, or broken, and I believed that if I spoke the truth to anyone about that night, I would surely do more harm to him than had already been done—by Mom *and* by me. I stayed silent to save face and save him, but I know now, and have for many years, that I should have spoken urgently, if confidentially, to someone—anyone—who had the knowledge and the skill to save her. But I did not. And I have lived every day since with the knowledge that my acquiescence and my inaction spoke volumes. I chose to protect our image rather than her life, and I have never forgiven myself.

Even these long years after, I can still see Dad's hands and hear the broken, half-whispered sound of his words, pressing me into service and falsehood. My silence did not, however, free me from the persistent, engrammic vision he was asking me to lie about; of Mom at her vanity, the blood flowing from her wrists, pleading with me not to tell my father. It has stayed with me since, etched in my memory, and there are still nights when it is crystal clear, as if it happened only yesterday.

Unintended and certainly unforeseen, Mom and I were now connected by another type of bond altogether, but not maternal, umbilical, or oedipal. Branded by our own actions—cavalier and desperate—we'd brought shame upon the family. A wary eye was kept on us both, and neither of us would be fully trusted ever again. We had joined ranks with Dad's brother, Stanley, and become the new skeletons that had to be kept in the closet.

Though they could not be completely put out of mind, each of the crises that had so changed our family was conveniently placed out of sight, lest they sully the name and image of Ernie Ford. This was the wife and son of a legend, for God's sake, a man who represented all that was good and decent in the world. A man who stood for everything righteous—for God and for country. For such a man to be the father of a son so aberrant, so divergent from normalcy, was unthinkable. For the bride of such a man to resort to suicide while in the depths of a depression soaked in alcoholism and magnified by drug addiction was impossible. Not this family, not this couple . . . not Ernie Ford and his lovely wife, Betty.

Although it was never something that came up in conversation, never a subject we conspiratorially commiserated over, everyone, including Mom and me, knew it would be suicide of another sort altogether if our misadventures became public knowledge—if the skeletons were taken out of the closet. We could bring ruin upon us all. And so, *denial* was the word . . . but we never spoke it; we just practiced it.

Perhaps they both sensed how fragile the bonds had become that once made them so strong. It's possible that they could see how tenuous things were; how close Mom had come to death, and how hollow the space between them was . . . I can't say. But for one of those reasons or another, they began to take stock of their lives over the next several years and to take steps—though not demonstratively—to remedy and heal themselves. Mom began to eat more, and to eat with more regularity. She appeared to level off the bottle somewhat and reduce her intake of pharmaceuticals. For his part, Dad appeared to pay more attention to her, to take a more genuinely compassionate interest in not only what she was but who she'd become. She put on weight; he cut back his road schedule. She insulted him less frequently;

he complimented her honestly, not just out of habit. They took trips together again—a cruise here, a flight there—and by all accounts they were happy to be with and to be seen with each other again.

They bought a small condo in Palm Springs, and in the weeks just after the closing shopped for furniture, art, and decor together. He demurred to her tastes, did not mind the modern art, and she allowed him a Remington bronze. They socialized occasionally with Sinatra and his crew, chatted every once in a while with Bob and Dolores Hope, and became fast friends with Gerald and (the other) Betty Ford. Dad played a lot of golf, and Jack Fascinato did his best to get him into tennis. Jack's wife, Loras, introduced Mom to the Palm Springs social scene, and she got to know the doorman at Saks on a first-name basis. Life was good. Well . . . it was better.

In addition to a reduced tour itinerary, Dad did two specials for NBC and concluded his deal with them, declining to renew. The second—and last—show very nearly didn't happen and very nearly resulted in a lawsuit brought against the network. It was called *Sing America Beautiful*, and while laden with some of the usual seventies-era, overproduced music, off-the-radar wardrobe decisions, and less than inspired writing, it somehow managed to include Danny Thomas, Diahann Carroll, the Marine Corps Marching Band, the International Children's Choir and the Smothers Brothers in the lineup, and avoided any disruptive politics or censorship, or fistfights in the process. It was, apparently, just strange enough to work, because it got huge Nielsens and great reviews.

It was originally scheduled to air on a Friday night, following NBC's special on the opening of Disney World—as plum a time slot as anyone in programming could hope for—but someone in New York with a pet miniseries project called *The Funny Side* decided to change the lineup three days before airing. At the time, *The Funny Side* was the lowest rated show on the network, but the favorite of one or two executive dweebs who thought it had promise. All that was required was the right audience to give its ratings the boost the show needed. Let's see . . . what can we bump. Ah—here we go—that old fart, Tennessee Ernie Ford. It's his last special under his current deal with us anyway; let's cancel it and replace it with *Funny Side*. We'll let him know when he comes out to L.A. to watch the final cut. . . .

When Dad, BetFord, and the cast and crew were informed, the shit hit the fan. When the press was informed, it hit it again—in the national media. BetFord threatened an action that would have punctured NBC's public relations division and soaked them financially. That old fart Ernie Ford was pissed off, and it wasn't nice to fool with a pissed-off old fart.

The network recapitulated and rescheduled the special for the following week. The time slot wasn't nearly as prime as following the Disney World special, but the numbers that came in were still way more than respectable. When the network geeks came around all smiles with a renewal option for three more specials, they were given an anatomical map and shown where they could shove their option. It was the end of Ernie Ford's sixteen-year marriage with NBC, and the divorce was anything but amicable. Dad couldn't have cared less. His alimony check was one of the biggest the network had ever paid out.

At about the same time the curtain came down on his run with NBC, Dad began a twenty-five-year association with Martha White Mills, one of the country's leading baked-goods manufacturers, based in Nashville. Its chairman and CEO, Cohen Williams, was the outspoken patriarch of one of the city's most legendary old-money families, and one of its most influential.

The connection between Dad and Cohen was almost immediate; they became instant, mutual fans, and Dad became the face and voice of the company as their new spokesman. The cream of Nashville society was thrilled, welcoming the long-lost favorite son of Tennessee back into the fold. Cohen and Martha White were involved in everything that had to do with country music or money in Nashville, and he saw to it that Dad was just as involved. He began making scores of trips to town for still shoots, television commercials, radio spots, company parties and conventions, and walk-on appearances at the Opry, the latter resulting in near-pandemonium every time he stepped onstage.

The business arrangement between Dad and Martha White was more than profitable financially, and the repercussive gigs that came in the wake of his popularity and visibility as their spokesman were equally so. They took up the slackening and seemingly inexorable decline in record sales under Capitol's inept marketing, as well as the reduction of regular television residuals, save for fees that were negotiated for occasional guest appearances on *Dinah*, *Laugh-In*, *Sonny and Cher*, *The Mandrell Sisters* show, and a few other forgettable, seventies-era series. The long-range guarantees in the Martha White deal had buttressed and shored up the financial underpinnings of the family and BetFord Corporation, and Dad was not reserved in his gratitude. He glommed on to Cohen, his wife, Naomi, and their daughters and sons-in-law, and they in turn showered him with starstruck adulation, creating their very own mutual ingratiation society.

Within a few years they were integrally involved in some way in virtually every aspect of Dad's career and his life, an involvement he welcomed and believed held great promise—and not just for himself.

Somehow I had failed the test; I'd bitten the hand that fed me and was, perhaps, beyond salvaging. I was living God knew where, doing God knew what, with God knew who. I was beyond his reach and his control. Not so, Brion. There was still hope . . . Dad still had one redeemable son left.

After he graduated from Stevenson, Brion had joined Dad for two road dates and a Capitol session; not as a roadie as my task had been several years earlier, but as a singer. Fearful that he'd perhaps fall under the influence of his wayward older brother, Dad kept him on a tight leash, bringing him on tour that summer and giving him a walk-on for two dates, to do a duet together of the contemporary folk standard, "Today" ("while the blossoms still cling to the *vine*"). Brion ate it up, and with no college plans in the offing, he stayed close to home and closely connected to Dad, hoping for more work and a coattail entrée into the business. He appeared to move a step closer to getting just that when Dad agreed to have him do one side on his *Folk Album* release in October of that year; a duet of the old standard "Cotton Fields." The back cover featured a shot of Brion and Dad together, and the liner notes announced his recording debut, which, unknown to anyone at the time, was also his swan song with the label. The album tanked, for lack of a better term, and Brion's future as a cast member of the Ernie Ford Show was in doubt. For that matter, his future— period—was in doubt, in Dad's eyes, anyway. He'd eschewed the military, his grades from Stevenson did not have universities clamoring for his attendance, and he wasn't exactly building a repertoire of employable basic skills.

Cue the Martha White theme. A couple of phone calls from Dad to Cohen Williams, and Brion had a future—guaranteed and dusted with flour. It was a marriage made in Hot Rize Heaven; the son of the spokesman for one of the South's oldest dynasties takes his rightful place and begins his training as heir apparent. Dad was ecstatic. He saw his son gainfully employed, and the corporate powers saw their spokesman for the next generation. Brion, however, saw his dreams of stardom sidelined, and saw himself shoehorned into a job about which he felt less than gung ho.

What Brion wanted never really mattered, though. What mattered was what Ernie Ford wanted *for* him, needed for him, and, most important, needed for himself; the knowledge that this son would not fail, that his future was secure. That he was finally out of the house.

By mid 1973, Brion's life had been mapped out for him. Dad moved him back to Nashville, bought him a truck, set him up in a two-bedroom condo, and brought him to Cohen Williams for baptism. Paired with one of their area reps who was nearing retirement, Brion started work for the company in an entry-level sales position, delivering product to midsize markets and small country stores. He was perfect. Engaging, friendly, right shrewd with the local folks, he learned the routes and the names quickly, winning every account over with his infectious personality and his ability to get along, it seemed, with anybody. It was only a matter of time before every grocery manager from Smyrna to Portland learned whose son he was, and when that word got out, Brion's dream of stardom came true. His audiences may not have been filling an auditorium or glued in front of their televisions, but in the eyes of every Piggly Wiggly and Food Town supervisor in middle Tennessee, he was the next best thing to show-business royalty. People loved him, and while he knew the real reason they loved him, he savored the attention anyway.

Grocery stardom notwithstanding, the attention coming Brion's way had not yet dulled his senses or clouded his vision. After a few short months on the job, he was being considered for a raise and a promotion to a position that the salesman who'd been his mentor had worked toward for years but not merited. He began to realize that he was being given preferential treatment, and he had the distinct impression he was being groomed for an entry-level position into the Williams family itself.

And while the salesman assigned to guide him through the basics was affable enough, Brion could sense a swelling undercurrent of resentment from this old-line company man, knowing he was being passed over in favor of this kid from California whose name had landed him on this route and put him in line for that promotion. To his credit, Brion placed the future of that man above his own, and before he'd been with the company for a year, he abruptly quit.

That, at any rate, is the story as Brion told it many times. In fairness, more than one person had a somewhat different recollection of the reasons behind his severance from Martha White, but I'm choosing here and now to give my brother the benefit of the doubt.

While disappointed and with, perhaps, just a smidgen of egg on his face, Dad could not let Brion's departure from the corporate security he'd planned for him affect his own direction or business plan. Nor would Cohen Williams.

In the ensuing months since relocating Brion to Twang Town, Dad had become far more attached to the Martha White machine, and to much more than simply the company's spokesperson. For all practical purposes, Cohen and Naomi's Belle Meade manse became his second home, one of its many guest rooms perennially reserved for him. Cohen and his son in-law, Bobby Dale (Martha White's president), and grandson, Jim King, were not only welcomed into but also given key arcs in the coveted Ernie Ford inner circle. They orbited around him 24-7, 365; advising him, counseling him, fishing with him, golfing with him, investing with him, drinking with him, touring with him. They became his new de facto managers; unofficially tag-teaming with Jim Loakes and Peter Brown, protecting their investment and casting themselves as essentially the Nashville Division of Ernie Ford, Inc.

It reached a point of complete absurdity in 1977, when Dad was in town cutting some regional radio spots and Brion and I were literally barred from the studio by Jim King before we could even get to Jim Loakes and schedule a few minutes with Dad before he left the city. Admittedly, neither of us was on the short list in those days, and one or both of us were usually on the dole, which usually put Dad on edge, which usually didn't make for a relaxed session in the studio. Nevertheless, I was unequivocal in my promise to Dad in a phone call the next day, that if Jim King, or anyone, ever attempted to bar me from seeing my own father, he'd be doing so from the ground, bleeding. I was that angry. And although things were not what one might call warm and fuzzy with us then, I think my indignation and threat of physical response struck some sort of manly chord in Dad, and whether out of fatherly pride or in a spirit of mediation, we were never denied a backstage pass, as it were, again.

In a few short years, the Martha White contingent had gone from being business partners with Ernie Ford to something else entirely. They had become nothing less than his second family. And it was not long before he quietly, carefully, but openly confided in them the angst-ridden, frustrating, and discouraging histories plaguing his own. They listened, they understood the poor man, and they offered him the respite, succor, harborage, and scotch he obviously—desperately, at times—needed so badly. They opened their hearts and their home to him, freely giving him all the things that he wasn't receiving or couldn't or hadn't received in God knew how long from within his own home; the respect, honor, fealty, and love a husband and father of his caliber *should* receive. There was no chance in hell any of these loyal children would ever be arrested for smoking dope, or that any of these beautiful, doting wives would ever stoop to attempt suicide, bringing shame upon their name and their house. This was the way a family—his family—was *supposed* to be.

As the years progressed and Dad's relationship with the Williamses and Martha White flourished, more than one observer on the perimeter of this circle had the distinct impression that of the two families he now had, he favored the latter over the former. One of those people was at home in Portola Valley.

This new ménage, this confederation of "throwbacks to the Old South" (one of her favorite profiles when the subject came up), was glued to Ernie Ford at his hip like groupies—wherever he was. Except when he was at home with Mom. They did not venture there, and in the twenty years that marked the Martha White association, she set foot in Cohen and Naomi Williams's home only twice, and, save for one instance, did not deign to accompany Dad on any trips or junkets if they or any of their brood were included. She felt—and said as much on more than one occasion—that she and Brion and I were being supplanted.

In fairness, I did not and do not believe that any of the Martha White crew were bad people, or that they sought to drive any kind of wedge into or exploit the fissures that had begun appearing in our family facade. It may have been nothing more than a case of regrettable kismet, of unfortunate coincidence, but the personal relationships that grew and thrived out of the Martha White arrangement ran parallel to a reversal of the healing between Mom and Dad that had begun early in the decade.

While it was not immediate, Mom began withdrawing again, withering; her body weight dropped, and her bill at the liquor store increased. She went to the condo in Palm Springs by herself, and to the penthouse in Honolulu with her friends. Walls that had been nearly dismantled were erected again, and it would be some time before there were chinks wide enough to allow even the thinnest shafts of light to pass through from either side. In dwindling moments of clarity, Mom began to suggest that she and Dad seek counseling, a recommendation he dismissed disdainfully, but one she would propose repeatedly over the next ten years.

In response, perhaps out of frustration, a sense that he had failed somehow, somewhere—or simply in a bid to forget, Dad himself began to drink heavily, doubling, sometimes tripling his normal intake for the day. It was not unusual for him to begin the day with a Coors Tall Boy. "Doctor said it'll help me keep my weight down," was the logic. "It fills me up, so I don't eat so much." Umm-hmm. His bottled preferences swung from Cutty to Smirnoff, but he favored the former. He began carrying a briefcase, for Christ's sake; a big leather, accordion-bottomed valise engraved with his initials below the gold-plated hasp. Very professional, you know. And expandable to boot, providing just enough depth and width to haul and hide the bottle of scotch that had become as crucial a component of his daily gear as his golf clubs and pipe.

Unlike Mom, however, you couldn't really tell when he'd been in the bag. Whether it was his molecular structure, his resistance level, his conscious awareness of the importance of his image, or simply his ability to carry it, he hid it well—for a few years, anyway. By the mid-seventies, though, even he was not able to mask all the effects. It began to affect his work, and it began to gradually affect his appearance. A paunch began to form just above his belt, and not because he was gaining weight. His facial features and muscle tone began to lose their tautness, and his complexion began to fade. The effects were not overtly noticeable at first, but as the years progressed they became more pronounced, more difficult to conceal, and people began to talk—quietly, to be sure, but they began to talk. And one voice among the chorus was none other than that of Betty Ford, who, by 1977, was letting me know, none too quietly, that she was worried "about your father's drinking habits. And he refuses to listen to me. For God's sake, talk to him, Buck."

She was usually smashed when she called me.

* * *

In August 1974, Capitol released a pair of two-disc albums marking Dad's twenty-fifth year with the label. The packaging was beautifully done; tasteful and classy, each cover centered with a simple embossed-cameo profile. Very cool. One set chronicled a collection of twenty-four tracks of his straight stuff, the other, twenty-two of his inspirational sides—forty-six tracks in all. Both releases were met with critical acclaim, celebrating, as the trades quoted Capitol's president, "the silver anniversary of a legendary American singer, and one of Capitol Records' preeminent artists of the twentieth century."

Exactly two years later, after twenty-seven years with the label, spending more than a thousand hours in the studio, recording more than six hundred tracks that earned the company millions upon tens of millions of dollars; six weeks before going into the studio for his eighty-third session, Capitol assigned an under-assistant to an associate office manager in the catalog division to notify their legendary American singer and preeminent artist of the twentieth *century* that they were not going to renew his contract. A two-paragraph letter after nearly thirty years. The last song on the last day of the last session was a Glenn McGuirt track called "Ain't Goin' Down in the Ground Before My Time." A fitting end, don't you think?

He was picked up almost immediately by Word Records, a label geared exclusively for inspirational releases, and which, initially, seemed to be a good fit. But sales were slow and low, and after just six albums over eight years, the Word deal had run its course.

It's possible that his contract with Word could have had a longer life, but all things considered, it simply wasn't possible any longer—not in the state of health and voice he'd allowed himself to sink to. By the second session with Word, the timbre of his once-powerful voice was thinning, and his breathing was labored. He was *talking* the songs more than singing them, gradually losing his ability to hit or sustain the big notes any longer.

I do not lay his weakening solely at the doorstep of age; indeed, in 1977 he was only fifty-eight—far too young for his lungs to be failing him as noticeably as they were, and yet his condition was beginning to show as early on as the second LP for the label, called *Swing Wide Your Golden Gate*, an effort to reunite him with the Jordanaires. I was saddened, but not surprised when Gordon Stoker, the group's manager and one of its founding members, expressed dismay when I ran into

him at the Nashville AFTRA offices one afternoon just after recording for the album had wrapped.

"He's coming into the sessions half crocked, and he's drinking all
day," he told me quietly. "We tried, you know . . . but it's not the best
thing he's done. His mind wasn't on the session at all, and it didn't
seem like his heart was in it. *Any* of it. You need to talk to him, Buck."

Again with the You need to talk to *him*.

Although Dad's chops were not what they had been, his presence still
had power, and his name could still carry a marquee. Both were
enough to set the stage for a series of specials with PBS that were inau-
gurated the next year, in November 1978.

Helmed by Paul Corbin, who was then the senior VP of programming for KOCE in Huntington Beach—one of the network's flagship
stations on the West Coast—the series began with a concept for one
show, a show that was, in '78, a radical concept, even for PBS. Actually, *especially* for PBS.

"I was developing programming that I thought had the potential for
being nationally significant as specials or series for PBS," Corbin
recalled, "and I met with Tom Grasso, who worked as a producer in
the Midwest and California, and was affiliated with Cliffie Stone and
Dale Sheets, who had been one of Ernie's agents at MCA. Grasso
brought up Ernie Ford, and when he ran the concept by me, my radar
screen kind of lit up."

The idea was essentially Dad's, but one he credited to Cliffie and
Dale Sheets. It was an idea borne of denial, and one that would not
only make history, but would also set the stage for a trend in programming that is reaching its zenith today. The idea was to do a show that
the Big Three—ABC, NBC, and CBS—had long refused to even consider, deeming it far too exclusive, restrictive, and apt to alienate viewers rather than attract them.

The idea was an entire show of nothing but gospel music.

It took Paul about *that* long to be in. And it took him about the
same amount of time to sell it to the network. Within days of delivering the pitch, the network came back with a fully funded grant, and
That Great American Gospel Sound was officially in preproduction.

Four months later, Dad, Della Reese, the Fisk Jubilee Singers, and
the Happy Goodman Family took a final bow together on the stage of

the Grand Ole Opry House in Nashville in front of a capacity crowd of more than four thousand, all of whom were on their feet. The ovations were deafening—one after another, after another—ovations that were drowned out, however, the next day by the collective sound of two distinctly different but simultaneous reports: the Big Three kicking themselves, and PBS stations across the country applauding themselves. For good reason; when the numbers came in, the show became the highest rated pledge vehicle ever produced for PBS, earning ratings that literally swallowed everything on television from coast to coast that night.

It was clear that Ernie Ford was still very much a force to be reckoned with, and it took PBS about *that* long to commit to two more specials over the next two years—*Songs of This Lusty Land*, with Tom T. Hall and Merle Haggard; and *More of That Great American Gospel Sound*, with Della again and Andrae Crouch—extending the success, but more important for Dad, extending and strengthening the partnership and friendship he'd formed with Paul Corbin, who would go on to become one of the music industry's most influential executives and, in 1994, president of our family company, Tennessee Ernie Ford Enterprises; both outgrowths of that enduring partnership and friendship that began with an idea.

But the force could not be sustained. The excitement and success of the new relationship with PBS brought a sense of renewal to his voice and his outlook, but by the end of 1981 a weariness began to overtake him, and his resumption of drinking escalated.

At the time, I was working off and on as a songwriter and demo singer, attached to what was then Chappell Music Publishing in Nashville. One of the cats I regularly wrote and demo'd material with was Jerry Gillespie, who had huge hits with Terri Gibbs's smash "Somebody's Knockin'," and "Heaven's Just a Sin Away," by the father-daughter duo the Kendalls. He'd also been instrumental (no pun intended) in some of Anne Murray's hits and a couple of sides by the Bellamy Brothers.

Seeing Dad begin to slide backward in the aftermath of the PBS specials, I felt strongly that if he had another project he could get equally as excited about, he might reverse his backsliding and get his head above water again. I had little to no experience in television production, but I felt strongly that the writers I was regularly working around on Music Row could craft material tailored to him and his voice. I knew the song pluggers at nearly every major publishing house and had sung demos in half the town's studios. I knew the best studio players in the business, and I knew they'd jump at the chance to work on an Ernie Ford record. A new Ernie Ford record. A record that would pair him with the best writers, pickers, and creative people in Nashville. A record that would maybe put him back on the charts—with a new label—a label that would actually do the right thing by him.

And, of course, it would be a record I'd use to further my own career. What I needed was a partner; someone with strong enough credits to guarantee financing and the industry's interest. It took Jerry Gillespie about five seconds to jump on board. All I had to do now was convince Dad and find the financing to pull it off. I reversed those two requirements, arranging a meeting with Peter Brown when he came to town on business for Merle Haggard in the fall of 1981. I'd come prepared with a complete proposal and a budget, but neither was taken out of their report cover. He was in immediately, committing Eagle Banner Productions—a BetFord subsidiary—to bankrolling the entire project. With Brown's commitment in hand, I had no difficulty in securing Dad's agreement.

When the word went out, Jerry and I were overwhelmed by the sheer number of songs pitched for the album and by the names pitching them. We listened to songs written by Elton John and songs from the pens of Tom T. Hall and Hoagy Carmichael. We spent week after week plowing our way through hundreds of tracks sent from all over the world, eventually settling on ten, including one that I'd written as a gift for his and Mom's fortieth anniversary. It came close to not making the cut; not because it wasn't necessarily a good song or because it didn't fit thematically with the rest of tracks we'd picked, but because Dad found it increasingly difficult to listen to, let alone sing.

He heard the song for the first time in a motel room in St. Louis, where Loakes and I had arranged a meeting specifically to hear all ten tracks and then leave him a cassette so he could begin learning the songs in preparation for the first session. I'd couched it about two-thirds of the way through the group, but, in retrospect, I should have made it the final track.

I'd written it as a waltz and cut the demo as simply as I could—just me and an acoustic guitar, no overdubs, no harmonies—on an older four-track machine in Chappell's writers' studio off Sixteenth Avenue in Nashville. It was called, "Tell Me You Remember, Betty Jean."

With the tracks on the cassette that preceded it, I'd stopped the machine and given Dad and Loakes a chance to comment on the song they'd just heard, and then I'd given them a little information on the track they were about to hear. But with "Betty Jean," I didn't go into a lot of detail, and I didn't let on that I'd written it. I simply said, "This is for you and Mom, Dad," and punched the Start button on the little Sony cassette player. But after the first verse and the chorus, I had to press the Stop button.

Betty Jean, do you remember 1942?
Before we had the babies, and it was only me and you
You know, I can still hear you saying, "I Do"
Do you remember, Betty Jean?

Then tell me you haven't forgotten.
Tell me you still feel the same
Tell me the years haven't faded your love
Tell me you remember, Betty Jean.

When I looked up from the player, Dad had buried his face in his hands, tears streaming from behind his palms. I stopped the player and put my arms around him, his tears dampening the shoulder of my jacket. From the corner of my eye, I could see Jim across the room, turned toward the suite's picture windows, wiping his eyes with the backs of his hands.

As he stood, Dad pulled a leaf of Kleenex from the dispenser on the end table next to him and, still crying, walked slowly to the vanity, his head bowed. "I'm sorry, son," he said, his words halting and wet. "I don't know what to do anymore. I love her so much, but I don't know what to do."

I returned to my chair and left him alone. And as the sound of his crying subsided, it was replaced by the unmistakable tones of ice cubes dropping into a glass, and the scent of scotch being poured.

Over the next two months I checked in repeatedly, calling home to make sure he was learning the material. The first couple of calls were strong; he loved everything and couldn't wait to get in the studio. But as the weeks passed, each call went progressively downhill, and his interest level for the session with it.

Three sessions were booked for the project, all at LSI Studios on Sixteenth Avenue. Gillespie and I had hired a team of A-list players for each, and a small string ensemble to add some layering after we'd wrapped Dad and his parts. The plan was to cut everything but the strings live; Dad, the background vocalists, and all the accompanists. The weeks before the session were spent in rehearsals and drafting number-sheets so each picker would be 100 percent fluent on each track. It was an economical and efficient plan, one that would allow us to turn the project around in a relatively short period of time and come in under budget. The plan's success hinged on Dad's having learned the songs in the keys he'd selected. He'd come in, we'd set up, he'd meet the crew, step into his booth, and do what he'd done for thirty years—sing.

But the best-laid plans . . .

Loakes and Dad got into town the day before the first session on a late flight from home. No time to get together that night, but Dad wanted to have lunch before the two o'clock call the next day. Great. Jerry and I suggested a little place called Third Coast near Vanderbilt at noon; this would give us time for a leisurely bite and also allow time for Dad to get comfortable with Jerry, whom he'd yet to formally meet.

Jerry and I were ten minutes late. When we got to the restaurant, Dad and Jim were ensconced at a center table, along with Cohen Williams, Jim King, and Bobby Dale of Martha White. Dad was completely wrecked and in the process of ordering another screwdriver when we walked in the door. The fajitas and arroz con pollo didn't help—didn't absorb and level him off, primarily because he drank during the entire meal. When we left ten minutes before the session was to have begun, he'd convinced our starstruck waiter to let him leave with the drink he'd just ordered.

The ride to the studio should have been buoyant, but I was petrified. For his part, Gillespie was unaware that a problem might exist; he knew Dad'd had a few, but, like me, he'd worked with more than one cat who'd needed something to drink—or smoke, or snort—and actually performed better when they were lubricated, or whatever. It was a well-known fact that, in many cases, these "needs" were actually built into the budget for some stars, a factoid that might have shocked Ernie Ford, who was smashed by the time we walked into the studio.

Two tracks into the session, we had to stop. Before we'd even reached that point, the expressions on the faces of the musicians and singers had slowly gone from "Wow, I'm cutting tracks with a legend" to "Holy shit, the legend can't sing anymore." Billy Strange, who was on hand and would be writing the string parts later, suggested we "stop the session now. Before he collapses." Charlie Black, our rhythm guitar player, quietly suggested during a break that maybe my voice might be technologically altered just enough so "nobody would know it wasn't really your dad."

The problem was not simply that he was too crocked to sing. It was clear that he had not learned even one of the songs he'd had with him for almost three months. I was furious and did not make an attempt to hide it. I called the session, released the players and singers, enlisted Loakes to get rid of the Martha White contingent, and locked the doors to the control room, sealing me, Dad, Gillespie, and Loakes inside.

We went over the songs time and time again, but it became clear sooner rather than later that no matter how many times we went over them, nothing worth keeping was going to get cut that day. We canceled, and Dad left with Loakes to get ready for a walk-on at the Opry that night. I knew by the stride of his gait as I watched him walk to the car that he was mollified and angry. I mistakenly thought, however, that he was angry with himself.

Later that evening, against my better judgment but electing not to deviate from the itinerary Loakes had prepared, I drove to the Opry House to join Dad backstage before his curtain call. I checked the greenroom, he wasn't there. His dressing room was empty. He wasn't in makeup. Adding to my concern, with his introduction less than fifteen minutes away, was that Loakes was nowhere in sight, either. I was preparing to leave, thinking that maybe I'd misread the itinerary, maybe he'd canceled at the last minute . . . when I saw him standing in the wings, behind a fold in the curtains just off stage right. He was watching me, looking for him. When I started toward him, he pretended not to see me and walked across the gangway to the opposite side of the stage. When he saw that I'd changed direction and followed him, he turned around and went back the way he came. At first I thought perhaps he was pacing before his appearance, but he'd never paced before an appearance in his life.

He was avoiding me.

I was embarrassed and struck by a number of other emotions I couldn't identify. They were all new and all unpleasant. I persisted, however, and, with just minutes remaining before his introduction, I cornered him. I apologized for maybe being too hard on him at the studio, and for the day being unproductive. I let him know I'd find a way to make the next session more Dad-friendly, and easier to get into. He never so much as looked at me, let alone acknowledged anything I'd said. His hairline was tightening, though, so I knew he was angry. When he spoke, his words were clipped, and his tone final.

"Don't try to make me into something I'm not, Buck."

As if on cue, Loakes appeared out of nowhere and then Dad was gone, his name echoing through the auditorium, the crowd rising to its feet, as he strode across the stage, smiling and waving to an ecstatic audience. I watched for a few minutes from the curtain folds, glad to be in the shadows—a place I could hide until my eyes were dry.

Two days later I called Jim at the office to discuss plans for the next session.

"Right now your Dad is 70 percent no, 30 percent maybe," he said.

"He was smashed, Jim. Jesus, this wasn't my fault. If he'd been sober and known the material, we wouldn't be having this conversation right now."

"You might be right," he said. "And it might be a problem. You might want to talk to him."

And *again* with the *You need to talk to him.*

Had I thought for even the briefest of moments that he would actually have listened to me, I would have done just that. But in 1982, I had crawled so far up my own ass that seeing my way clear to speak honestly to my father about a drinking problem would have required that I put my own problems aside long enough to do so.

Relatively new to Nashville, newly married, our first child just three years old, I was struggling to find a niche as a writer, a singer, a performer—as anything that would keep me in the business—and my meetings with Dad during his trips to town were brief, hurried, and usually involved needing money. It was easier for me to have a drink with him, plying him as convincingly as I could, before I told him the electricity or the phone was about to be cut off, or that I was short on rent money that month. I'd put on my best bullshit face, tell him about all the auditions I was (or wasn't) going on, about all the songs I was writing that weren't getting cut, and how every time I went out for a straight job interview, I'd get a call for an audition, or a session . . . and "I just couldn't pass up the opportunity, Dad . . . It might be the break, you know . . . my break—*my* chance to grab the ring."

He'd listen, top off our glasses, add a cube of ice, tell Jim to get his checkbook, write me a lifesaver, hug me—sort of—and get on the plane to go home.

Eventually the album was completed, but we had little success shopping it. None of the majors were interested, and it lay dormant until it was finally picked up for distribution by Artie Mogull's independent label, Applause Records. In keeping with Murphy's Law, Applause went bankrupt two months after releasing the album to a limited market. The advance I'd received was gone, and I was looking for the next ticket. I was still several years away from hitting the first strides of success as an actor, but, still convinced that I was going to strike some kind of gold in the music business, I held fast to an unrealistic, unattainable dream and sought financial succor from home in the interim.

It would be several more years before I realized how badly I was fooling myself and how badly I was disappointing Dad. Contrary to everything he'd hoped and planned for, escaped from Hollywood to get away from, tried vainly to steer me away from, I had disavowed and turned my back on the life he'd worked so hard to make for me and, instead, had become a profligate dreamer, my hand in his pocket, seeking success in the same business he had thrived in publicly, but decried so vehemently in private.

Where in the hell had he gone wrong?

Back home, the woman he'd fallen in love with and married thirty-six years earlier had turned into someone he no longer understood, someone he stayed married to because (as he put it several years later, in a rare, unguarded admission) it was his "lot in life." She'd become someone who no longer wanted him around her but who needed watching, needed monitoring, needed to be kept away from sharp instruments and prescription bottles.

Across Oregon and Nevada, Dad's dreams of a ranch had mutated into grotesque landholdings he'd never seen, that had cost him hundreds of thousands of dollars, and that had never made him a dime.

Adding insult to his injuries, the record label he'd helped put on the map; its shining, tall tower in Hollywood built with the money he'd made for them, had left him.

Where in the hell had he gone wrong?

Outwardly, one unfamiliar with him would not have noticed the wounds or the pain. He did not betray such things. Under the surface, though, behind the facade, he was fighting for air. For nearly twenty years he'd kept everyone around him afloat, but the weight of so many standing on his shoulders for so long was becoming too hard to bear. He was treading water, and he desperately needed a lifeline.

In the early eighties he bought one—a small A-frame in the Sawtooth Mountains of Idaho, about two and a half hours northeast of Boise. Tucked into a grove of lodgepole pine and quaking aspen, a few hundred yards from one of the main streams flowing into the Payette River, the Wapiti Creek cabin was isolated, rugged, and about as far removed as you could get from a world that had become increasingly complex, stressful, and painful for Dad. It became his refuge, his sanctuary; the one place he could retreat to when escape was necessary.

As he had done when he bought Long Valley Ranch in 1956, he began planning his entire year around going to the property. Any work—including his obligations with Martha White—was simply a means to end up at the cabin. He talked about it constantly and couldn't wait to show it off. He was selective in who made the trip, who was allowed within the circle. No business of any kind was to be discussed, no conversations about work, no reminders of the world that lay beyond its borders. You were here to breathe, eat, drink, fish, drink, eat, sleep, drink, and forget what awaited you back in the world.

It was the lifeline he'd so sorely needed, and once he grasped it, he began breathing almost immediately again. It did not come cheap, however, and to keep breathing, to maintain his hold on this tether, he needed to cut ties elsewhere, to sever connections to other dreams. In the spring of the second year after he acquired the place, he took Peter Brown with him, and, violating his credo of not conducting business, he holed himself up and, over three days, sold Eagle Banner Ranches. The Alturas property went first, followed by the Modoc Ranch, and finally the Eagleville spread. A total of 220,000 acres were moved to the hands of new stewards in a matter of hours. But while he'd freed himself from the properties themselves, his haste to sell had made it a buyer's market, and the consortiums that acquired each of the ranches did so at values far below what they should have brought. He was free of the land, but, thanks to the wisdom and foresight of Peter Brown ten years earlier, he was not free from all of the original debt.

Some two years after buying the Wapiti Creek property, he took Mom on the first of only two trips she would make there. The journey tired her quickly, and although he tried his best to open her eyes to the beauty of the mountains and the serenity he'd found there, she could not be persuaded. A cabin in Idaho 110 miles from the nearest depot of civilization was not Betty Ford's idea of fun, and being cooped up in an A-frame 110 miles from the nearest depot of civilization with Ernie Ford was nowhere near her idea of a relaxing getaway. In a letter to my wife, Murphy, from July 1984, she left no doubt as to how she felt about it.

"I hate that place with a passion," she wrote. "You are so damned stranded—100 miles from nowhere. The cretins who traverse up there from Boise on the weekend are just plain nuts. Ern seems obsessed by the place. I dread to think of the money and manpower that have gone into a place that's already falling apart after just a few years. The last time I was there—sick the whole time—the shower door fell off the track every time I tried to take a shower. God forbid you turn on a light because the propane is so expensive. Don't flush the toilets too often, don't run the washing machine, never touch the dryer because it doesn't work. God forbid—don't use the dishwasher, because it might tilt and throw all the dishes out. Ford and his pals can stay in Idaho until hell freezes over. Give me Honolulu, or Palm Springs."

Within two years of that letter, however, neither the penthouse nor the condo in the desert would be theirs any longer.

Later that same summer, Dad hired a local Boise architect, Victor Hosford, to remodel the entire place, adding two wings in the process. The cost was more than he'd anticipated, but doable. Within weeks of paying for the remodel, however, Wells Fargo and two other banks called two notes on development properties outside Reno that Peter Brown had advised him to invest in at the same time he'd bought into the Alturas spread. As fall gave way to winter and the interest rates on the notes accumulated daily, Brown advised Dad there was no recourse but to sell penthouse 9 at the Colony Surf in Honolulu. Mom was three weeks from packing for an extended stay when Brown called the house and gave her the news. Dad was not home. He was at the cabin.

Dad's refuge in the mountains was secured fast, but Mom's safe harbor by the ocean was gone.

FOURTEEN

CONTRARY TO POPULAR BELIEF, Ernie Ford was not a particularly religious man. No more than the next person is, anyway. We were not a faith-based family. Religion did not dictate our habits or customs, it did not govern our lives, and we did not live by the lyrics of the hymns that provided the income we lived on.

We did not go to church every Sunday. In the North Hollywood years, we attended the First Methodist Church on Alameda occasionally, but it was not customary. What *was* customary was getting takeout from the Kosherama delicatessen on Olive after the service. Greatest corned beef on rye in Burbank. Not wanting to offend anyone, we sang with the Christians and ate with the Jews.

We said grace at the table, but not every night. Brion and I knelt by our beds and said our prayers, but not every night. More often than not, we prayed that Mom would not come in with a belt after having several of another sort. If she did, we prayed her aim would be accurate, because the leather falling on our legs or our backs was way worse than on our backsides. And we prayed that Dad would take pity on us and intervene sooner and not later.

When we moved to the Bay Area, even our sporadic church attendance stopped after only a few Sundays. I suspect that Fame had something to do with that; I have fragmented memories of Dad's unease and embarrassment, surrounded by an infatuated congregation paying more attention to him than the sermon and the pastor giving it. I suspect

Mom also had something to do with it; services traditionally began at eleven, and Sunday or not, she'd usually had a glass or two of tomato or orange juice by then—mixed generously, of course, with a healthy splash of Smirnoff. Add just a dash of unpredictability, and an ever-so-slight pinch of unexpected caprice, and God only knew—literally—what wondrous thing one might behold or hear from Betty Ford, wedged into a pew between her seditious sons and her pious-in-the-eyes-of-the-public husband.

Confliction and faith existed side by side in our house, and while I believe that Dad was for the most part secure in the beliefs practiced historically in his family, faith neither offered, promised, nor provided any such covenants for Mom. While her mother, Jesse, was raised a strict Irish Catholic, and her father, Charlie, was brought up by iron-fisted Dust Bowl Presbyterians, their daughter took no refuge in the Scriptures or strength from the prayers of either doctrine. On the contrary, she recoiled from the whole idea, carrying a distaste and distrust of dogmatic ritual with her throughout her life.

That aversion was never more evident than in a letter from April 1979, when Jesse passed away at age ninety-two: "Ernie is gone to Vegas. Wouldn't you know Mother picked this week to die. Didn't go to the funeral, as I feel they are heathen and barbaric. . . ."

Her Christmas letter that same year included a sketch she'd done of herself, suspended from a cross, crowned in thorns, blood and tears staining her face.

I have no memory of ever hearing Mom profess alliance with any denomination, let alone those of her parentage, and I am ashamed I never asked her as much. In my youth, asking such a question was unthinkable. Not unpardonable—just unthinkable—I simply never thought to ask. Growing up, I assumed that she was what Dad said we all were, Methodist. And I never questioned my assumption, choosing instead to believe in the word of Dad.

While I don't believe Mom was agnostic, and certainly not atheistic, she was normally noncommittal when the matter of faith came up, and she usually changed the subject, feigned boredom, or busied herself with some innocuous task until the subject changed itself. Pressed into a corner, however, she rarely failed to make the moment memorable.

Not long after moving to North Hollywood, *Look* magazine arranged to come to the house for a cover story, feature interview, and photo spread, hoping to capture the "real" Ernie Ford and family. When the editor on hand suggested a shot of all of us at the kitchen table saying grace, he got way more *real* than he ever anticipated.

Excusing herself, Mom withdrew to her dressing room upstairs. When she returned, she'd changed into old capris, a dowdy sweater, and strategically placed about seven oversized hair clips around her head. Adding the pièce de résistance to her homely ensemble, she breezed over to the pantry and slipped an even older apron around her neck.

No one said a thing, but had anyone wanted to there was plenty of room—the silence was deafening.

Looking at the picture today, it speaks as loudly now as her actions spoke that morning. Seated at the rectangular table in the kitchen, Brion, Dad, and I are in earnest prayer; our eyes closed penitently. To my left, Mom sits forlornly, hair clips and all, her eyes wide open, staring blankly at the Formica patterns on the surface of the table.

All this is not to imply that we did not observe or acknowledge Christian tenets as a family—we did. But the truth is, we observed them less because they gave order and foundation to our lives and more because we were expected to; the public expected Dad to live by that image, and Dad expected his family to reflect it or, at the very least, not to tarnish it.

Expectations and imagery notwithstanding, our observance was practiced more often seasonally than regularly, and most often at Christmastime.

Oddly, I have no memory of Christmas before we moved to the Bay Area. I'm certain that we celebrated it in North Hollywood, and several early snapshots from the Whittier years confirm our commemoration while we were living there. Nevertheless, my holiday memory banks from those years are empty. Weird.

Few days of the year were as important to Dad; he reveled in the preparation, the decoration, and the anticipation (Jesus, that sounds like Jesse Jackson, doesn't it?).

He ordered enormous hams from a Virginia smokehouse and bought immense turkeys that cooked, seemingly, for days, taking an almost perverse delight in the art of basting. He baked golden pones of stone-ground corn bread in iron skillets, and labored over his cornmeal-and-sausage dressing—a master's recipe I vainly try to reproduce each year.

He rose early during the season, long before everyone else, and built great fires in each of the fireplaces, waking us slowly and peacefully with the sound of oak hissing and the smell of cedar burning on the hearth. Like an older brother, he counted the days until school ended, waiting in the parking lot for Brion and me on the last day, the station wagon warm, carols on the radio, pipe in his teeth, waving us to the car and into his embrace. Like a Rockwell scene come to life, we motored home, tree strapped to the roof, Dad, Brion, and I, singing "Little Drummer Boy" along with Bing.

Alas, my memories of Mom during Christmas are less idyllic, though they are no less evocative.

Of the hundreds—the thousands—of pictures chronicling our lives, I have only four taken during the holiday that include Mom. One is from 1950, her and Dad in front of their tree in Monterey Park, both of them smiling, but her eyes are closed. Jump ahead eleven years to '61, when we traveled back to Bristol to spend the holiday with Dad's folks. Here's a black-and-white of Dad standing between his mother and Mom, looking for all the world like a worried referee; Maude to his right, her eyes on her son, beseeching and . . . fearful? On his left is Mom, her jaw clenched, eyes riveted on the table, where, for all the world, she appears to be beating the living hell out of a defenseless ham. The last two were taken on Christmas morning of '82, just minutes, maybe only seconds, apart; Mom sitting on the steps of the living room, frail and thin in a faded pink housecoat, a Bloody Mary on the tile floor next to her, a wan smile gracing her face.

I believe that Mom wanted Christmas to be merry, but I do not believe it was ever so for her. The holidays I remember are wrapped in very few memories of her being truly happy during the season. Save for one year.

It was the only year I remember she accompanied Dad and Brion and me to select the tree, and she came only because she was promised the selection would be hers. No interference from Dad, no meddling or griping from Brion or me.

The lot was not far from Stanford, and the night was cold, even by Bay Area standards. We'd been customers of the sawyer for a number of years, so he naturally began the tour of the trees with the blue spruces; regal, tall, and redolent with the scent of evergreen. They were beautiful, and perfect for the sixteen-foot ceilings in the living room.

They were also in a completely different part of the lot than Mom.

She'd simply disappeared into the forest. Not knowing what to expect (she'd had a few drinks before we left the house), we split up and initiated a search.

It was Brion who found her first, alone in the back of the lot, where the stunted trees were tossed after being discarded from the truck as undesirable. They lay there in a pile, boughs bent, stacked like so much cordwood.

Amid this refuse stood Mom, holding a tiny, nettle-bare pine not three feet tall. It looked like it had the flu, if trees could catch the flu. She'd placed it on a stump used by the sawyer for trimming, and was waiting for us.

"I found it," she said.

Later that night, a fire burning brightly on the hearth in the living room, Betty Jean finished putting the last ornament on the little tree, on top of the round federal table near the window. As she slid the star over the tiny evergreen's tip, the weight of the ornament was too much and bent the tree to one side. But the star did not fall. Brion moved to right it, but Mom stopped him.

"It looks sad, Mom."

"I know," she said. "I'm going to call it my Charlie Brown Christmas tree."

"Why?" Brion asked.

"Because Charlie Brown's Christmases were always sad," she answered.

The big back log in the fireplace hissed and rolled forward, sending Dad to the hearth for the poker. Mom laughed a small laugh, took a sip from her drink, and we all took turns placing presents under that year's tree.

FIFTEEN

I MET MY WIFE, Murphy, in the
spring of 1977, less than a year
after I'd moved from Colorado
to Nashville. It was a summer
evening at a small club called
the Gold Rush on Elliston
Place—a regular haunt for
me and my running buddy at
the time, Jody Maphis,
youngest son of guitar legend Joe Maphis and his
wife, Rose Lee. It was late,
the place was packed, and Murphy was
standing behind her escort for the evening, who was sitting at
the bar, oblivious of his bad manners. I offered her my chair, and less
than a month later we were married in a small civil service. As I write
this, we are just five months away from marking thirty years together.

I am certain that I would be close to death, or quite possibly have
already reached that point by now, had she not taken pity on me and
seen her way clear to salvage what she could from the wreckage my
life was on its way to becoming. I won't say, "I can't imagine what my
life would be like without her," because I *have* imagined what my life
would be like without her, and the sheer terror of the image moves me
first to nausea and then to my knees, where I fervently pray that God
would keep her ignorant of how much better she could have done.

From their first contact, Mom and Dad both fell hard for Murph,
and the connection was mutual. But while she felt somewhat distanced
from Dad, the bond between her and Mom was immediate and grew
stronger as the years passed. Betty Ford had found the daughter she'd

dreamed of having, and Murphy found a tireless champion in Mom.

Between 1977 and 1989, only four occasions arose allowing Mom and Murph to actually see each other, but the miles between them were inconsequential. They were inseparable regardless of the distance—a distance lessened by a correspondence between them that lasted nearly eleven years, ending just two weeks before Mom's death. Over that time she wrote more than a hundred letters, chronicling the last decade of her life. During the same period of time, Dad wrote three, two of them postscripts to letters already written by Mom. Murphy kept them all, banded and boxed, and from them—through them, in them—I hear the voice of Betty Ford.

She wrote about everything—the books she was reading, her surgeries, the maid's foibles, the gardener's death, the neighbors' eccentricities, and her own genius. She wrote smashed; she wrote straight. She wrote in tears, staining some letters; in an anger that threatens to ignite the stationery, and with the same wry sarcasm that had earned her dubious fame in earlier years, honed so finely now as to give a whole new meaning to the term "paper cut."

Each letter was composed like a mini-novel, threaded with narrative that reads like Eudora Welty writing as Nora Ephron. Biting, beautiful, insightful and damning, hilarious and tragic, she reported unflinchingly and recounted unflappably, creating a memoir written in her own hand, a diary of a once-brilliant life, its author unable to hold back the encroaching darkness she sees enveloping her with the passage of each day, but still finding the courage to record its inexorable approach—as only Betty Ford could.

She gripes about Dad's trips to Idaho. She pines in passages over the loss of the penthouse in Honolulu. She bitches about her declining health, Dad's addiction to television, and the dwindling embers of passion between them. She glows with pride when he is awarded the Presidential Medal of Freedom in 1984, and she damns him for the trust he's placed in Peter Brown, the trust he no longer has in her, and the reversal of fortune that has befallen them; a reversal she lays at Dad's feet and Brown's doorstep.

She narrates brief family histories and urges me to write our story. She accuses the nineteen-year-old maid she hired of stealing her jewelry and flirting with Dad. She gossips about Adnan Khashoggi's ex-wife moving next door, and Brion's ex-wife moving him out. She counsels Murph on the finer points of Waterford crystal, and the proper china to accompany it. She writes excitedly about her cruise with Dad to Mexico, and lengthily about her boredom on their cruise to Alaska. She nauseates over life "with an aging star," but worries the pages with concern over his stress. She cries for help when his own liver begins failing, striking him down and sending him into a coma in 1987. She calls up the ghosts of her brother, Wallace, and her sister, Vayle, and foresees her own death two weeks before she overdosed for the last time.

On a sleepless night several months ago, I dreamed I was watching the documentary *Grey Gardens*, Albert and John Maysles' disturbing and often hilarious but nauseatingly beautiful 1976 film about the lives of Edith Bouvier Beale and her daughter, Little Edie, first cousin of Jacqueline Bouvier and daughter of the celebrated Manhattan attorney Phelan Beale.

In my dream I'm watching the sequence of Little Edie swimming in the Atlantic waters just beyond Grey Gardens, the decaying, dilapidated, once-grand East Hampton manse that warehouses her and her ailing mother. Like the life we see on the screen, and the life we learn she lived before coming to the point in time the film centers on, her movement through the choppy, cold waters of the Atlantic is sublime, graceful, fluid, and contrary to the current of the sea.

Swells rise and fall around her, whitecaps forming just at the surface, only hinting at the troubled eddies of the water. These are not calm seas. Yet she swims through them, cutting the swells with her lithe, still-strong—"staunch!"—body, as if this task alone serves to center the chaotic, turbulent, and squalid life she has chosen to share with her mother.

She is dressed in a black, vintage seventies-era one-piece suit, betraying too much of her cascading but surely once-proud cleavage behind a gauzy net, opened in a V to her navel, and an off-white rubber swimmer's cap, ruffled across its surface with layers of feathered latex.

In my dream I'm riveted by this scene, transfixed, hitting the Rewind button on the remote repeatedly. Edie swimming . . . Edie swimming . . . Edie swimming. Murphy takes the remote from me and I watch as Edie comes out of the water, striding through the shore break. But it's no longer Edie, and someone has emerged from the sea with her.

It's Mom. And at her side is Dad.

Since beginning this memoir, many nights have been much the same. I have flashes of brilliantly illuminated memories of my parents minutes—seconds—before sleep claims me. I lay there, curse the book, and damn my obsession to record their lives. I tell myself I'll still possess this recollection in the morning, but with each subsequent intake of breath, each yawn, the image begins to fade.

In that netherworld between wakefulness and dream, I struggle with a kind of madness to reclaim memories of a life no longer mine. I see us on the *Zephyr*, on the deck of the *Lurline*, walking Ka'anapali on Maui, sipping iced teas on the Hau Terrace at the Outrigger Club. I see us in the *Ski Bird* on Clear Lake, gliding across the tranquil, glass-blue surface, undisturbed by whitecaps and troubled waters. I see a family. I see us all together again.

And then I see the Portola Valley house—the last house—grand and hollow. I see Mom alone, her companions to her right—Bloody Mary, Pall Mall, and Medihaler—her face sallow and drawn with sadness or anger, I cannot tell which. From the den I hear the sound of Dad's pencil filling in tiny squares in his crossword book, and the muted drone of a golf tournament commentator on television. I hear his admonitions and recriminations from behind their closed doors late at night, countering her awkward plea for his companionship, for the romance she refuses to believe is gone from their lives.

Then, like the sound track of a film as it dissolves to black, their voices slowly fade away and I finally drift off to sleep, wondering in the last few seconds before the veil covers me if the images that flickered across the screen were memories or illusions.

William Somerset Maugham said, "It is dangerous to let the public behind the scenes. They are easily disillusioned and then they are angry with you, for it was the illusion they loved."

I expect there will be a sizable number of people who will take issue with one part or another of this book. There will be those who will contradict certain events, those who will disagree with my portrayal of certain people—fringe and central—and those who will question the wisdom of exposing certain aspects of the lives of Betty and Ernie Ford. They will see what I've done as a betrayal, and they will say so.

I can't help that. My intention in writing this book was not to shatter illusions, nor was it to preserve them. Moreover, my intention was not to write a memoir but, rather, to compile a journal; to record the passage of two ordinary people caught up in and changed forever by an extraordinary journey.

But as the weeks and then the months passed, I realized that I was not compiling a journal at all. I was making a map, drawn each day from the memories that were filling my waking hours and my deepest dreams. At some point, though I do not remember when, I stopped being a writer and became a navigator, charting a course I could not alter, in a ship I could not abandon, on a river of no return.

I had to tell the truth of who they were, so I might discover the truth of what they were, and face the truth of what they became.

I do not mean to imply or convey a sense that the later years of the lives of Ernie and Betty Ford were one long descent into an alcoholic and pharmaceutical hell—one long, lost weekend, if you will—because they were not. There were spans of time in that last decade, days of uninterrupted lucidity, when a kind of mutual sobriety was agreed to—unspoken, most likely, but agreed to nevertheless; bright interludes that began when they became grandparents.

Patrick was the first. He was born February 26, 1979, precisely ten years to the day before Mom's death. From the moment he was born, her life changed. Her letters became great texts on the pleasures and myths of motherhood, the idiocy of people who glamorize childbirth, and the value of having enough hand towels in the house. As he grew, she would invariably enclose a separate letter to Pack, written in block printing, filling him in on the doings that week as reported by his pen pal, Grandma Bet.

The two postscripts from Dad written over those ten years are both written to Patrick, and while I have no doubt that Mom forced him to sit at the kitchen table, put the letterhead in front of him and a pen in his hand, I cherish them nonetheless. Although Dad earned great notoriety in many arenas throughout his life, he was never known for his skills as a correspondent, making those two missives rare keepsakes, indeed. Truth be told, Mom probably dictated them, but I treasure them anyway.

Brion's only son, Jarrod, was born just three weeks later, but his arrival was not enough to rekindle the love between him and his estranged wife, Bettilynn, or to salvage their marriage or the growing division from the family. In just a few short years after his birth and their bitter divorce, she and Jarrod separated themselves for all practical purposes from all things Ford.

Seven years after Patrick's birth, our daughter, Jesse, was born. Thanks to the wizardry of ultrasound, we knew we were having a girl, and if the prospect of being grandparents had brightened Betty and Ernie Ford's lives the first time around, preparing for the arrival of the first daughter born in the Ford family in three generations positively illuminated them. They were incandescent, beaming. Hell, in the night sky above Nashville I swore I could see the aurora borealis emanating from Portola Valley. And while he did not convey it in any long, or even short, letters, the brightest light came from Dad. He was smitten, and acted like a complete idiot around her. In the early morning hours before I called home with the news of her birth, he left the house, Mom fast asleep, and drove to the Rexall in Woodside, where he emptied the store of its party inventory. When Mom awakened, she arose to a house filled with pink ribbons, pink papier-mâché streamers, and pink balloons; decorations courtesy of Ernest Ford. For the first time in probably twenty years, Betty Ford smiled when she opened her eyes that morning, and she smiled at her husband.

Murphy and I would be blessed with two more sons: Tucker and James, but Mom would not live long enough to be a part of either of their lives, and Dad was gone two years before James's birth.

Eight years after Dad's death in 1991, Patrick was killed when his Mercury Marquis left the road outside Nashville. Mere hours earlier, he'd been by my side on the front porch of Murphy's family home in Smithville, each of us in one of the big white rockers, my heart filling with pride as he told me of his plans for the coming year. In an instant he was gone.

In the days immediately after, I sat alone at the dining room table, answering letters and cards, the task too painful for Murph. As I wrote, trying hard to keep each thank-you note dry, I would search for words original for each, not wanting the message to anyone to sound stamped, my emotions rising and falling as I read the messages from so many whose lives Patrick had touched. Fighting tears, and losing, I turned away from the task at hand, and my eyes fell on the life-size portrait of Mom that hung on the wall above the buffet.

It was an oil done in 1958 by a well-known Hollywood portrait artist named David Immerman, who'd been commissioned by Ralph Edwards for the purpose of painting individual portraits of both her and Dad. Of the two, Immerman captured her perfectly. She is radiant, dressed in black capris and a salmon pullover sweater; her hair cut in the usual pageboy, glistening like ebony.

But as I looked at the painting now, I was forced to look away almost immediately and wipe, then rub, my eyes, then my glasses, which I thought must have become fogged from the moisture behind them. I'd long since used all the Kleenex, so, violating the lesson of eyeglass etiquette Murphy regularly cited me for, I pulled out my shirt-tail and cleaned the lenses as best I could, put them back on, and turned once again to Mom's portrait.

Grief and death are powerful forces in life. Most accept the inevitability that we will experience both at some time during our lives. We are born, we live, we die. But in accepting that inevitability, we presume—we believe—that the cycle will hold true; that having preceded our children in life, we will precede them in death. When that cycle is broken, you are changed forever, your life is never the same, and you walk in two worlds, thanking God for each day, each hour, each minute, each breath, but no longer afraid of death because part of you has already passed, bringing you that much closer to those who have gone on before you.

That truth was made clear to me when I looked back at Mom's portrait and knew I was seeing tears in her eyes. I did not cry out, though; I did not run to tell Murphy, or Jesse or Tucker or James, not certain if the same image would be visible to them. A distinct calm came over me, and I knew without any doubt that Mom was in the room with me, and that people cry in heaven, too.

Then, several hours later, as I finished the last of the cards, Murphy's sister, Jo Lynn, arrived to spend a few days as a shoulder and an extra pair of hands. Both would be sorely needed. I stood from my chair at the dining room table to embrace her as she came toward me. She was crying but bravely trying to put on a strong face. She put her arms around me but then stepped back almost immediately, her hand covering her mouth, her expression one of complete disbelief. Her eyes were riveted on Mom's portrait.

"Oh my God," she said through her tears. "Your mom . . . she's crying."

SIXTEEN

MY FLIGHT ARRIVED AT SFO at ten o'clock, the night of February 25, 1989. At the gate, Jim was waiting, his face drawn and gray. "We need to hurry," was all he said.

We arrived home just before eleven, pulling into the garage as Dad was coming out the back door with Tom Herbert, neighbor, friend, and counselor. Dad did not expect to see me and immediately put both arms around me.

"Your mom needs us, son. We may not have much time." With Tom at the wheel, we climbed into the station wagon and rode the ten minutes to Stanford. Neither of us spoke, but from the driveway to the entrance of the hospital, Dad never let go of my hand, squeezing it tighter as we approached the entrance.

The hospital room was small, and only one small light burned at its far corner, a wall-mounted brass sconce over an end table, casting a copper-tinted and diffused hue that faded before it reached the single bed along the wall by the door.

Standing at the railing of the bed was Tom's wife, Mary Ann, who'd been at Mom's side for the evening, though it's doubtful Mom knew that she'd been there. She looked up slowly as we stepped into the room, our footfalls silent on the white tile floor. "Oh, Buck . . . she'd be so happy," she said. "Her breathing is . . . shallow now—very weak since they removed the oxygen. It's good you're here." Dad took my hand again and motioned me toward the bed. "Go to your mom, son," he said.

He released my hand and I walked to the bed, my feet not wanting to move, and my eyes not wanting to see.

The slight rise and fall of the sheet she was under told me she was
breathing, but as I placed my hand on her, I could feel each breath
weakening, her life slowly ebbing.

My eyes fell on her face, turned sideways on her pillow, and for a
moment, it seemed all the years and the pain and the sickness were
gone. She was just asleep. From the bedside table I picked up her
brush, and as I gently stroked her beautiful hair, Dad put his hand on
my shoulder and his other hand on her head. Behind us, I could hear
the sound of Jim crying.

Beside me, Dad's will was failing, and I could feel his own strength
draining. He looked toward me briefly and then back at Mom.

"Son . . . I can't stay here. Please come home with me," he said.

I was torn, wanting—needing—to stay with Mom, but knowing
that Dad needed me right then more than she did. That instinct
proved to be true, but its truth did not and has not lessened the guilt
I still feel today at leaving my mother's bedside at the time of her
death. At that last moment, that last breath, I was not there with her.
I was not there for her.

Dad simply did not have the strength to watch her die, and I
believed that my place was by his side, should he, too, fall and need
his son to carry him.

At twelve forty-five that morning, half an hour after Tom had
dropped Dad, Jim, and me at the house, Mary Ann called from Stanford. Mom was gone.

The next day I found the last letter she'd written—addressed to
Dad and composed on a note card from her Metropolitan Museum of
Art collection, a John Gould lithograph from 1855 on the front. After
emptying a bottle of Valium, Seconal, and two other prescriptions with
names I could not pronounce, and washing everything down with a
Bloody Mary—the remains still in her glass by the sink—she'd placed
the note in its envelope and pushed it under the cushion of her vanity settee before her spinal cord was shocked by the massive infusion
of drugs she'd taken, paralyzing her.

Judy Fleming, hired just months earlier as a companion, cook, and
housekeeper, found her first, giving what menial care she could, carrying Mom—who was still conscious enough to curse her immobility—
to the bed before calling Dad at the club. Together, they carried her

to the car when he returned home, and then to Stanford, where he placed the first call to me from her doctor's office.

Two days later, against his wishes, but at Jim's earnest and urgent advice, I was on an American DC-10 nonstop to San Francisco.

Until this moment, as I write these last lines, only two others besides me knew about her last letter, and Dad was not one of that pair. I kept it hidden from him, never betraying its existence and never revealing the depth of pain in its bitter passages. The love of his life was gone now, and the pain and the bitterness that had threatened that love had gone with her, leaving, I prayed, the better memories of the love and light that had once bound them together—from that first day on a dusty airfield in Victorville a lifetime ago.

On the crest of the hill around the house stood a small break of California pines; tall and green, each one planted by Mom's hand over the years in memory of a family member who'd died. She'd dug each hole herself, set each sapling, and watered each over the years, watching them grow and sink their roots deep into the ground. Three days after she'd gone, I knelt by the last of those tall pines with Dad, our hands darkened with the loamy dirt that surrounded their trunks. At each tree, we'd carefully dug the top layer away, and where the roots lay, we placed her ashes, gently covering the dust and bones with the soft earth from the hill she'd called home for so long.

As we stood after finishing the last tree, a lone hawk circled through the valley below us, the drafts of a light breeze lifting it up under its outstretched wings and carrying it soaring past us. As it disappeared over the eaves of the house, the wind stopped. Opening the vase under his arms, Dad poured its contents into his hands, and threw the ashes across the hill. "She'll always be here now," he said.

Sealing the vase, he brushed his hands together, put his arm on my shoulder, and looked out across the valley. The wind was picking up again and, on it, I thought I could just catch the scent of an ocean breeze as we turned toward the house.

EPILOGUE

Three months and ten days after scattering Mom's ashes, Dad was in a Nevada courthouse marrying Beverly Wood Smith, the sixty-six-year-old daughter of a once-prominent Bay Area surgeon, and one of our family's oldest acquaintances. He was in the advanced stages of liver disease by then and in advanced denial of his illness, drinking daily, eating handfuls of Zantac to curb the increasing pain in his gut, and dismissing the progressive spells of disorientation that were occurring more frequently and alarming others around him. Beverly was acutely aware of his condition, though, and we were hopeful, convinced in the beginning that her intentions were of the best sort and gladdened that he would not be alone.

Twenty-six months later, our hope and Dad were gone, and Beverly's intentions clarified. In that short span of time, her attorneys replaced Dad's lifelong advisers, she assumed his management and named her daughter as his publicist, his doctor of fifteen years was summarily relieved, his children and grandchildren were disinherited—twice, she altered the dates on two life insurance policies with a used ribbon of correcting tape and a twenty-year-old typewriter, and she arranged for his first face-lift. "To erase a few lines," was how he put it.

In the four years following his death, she spent just over a million dollars in funds from Dad's estate on six law firms in five states trying in vain to erase something else altogether: the memory of Betty Jean Ford and the life she and Ernest Jennings had shared for nearly fifty years.

She failed. But not before she had forced us to spend very nearly the same amount of money in our fight to defend that memory. Greed is a powerful impeller, but no less so than blood.

The legacy of Betty and Ernie Ford was saved but at great cost, cutting the family deeply and wounding us permanently. We hemorrhaged money, paying hundreds of thousands of dollars to attorneys we would never meet personally. I was denied any time to grieve; every waking hour spent devising strategy, filing counterclaims, drafting interrogatories, and reading vile hearsay. We accepted the proffered help of people we believed were allies; friends we hoped would help stanch the flow of blood and finances; friends to whom we willingly gave power, authority, and money, blindly inviting treachery from within our own ranks. Treachery that grew in darkness, from seeds of avarice planted, perhaps, by my own hand. Treachery my children may very well be paying for even after I'm gone.

All of it . . . all the lawsuits; all the money; all the bitterness, division, and rancor; all the memories; all the tears; all the pain and all the laughter—all of it is a testament unto itself. A testament of the lives of two simple people who saw a handful of dreams that bound them together in the beginning turn into ropes that bound them to a life they lost all control over. And it is a testament to the power our lives can continue to have over others long after they have ended.

Jesus, I miss them.

I'm not certain there's a moral here. And if there is, I'm not so vain as to suggest it be a lesson to anyone, save perhaps for me and my own. I would tell my children that things are rarely what they seem, and appearances are deceptive. That life is short.

I will tell them that all things exist in opposites. For there to be goodness in the world, there must be evil. We recognize light because it dispels darkness. Without knowing hate, we can never fully appreciate love. I will try to teach them that our lives balance between these opposites, and the beam upon which we stand is narrow.

I will try never to let a day pass without telling them I love them. That they must look out for one another.

I will teach them that family is everything.

INDEX

ABC, 46, 58, 156–57, 165–66, 168, 173, 220

ABC Radio, 46, 58

Adams, Berle, 86–87, 152, 154

Adderley, Nat, 98

Admirals Club, 13

AFTRA, 84, 220

"Ain't Goin' Down in the Ground Before My Time," 219

Air Corps, 23, 28, 30, 33, 40, 42–43, 46, 119, 181

Air Force Academy, 193

Allen, Steve, 89

"Anticipation Blues," 68

Apaka, Alfred, 137

Applause Records, 227

Apple Valley, 29

Armed Forces Radio Network (AFRN), 39, 46, 95

Arnold, Danny, 88

Arquette, Cliff, 93, 154–55

Atkins, Chet, 108

Ausden, Peter, 119

Autry, Gene, 46

Auxiliary League, 52

Award, Minnie Pearl, 124

Axelrod, David, 98

Back Porch Majority, 189

Baez, Joan, 108, 182

"Ballad of Davy Crockett, The," 153

"Barbara Allen," 108

Barnet, Charlie, 105

Barney Miller, 88

Bar Nothing Ranch, 48–51, 53, 60

Beale, Edith Bouvier, 239

Beale, Phelan, 239

Bellamy Brothers, 221

Bennett, Tony, 103, 141

Benny, Jack, 85, 166

Berle, Milton, 82

BetFord Corporation, 63, 126, 141, 157, 166, 169–71, 212–14

BetFord Production, 166

Billboard charts, 101

Bishop, Joey, 172

"Blackberry Boogie," 79

Black, Charlie, 225

Black, Shirley Temple, 157

Bohemian Club, 187–89, 195

Boone, Pat, 85

Bouvier, Jacqueline, 239

Brigman, Anne, 184

Bristol, Tennessee, 25, 28–29, 39, 43–45, 101, 119, 234

Brokaw, Norman, 172

Brooks, Steven, 183

Brown, Charles, 169, 171

Brown, Peter, 169, 171, 216, 222, 228–29, 238

Bruns, George, 96

Bryant, Jimmy, 59, 96

Bryner, Sharpe, 66–67

Brynner, Yul, 187

Burch, Bill, 166–67

Burnette, Johnny, 144, 173

Bush, Barbara, 13

Campbell, Glen, 104

Campbell-Ewald, 89

Capitol Records, 22, 58–61, 68–69, 79–80, 97–99, 101–10, 131, 170, 172, 213–14, 219

Carmichael, Hoagy, 96, 99, 222

Carroll, Bob, 39

Carroll, Diahann, 212

Cash, Johnny, 92

Cavanaugh, David, 98

CBS, 58, 68, 79, 91, 120–22, 172, 220

Channing, Carol, 92

Chappell Music Publishing, 221–22

Cincinnati Conservatory of Music, 28, 181

Clearlake, California, 140, 143, 145, 156, 169

Clooney, George, 121, 123

Clooney, Rosemary, 85, 107

Clough, Eric, 157

Coast Recorders, 103

Cole, Nat King, 96

Colgate Comedy Hour, The, 84

Como, Perry, 89

Cooley, Spade, 48, 59

Cooper, Gary, 142

Cooper, Gene, 142, 144

Copeland, Allan, 106

Corbin, Paul, 18, 20, 95, 220–21

Costello, Frank, 133

"Cotton Fields," 214

Courtneidge, Cicely, 81

Country Hits . . . Feelin' Blue, 103–4

Crawford, Joan, 126

Crazy Gang, 81

Crosby, Bing, 60, 81, 157, 234

Crosby, John, 90, 118

Cross, Douglass, 141

Cross, May, 140–41

Crouch, Andrae, 221

Dale, Bobby, 14, 216, 224

Darby, Kenneth, 7

Dating Game, The, 165

Davis, Bette, 126

De Paolo, Tom, 154

Dermott, Chuck, 119

Dinah Shore Chevy Show, The, 86, 89, 100

Disney Studios, 113

Donegan, John, 185

Doodletown Pipers, 188

Dorsey, Tommy, 44

Douglas, Mike, 172

Dylan, Bob, 108, 182–83

Eagle Banner Corporation, 169

Eagle Banner Productions, 222

Eagle Banner Ranches, 228

Eastwood, Clint, 127, 182

Edwards, Ralph, 118, 122, 242

Eikenberry, Arthur, 183

El Capitan Theater, 83–84, 89, 100, 109, 126, 142, 152, 165

El Monte Legion Stadium, 63, 100

Ephraim, Lon, 207–8

Ernie Sings & Glen Picks, 104

Evers, Jason, 166

Everything Is Beautiful, 98

Fairbanks, Douglas Jr., 92

Farina, Richard, 182

Farm Services Agency, 49

Fascinato, Jack, 86, 101, 106–7, 109, 118, 141, 174, 212

Fenton, Jerome, 183

Fisk Jubilee Singers, 220

Fleming, Judy, 246

Flower, Mary, 207–8

Folk Songs of the Hills, 108

Ford, Bettilynn, 241

Ford, Brion, 17–21, 31, 33, 63, 69–75, 78–80, 93, 113–14, 116–17, 119–20, 122–23, 125–28, 131, 134–35, 137–40, 142–45, 149–50, 156, 159, 161–63, 176, 180, 184, 189, 202, 205, 214–17, 231, 233–35, 238, 241

Ford, Clarence (T.C.), 25–26, 29, 45, 119, 181
Ford, Donald S., 23
Ford, Gerald, 212
Ford, James, 242
Ford, Jarrod, 241–42
Ford, Jesse, 242
Ford, Maude Lee, 25–26, 29, 45, 119, 181
Ford Motor Company, 84, 86, 91, 100, 153–56
Ford, Murphy, 19, 22, 229, 237–39, 242–43
Ford, Patrick, 241–42
Ford Show, The. See Tennessee Ernie Ford Show, The
Ford, Stanley Haskell, 25–27, 43, 45, 62, 211
Ford, Tucker, 242
Four Preps, 83
Four Seasons, 173
Freeman, Mickey, 118, 161
Funny Side, The, 212

Gabor, Zsa Zsa, 92
Gardiner, Reginald, 88
Garland, Judy, 81, 125
Gatlin, Larry, 14
Gay, Don, 74
Gibbs, Terri, 221
Gillespie, Jerry, 221–22
Gillette, Lee, 58, 68, 98, 105, 107–8, 110
Gobel, George, 85, 166
Good Night, and Good Luck, 121
Goodman, Benny, 61
Goodsell, O. M., 28
Gordon, Anita, 165
Grade, Leslie, 81
Grade, Lew, 81
Grand Ole Opry, 68
Grand Ole Opry House, 213, 221, 225
Grasso, Tom, 220

Grateful Dead, 157, 188
Great Gospel Songs, 103
Green, Barry, 176–77
Griesedieck Brothers Beer, 96
Griffith, Andy, 172
Grossman, Albert, 64
Groves, General Leslie, 188
Guthrie, Woody, 107

H.M.S. Pinafore, 92
Hadley, John, 157
Haggard, Merle, 221–22
Hall, Tom T., 221–22
Halterman, Robert, 22
Handley, Randy, 207
Hapgood, John, 20
Happy Goodman Family, 220
Hawthorne, Jim, 60
Heminger, Alvin, 30
Heminger, Charles Dallas, 30–33, 37, 40, 181, 232
Heminger, Jesse Etheline, 30, 36, 128–29, 181, 232
Heminger, Vayle, 30–31, 33, 156
Heminger, Wallace, 31, 33
Hemmings, Fred, 137
Hensley, Harold, 96
Henson, Jim, 101
Herbert, Tom, 245
Hilgenstuhler, Ted, 54
Ho, Don, 137
Hockney, David, 184
Hoffman, Milt, 86
Hollywood Palace, 83
Hollywood Playhouse, 83
Hollywood Walk of Fame, 155
Hometown Jamboree, 50, 58–61, 63, 69–70, 79, 83, 100, 105, 108
Hoover, J. Edgar, 109
Hope, Bob, 85, 113, 115, 117, 149, 152, 173, 212
Hope, Dolores, 115, 212
Hopper, Hedda, 92, 118, 152
Hosford, Victor, 229

Huston, John, 142
Hutton, Betty, 96, 105–6
Hutton, Timothy, 148
Hymns, 99, 101–2, 105

"I Left My Heart in San Francisco," 141
"I'll Never Be Free," 105
I Love Lucy, 58, 83, 87
Immerman, David, 184, 242
Ives, Burl, 107–8

J. Walter Thompson, 78, 86–87, 89, 91, 100, 153–54, 156
Jackson, Corny, 86–87
Jedica, Chuckie, 114
Jeffers, Robinson, 182
John, Elton, 150, 222
Jones, Frank, 69
Jones, Hank, 165
Jordanaires, 103, 219

Kahanamoku, Duke, 137
Kaiser, Henry J., 136
Kaye, Danny, 81
Kay Kyser's Kollege of Musical Knowledge, 58, 87
Keane, Walter, 70, 184
Keillor, Garrison, 99
Kendalls, 221
Kennedy, Bobby, 166, 168
Kenton, Stan, 58
KFXM radio, 40, 46, 49, 51–53, 60
Kids Next Door, 189
Kienzle, Rich, 95
King, Carole, 99
King, Jim, 216, 224
King, Loyal, 52–53, 55, 58
Kristofferson, Kris, 104
KXLA radio, 52–53, 58–62, 69, 79–80
Kyser, Kay, 87

Lange, Dorothea, 49–51

Lange, Jim, 165
Larson, Glen, 83
Laughton, Charles, 92
Lear, Norman, 88
Lee, Peggy, 61
Leeds, Howard, 88
Lewis, Jerry, 84–86
Liebert, Billy, 96
Livingston, Alan, 105–6
Loakes, Jim, 18, 20, 63–64, 70, 88, 95, 118, 126, 131, 138, 154, 160, 178, 193, 216
London Palladium, 58, 69, 80–82
London, Julie, 85
Long Valley Ranch (California), 140–42, 146, 169, 171, 228
Long, Nancy, 26, 119
Long, Walter, 26
LSI Studios, 224
Luciano, Lucky, 133
Lynch, John, 31

Mandrell Sisters, 213
Maphis, Jody, 237
Marine Corps Marching Band, 212
Martha White Mills, 14, 213–14, 216–17, 224–25, 228
Martin, Bill, 166
Martin, Dean, 84–85, 107, 172
Martin, Frank, 170
Marvin, Lee, 92
Maugham, William Somerset, 240
May, Billy, 59, 105–6
Mayer, Louis B., 37
Maysles, John, 239
McCarthy, Joseph, 123
McGuirt, Glenn, 219
McKay, Jim, 72
McNulty, Barney, 126
McVay, Charles, 137
McVay, Kimo, 137
McVay, Kinau Wilder, 137
Merrill, Bob, 107
Messina, Jimmy, 102

Metalious, Grace, 184
Mikado, The, 90–92, 129
Mitchum, Robert, 106
Moffatt, Katy, 207
Mogull, Artie, 227
Monroe, Marilyn, 106, 133
Monterey Park, California, 57, 68, 78, 83, 234
Moore, Tom, 157
Moran, Diamond Jim, 132, 134
More of That Great American Gospel Sound, 221
Morse, Ella Mae, 105
Mosher, John, 103
Murray, Anne, 221
Murrow, Edward R., 120, 122–23
Myers, Farlon, 154
My Favorite Things, 141

Nabors, Jim, 172
Name That Tune, 118, 165
Nannini, Filaccina, 54
Nashville Network, 18
Nelson, Ricky, 144, 173–74
Newman, Lionel, 7
Nielsens ratings, 91, 212
Noel, Dick, 165, 167
Noonan, Chris, 114–15, 149
Norden, Carl, 33

"Oceans of Tears," 79
Oppenheimer, Robert, 188
Opry. *See Grand Ole Opry*
Opryland, USA, 74

Paley, William, 84
Parnell, Val, 81
Patterson, George, 157
pea picker, 50–52, 92
Pearl, Minnie, 14, 92, 124
Person to Person, 120–23
Peyton Place, 184
Phillips, Sister Mary, 132, 135
Pola, Ed, 106

Porter, Cole, 96
Prairie Home Companion, 99
Presley, Elvis, 123
Price, Ray, 104

Rawls, Lou, 98
Ray, Johnnie, 81
Reese, Della, 220
Resolution Trust Corporation, 170
"River of No Return," 7, 106
Revue Studios, 166
Robert Louis Stevenson School for Boys, 181–85, 192–94, 214
Rodgers, Jimmy, 107
Romero, Cesar, 92
Rose, David, 85–86
Ryan, Irene, 70

Sacks, Dave, 166
San Bernardino, California, 23, 30–32, 35–36, 38, 40, 43, 45–46, 48–49, 51–52, 58, 65, 181
Sands, Tommy, 123
Sarnoff, David, 84, 153
Sarnoff, Tom, 87, 153
Schulz, Charles, 168
Seeger, Pete, 107
Seymour, Danny, 87, 154–55
Shand, Terry, 107
Shankar, Ravi, 183
Shaver, Billy Joe, 105
Shields, David, 191
Shore, Dinah, 85–86, 89, 100, 172
Sinatra, Frank, 59, 86, 107, 212
Sing America Beautiful, 212
"Sixteen Tons," 18, 58, 74, 107–8, 110, 126, 173
"Somebody Bigger Than You and I," 106
Smith, Beatrice, 116–17, 124–26
Smith, Beverly Wood, 13, 16–22, 124, 249
Smith, Kate, 46, 86
Songs of This Lusty Land, 221

Sparks, Randy, 189
Spirituals, 101–2
Stacy, Eldred, 174
Starr, Kay, 79, 105
Stoker, Gordon, 219
Stone, Cliffie, 20–22, 59–62, 64,
    68–70, 79–80, 87–89, 95, 97,
    100–1, 104, 106–8, 110, 118–19,
    124, 126, 138, 155, 220
Stone, Steve, 104
Strange, Billy, 96, 103, 165, 225
Strathairn, David, 121, 123
Stratton, Gil, 88
Street, Baronne, 132
Swing Wide Your Golden Gate, 219

Taupin, Bernie, 150
TEF, Inc., 63
"Tell Me You Remember, Betty Jean,"
    223
Tennessee Ernie Ford Enterprises, 221
Tennessee Ernie Ford Show, The, 58,
    64, 83–84, 87, 89, 90–92, 95–96,
    100–2, 113, 118–19, 126, 131,
    144, 151–54, 156, 165–66
That Great American Gospel Sound,
    220–21
The Prophet, 198
Thetford, Bill, 71, 114, 149
This Is Your Life, 118
"This Must Be the Place," 106
Thomas, Danny, 92, 212
Thompson, Ken, 126–27, 132, 138,
    160, 178, 190
Tilford, Judy, 44, 46
Tillstrom, Burr, 101
Titov, Gherman, 166–68
Travis, Merle, 107–8, 111
Tucker, Sophie, 81

U.S. Army Air Corps. *See* Air Corps
Up with People, 188

Valencia, Johnny, 125

Van Horne, Harriet, 122
VandenBerg, Ron, 21
VanDevender, Karl, 14
Vasilakos, George, 135

Wakely, Jimmy, 60
Wasserman, Lew, 86, 152
Wells, Lloyd, 95, 97
Welty, Eudora, 238
Werblin, Sonny, 87, 152
Weston, Paul, 105
William Morris, 172
Williams, Andy, 168, 172
Williams, Cohen, 213–17, 224
Wills, Bob, 60–61
Wilson, Earl, 118, 152
Word Records, 219
Works Progress Administration, 30

Yorkin, Bud, 88
"You Don't Have to Be a Baby to
    Cry," 107